I0051605

David Arellano-Gault, Arturo del Castillo

The Promises and Perils of Compliance

David Arellano-Gault, Arturo del Castillo

The Promises and Perils of Compliance

Organizational factors in the success (or failure)
of compliance programs

DE GRUYTER

ISBN 978-3-11-074902-1
e-ISBN (PDF) 978-3-11-074911-3
e-ISBN (EPUB) 978-3-11-074921-2

Library of Congress Control Number: 2022946833

Bibliographic information published by the Deutsche Nationalbibliothek
The Deutsche Nationalbibliothek lists this publication in the Deutsche Nationalbibliografie;
detailed bibliographic data are available on the internet at http://dnb.dnb.de.

© 2023 Walter de Gruyter GmbH, Berlin/Boston
Cover image: cnythzl/DigitalVision Vectors/Getty Images
Typesetting: Integra Software Services Pvt. Ltd.
Printing and binding: CPI books GmbH, Leck

www.degruyter.com

Advance Praise for *The Promises and Perils of Compliance*

"There is an urgent need in the compliance profession for discussion about the underlying principles and expectations of what we do. This book provides an excellent explanation of why that discussion is needed and a solid opening for that discussion, combining organizational behaviour with practical experience. I recommend this book for anyone who questions why compliance professionals do what we do, and what we should do differently."

–**Brian Weihs**, Managing Director and Head of Kroll Mexico

"A realistic and integrative book that moves the study of compliance beyond the legal and rule-bound approach that has thwarted advances in the field, one of the fastest growing and inclusive professional sectors in the world. Once a country or sector receives a list of the rules, how does a compliance professional get employees to accountably follow them? Arellano-Gault and del Castillo have clearly responded to that question with essential knowledge and understanding of ethics, influence and negotiation, power, and organizational behavior. This is the one book that has it all and we need it."

–**Carole L. Jurkiewicz**, University of Colorado, Colorado Springs, School of Public Affairs

https://doi.org/10.1515/9783110749113-202

To the whole family Arellano-Gault, particularly to my mother, María, and my brothers Antonio and José, who prematurely left us in 2020. To Laura, Ana, and Ricardo, my enduring reasons to live.

David Arellano-Gault

To the many wonderful and generous people who have been invaluable in nurturing and shaping my professional career dedicated to the forensic investigation and teaching others about compliance in the corporate world. And especially to my dear wife, Nuria Ordax, who strengthens and inspires me every day with her brilliance, great character, and endless love. This book is dedicated to her.

Arturo del Castillo

Contents

Introduction

Today's era is one of increased regulation and renewed enforcement efforts. Unethical behavior and misconduct are a focus of concern among governments and regulators, investors, firms, employees, customers, and the public. Accordingly, compliance programs have gained prominence in the organizational agenda. The main promise of compliance is as follows: a properly designed and implemented compliance program provides crucial assurance for all stakeholders that an organization's personnel abide by all applicable regulations, internal ethical principles, codes of conduct, and other guidelines governing their actions.

However, experience has shown that compliance programs encounter numerous pitfalls in their design and implementation that make it challenging to achieve their stated goal. Many compliance programs fail to avert the misconduct they were intended to prevent. On the surface, a compliance program may appear to provide systems for identifying and mitigating risks such as money laundering, bribery and corruption, sexual harassment, cyber-attacks, and numerous other issues: In reality, however, the outcomes of compliance reforms are far away from being satisfactory.

Nevertheless, the design and implementation of a compliance program cannot be seen as a linear procedure of orders and systems that members of any organization will immediately adopt. A compliance program could be designed rationally, using the most effective administrative techniques and yet fail to be implemented and adapted in practice. Why? Like any organizational strategy or proposal, a compliance program is a political construction that will be interpreted, analyzed, and, if necessary, resisted by several people, groups, and coalitions inside and outside the organization.

An organization is not an orderly, monolithic creature. It comprises very different people in various positions of authority and leadership. Organizations can be described as a set of coalitions and groups that negotiate and struggle every day to enact accepted routines and practices. These practices and routines that produce the actual decisions and actions make an organization exist.

Assuming that a compliance program will be accepted and enacted because of its intrinsic rationality can be a big mistake. Assuming that one mandated by the highest echelons of the organization would suffice for the program to be accepted and internalized could prove to be an even bigger mistake. Like any major change in any organization, a compliance program will necessarily be interpreted, adapted, changed, and redefined in action. Moreover, if necessary, boycotted or, in many cases, formally adopted but just as a façade. A façade that allows the people and groups in the organization to continue undertaking their activities with no major transformation.

Watching an organization spend months or even years attempting to enact a compliance program is by no means unusual. Nor is it uncommon to see an organization committed to creating and legitimizing a compliance program through several

https://doi.org/10.1515/9783110749113-204

meetings and spending large amounts of money. It is not surprising to see compliance programs inaugurated with significant events and public presentations. The saddest thing is that it is not unusual to see these organizations, months after their big inauguration day, still struggling to show that their compliance programs have been adopted and internalized in the routines and culture of their members.

A compliance program involves an ambitious organizational change process. Furthermore, changing an organization requires strategic, tactical, and political abilities. Organizations are arenas of groups and coalitions which, through their interaction, negotiation, and conflicts, create the organizational routines and culture enacted. Changing a reality such as this, therefore, requires far more than goodwill and rational proposals. It requires critical steps to convince different people and groups that the proposed changes are viable and that all the actors in the organizations have a role to play. Change must be intelligible to the various parts of the organization. As in any change program, a compliance program requires a clear message that organizational groups can grasp and adopt to create intelligibility. However, a compliance program adds complexity to this picture.

Compliance programs have been created and developed to tackle a major problem in several (if not all) organizations: people in organizations can break the rules and even laws. They can act unethically. They can develop the ability to commit fraud, not only affecting the organizations they work for but also clients and even populations and society. Organizations can even become trapped by these unethical acts, which become routine. Indeed, organizations can normalize and rationalize what is tantamount to unethical practices.

How does one change such an intricate reality? What possible ways of *normalizing* habits and routines facilitate or even create fraud and corruption in an organization? Corruption and fraud are not accidents or exceptions in organizational life. For years, ACFE studies have shown that the existence of these acts is common and even continuous in organizational life worldwide (ACFE, 2021).

The task of a compliance program is to build the internal capacities of an organization to address this situation: an organization is not only capable of prosecuting wrongdoing but also of preventing it and producing the necessary organizational capabilities to transform the behavior of those in an organization to create a culture of compliance and integrity. However, this ambitious agenda has proven to be more difficult than expected.

Compliance is expected to achieve several complicated objectives. Expectations are high: an organization should have internal solid and governance capabilities not only to detect and punish wrongdoing but also to prevent it and create a whole new culture that will transform the behaviors of the organization and its member in the short term. In practice, a compliance program is a proposal that attempts to link various structures, rules, and procedures for different parts of an organization. It requires steps and phases to cope with different challenges and dangers.

Changing behaviors and relationships in an organization can take time. More-over, the end results might not be what was expected. Months or even years can elapse between the occurrence of an incident and its detection. Compliance programs often appear to be working when they are not. An organization may have all the pieces in place to show that it has a good compliance policy and controls until a felony or scandal is revealed. Only then will the organization discover that its compliance program was not as robust as it seemed.

A compliance program is primarily an organizational decision and action. In other words, organizations do not just launch compliance programs in a vacuum. Compliance programs are political decisions expressed through an array of discourses, designed not just to achieve formal objectives but also other nonexplicit, informal ends. Compliance strategies are formulated, designed, and implemented in a dynamic organizational setting. It is therefore critical to discuss the organizational factors that determine the effectiveness of compliance programs. A compliance program is generally defined as a rational system of processes, policies, procedures, and controls developed to ensure compliance with all the applicable rules, regulations, contracts, and policies governing the actions of the organization. However, the organizational logic underlying this type of rational process is substantial regarding the effects a compliance program is expected to achieve.

One promise of the compliance discourse is, therefore, that an effective program helps individuals within an organization to be aware of and understand the expectations of doing the right thing. But criminal acts, such as fraud, bribery, or embezzlement, are not just the result of "rotten apples." Misconduct happens in the context of a chain of behaviors within complex organizational situations. An unethical act may be performed by some other person who is aware of his or her irregular behavior. Moreover, another person might have unwittingly contributed to the situation without realizing she or he were violating a law. Some other persons might even believe they were following the rules of the organization.

Therefore, this book seeks to discuss compliance as not just another management tool but a collection of rules, norms, and controls embedded in an organizational environment that must be understood. Compliance programs run the risk of becoming an oversimplified instrument. Accordingly, practitioners and scholars can benefit from the deep understanding that ethical behavior is not just the outcome of disciplinary measures. Organizations are complex scenarios of people behaving in multiple situations, and it is essential to understand this complexity to develop a more realistic basis for compliance programs to be effective.

The book offers a pathway to understanding the organizational dynamics any compliance effort needs to consider, using a compliance program as a unit of analysis and a transformation project. In this vein, Chapter 1 explains the organizational logic of unethical behavior and misconduct. These phenomena have become a significant concern in organizations. Reputational scandals due to criminal issues began to appear not as exceptional incidents but as a common situation in organizations. In this context, compliance appeared to be an effective solution. Broadly defined as a formal program specifying an organization's policies, procedures, and actions within a process to help prevent and detect violations of laws and regulations, compliance emerged with the promise of protecting organizations from misconduct. This chapter aims to answer the following questions: What is a compliance program? What is the purpose of a compliance program? What are the promises of compliance discourse? What is the appeal of compliance discourse?

Chapter 2 observes organizations not as a monolith but as an arena. Organizations are a set of people engaging in various types of behavior. In other words, organizations are social spaces where social relationships are built on a day-to-day basis. It is therefore essential to understand that unethical behavior is not only an individual's deviant behavior from formal rules. It is also an outcome of the group and social dynamics in which an individual is embedded. Organizational context matters because the difference between behaving and misbehaving can be blurred. In an organizational context, people normalize, rationalize, and make sense of what appears to be appropriate. People are rationally bounded and, therefore, also ethically bounded. Understanding why people in organizational settings normalize unethical behaviors and rationalize practices that can lead an organization to make deviant decisions is an important step toward understanding the perils of compliance programs. This chapter aims to answer the following questions: Why do organizational dynamics matter in the implementation of compliance programs? To what extent are unethical behavior and misconduct driven by the organizational context? Why does organizational reality challenge the promises of compliance discourse?

Chapter 3 links the discussion in the two previous chapters, describing the path to creating and implementing a compliance program as long and winding. For organizations seeking to build a compliance program, the process of building is difficult and vague. First, there is not a single protocol or referral program to use or implement. However, many recommendations are available from the various government entities worldwide responsible for compliance investigations and enforcement. For example, in 2007, the US Department of Justice (DOJ) published its guidelines, Evaluation of Corporate Compliance Programs, updated in April 2020. These guidelines are designed "to assist prosecutors in making informed decisions as to whether, and to what extent, the corporation's compliance program was effective at the time of the offense" (DOJ, 2017). Organizations usually build their programs based on what is considered "best practices" or their own criteria. In any case, the process of building compliance programs is embedded in organizational dynamics, which largely determine the features (limitations and strengths) of compliance programs. This chapter aims to answer the following questions: How are compliance programs built? Are compliance programs as effective as they are intended to be? What are the actual purposes of compliance programs?

In Chapter 4, the main concern is to tackle the most common problems and organizational dynamics that might reduce the possibility of a compliance program becoming implemented and effective. Any compliance program aspires to provide assurance that personnel in the organization are behaving according to the regulations, policies, and code of conduct of the organization. The reality, however, is that many compliance programs fail to avert the unethical behavior they were designed to prevent. The failure of compliance programs is largely a result of the limits imposed by the organizational context on compliance efforts. An insufficient budget, lack of risk assessment, absence of political support from top management, and weak or dysfunctional leadership, among other factors, can jeopardize compliance efforts. Thus, compliance programs face various challenges, from design to implementation, which limits their effectiveness. In this context, compliance risks becoming a fad rather than an inspired solution to the significant problem of unethical behavior in organizations. Compliance cannot simply be a matter of narrowing the gap between formal rules and obedience. Compliance programs seek to address a broad range of unethical behavior, from individual misconduct to complex fraudulent organizational projects. Practitioners and scholars are increasingly aware that ethical behavior is a matter of continuous organizational commitment to creating and embedding new routines and normalized behaviors, rather than just an issue of enforcing norms and formal procedures. This chapter aims to answer the following questions: What are the most relevant organizational factors undermining compliance programs? What are the main strategies that must be adopted to transform the political discourse of compliance reform into action adapted to the culture of the organization where it is being implemented? What type of structure, symbols, and culture transformation might be required for a compliance program to become effective in practice?

In Chapter 5, the lessons offered throughout the book are summarized to identify the scenarios and minimal organizational and managerial conditions for transforming an organization involved in a compliance program. How would compliance programs be able to mitigate unethical behaviors in practice? How can they be implemented, without becoming just a new narrative, rich in new rules and instruments, yet not embedded in real life of organizations? Some critical elements considered dos and don'ts would seem to be the most honest and best way to guide a compliance program, rather than insisting on the compliance discourse, which states that ultimate integrity is possible with a few mechanisms or tools.

Lastly, in Chapter 6, in the conclusions, we stress that compliance programs can be necessary instruments for reducing unethical behaviors within organizations. However, this is just one facet of compliance. More importantly, compliance programs are also formal instruments able to transform the culture and behavior of leaders, managers, and personnel. In other words, they are a tool for creating an entire cultural system based on an integrity perspective. This book argues that a compliance program will only work if it is based on a realistic understanding of the organizational context and if there is a political strategy around it. A political strategy is important because a compliance program will affect different interests within the organization, modifying several power structures and authority figures. Accordingly, this final chapter proposes four critical steps to accomplishing a political strategy to drive a compliance program through the organizational complexity involved:

1. Build a legitimate coalition of different organizational groups to support the compliance program at all the design and implementation stages.
2. Define a realistic agenda for the different stages to be accomplished, emphasizing small gains so that organizational members can observe key changes.
3. Define the challenges and obstacles to modifying routines and practices to achieve the new behaviors that the compliance program requires to be successful.
4. Build a practical communication policy not only because of the need to "comply with the compliance program" but to define specific transformations in the cultural mindset of the organization and routines and processes.

Ultimately, any compliance program's success lies in the organization's transformation through its members' behavior. Furthermore, the aim is to become a more trustworthy group of people within a resilient organization.

Chapter 1
The Promise of Compliance Programs

1.1 Introduction

Unethical behavior and misconduct in organizations have become an issue of great concern. Reputational scandals due to criminal matters have emerged not as exceptional incidents but as commonplace in organizations.

In this context, compliance is framed as an effective solution for organizations. Broadly, compliance, defined as a formal program that specifies policies, procedures, and internal controls for preventing and detecting breaches of laws and unethical behavior, is developed with the promise of protecting organizations from misconduct and sanctions for regulatory failures. In this way, compliance is not a purely theoretical concept. On the contrary, compliance has been articulated more as a professional practice, with a growing influence on organization management. Nowadays, no organization, regardless of its type or industry, escapes the guidelines compliance has imposed on business management.

In this respect, it is essential to know what the promises are, in other words, the assumptions and aspirations of compliance as a new feature of organization management. The possibility of crime and misconduct within organizations is a constant. This begs the question of what set of solutions compliance proposes to address this reality. What assumptions does it make? What makes compliance so appealing in organization management?

The purpose of this chapter is to explain the promises that the dominant discourse in the field of compliance offers. The goal is clear: to enable organizations to mitigate the risks of committing regulatory compliance crimes or their employees and decision-makers engaging in unethical behavior. This is an ambitious goal, and the promises constitute an equally optimistic commitment to the capacity of the organizational instruments available to achieve it.

This chapter begins with a brief to provide a detailed analysis of the background of compliance practice with a historical outline of the concept of compliance. It explains how and where what is currently recognized as compliance in the literature and professional practice emerged. Based on this historical overview, an attempt is made to explain the context in which the various components now recognized as part of the discourse and practice of compliance emerged.

This is followed by a detailed analysis of the distinctive elements of compliance, namely the characteristics that constitute its main arguments and proposals. This part attempts to answer at least two key questions: How is the concept of compliance currently understood, and what is its purpose? The central concepts of the compliance discourse are discussed through the answers to these two questions.

https://doi.org/10.1515/9783110749113-001

On these bases, the central promises of compliance are set forth and explained. By promises, we mean the assumptions made to formulate the instruments and action tactics of the compliance practice. Given that compliance did not emerge as a theory (or at least, only as a theory), but rather as an instrument and a management practice, it is important to analyze its underlying assumptions to understand its objectives and theoretical and practical limits.

Finally, in the last section of this chapter, the features of the compliance discourse that make it particularly appealing are explained. Compliance has been framed as a solution to practical problems concerning the lack of ethics in organizations and corporate crimes. This section reflects on the characteristics of its discourse that make it so popular and widespread in organization management.

1.2 How has Compliance Evolved?

Compliance is not a strictly new practice or instrument; its current programs result from lengthy historical evolution. Throughout the 20th and the 21st centuries, compliance has acquired its current characteristics. A concise understanding of its evolution will shed light on various aspects of what is currently known as compliance.

Below is a brief chronicle of the transformation this perspective of organizational change has undergone from its origins to the present. This historical overview is divided into decades. This division is arbitrary and is intended to explain the events that have marked its evolution in an orderly manner as a timeline.

However, it should be noted that the historical events highlighted here may not be the only ones in the evolution of compliance. However, an attempt has been made to highlight those that have undoubtedly had a more decisive effect on the current understanding of this professional practice.

1.2.1 1900s – The Origins

The origin of compliance can be traced to the early 20th century in the United States, with the creation of Public Safety Agencies. The start of these federal agencies is interesting. The first agencies were created during the Progressive Era, a period of widespread social activism and political reform in the United States from the 1890s to the 1920s. The main goals of the progressive movement were to eliminate problems caused by industrialization, urbanization, immigration, and political corruption.

In this context, in 1906, the American journalist and novelist Upton Sinclair published the novel *The Jungle* (1985), in which he described the harsh living conditions and exploitation of immigrants in the United States. However, readers were dismayed by the novel's revelation of unsanitary practices in the meat industry in the early 20th century. *The Jungle* became a bestseller and caused a huge international outcry.

As a result, President Theodore Roosevelt introduced the Pure Food and Drugs Act (Greeley, 1907), authorizing the federal government to inspect food companies and force manufacturers to detail the list of ingredients to ensure the quality of food produced for human consumption. This law also created the powers of what would soon become the US Food and Drug Administration (FDA).

Thereafter, various federal public security agencies emerged to enforce laws and regulations in various economic fields and industries. This is where the notion of compliance arose as the obligation to comply with regulations that affect company activities.

The compliance model that emerged at that time and remained in force for seven decades focused on the ability of government agencies to monitor and enforce the laws regulating the obligations of companies in various areas, such as finance, health, and work. It was an exogenous oversight model (for firms), constrained by the government, financial, and human resources available to exercise oversight. And it was not only limited by the resources, but also by the skills and objectives these government organizations were able to obtain to achieve their own goals.

This model has not really disappeared. On the contrary, it remains in force and can be observed every time a new public security agency is created or new powers or mandates are granted to existing agencies. In this respect, what could be called exogenous and strict regulatory compliance endures insofar as it implies the capacity of the state to impose regulations – rules, laws, norms – on individuals in the interaction of their businesses.

However, as will be seen below, this regulatory model has evolved to acquire distinctive new features.

1.2.2 1970s – The Transformation

The 1970s saw the transformation of the exogenous, strictly regulatory model of compliance. During this decade, there was a shift from a type of organizational action focused on the government's ability to oversee companies to one where the responsibility for compliance was transferred to them, from an exogenous logic to one that makes compliance an endogenous duty of organizations. Several events explain this change in the way compliance is understood, which created the bases for what is now the dominant paradigm in the activity today, predicated on a different, sophisticated, and ambitious organizational model.

In 1973, in the wake of the Watergate scandal, the Special Prosecutor's Office, in collaboration with the US Securities and Exchange Commission (SEC) and the Subcommittee on Multinational Corporations, directed by Senator Frank Church (The Church Committee), released a report (Church Committee, 1976) identifying various corporations and top managers of companies that funds from their companies to make illegal contributions to governments and political campaigns abroad. These illegal contributions and payments were primarily to obtain or retain contracts with foreign governments.

The evidence presented in this report was a cause of great concern for various reasons:

– The distortions US foreign policy might experience with countries with bribed governments
– Imbalances were created in market prices and the rates of return on companies' investment
– It could be perceived as a morally questionable matter by the American public due to the environment generated by Watergate

Henceforth, this report, known as the Report on Questionable and Illegal Corporate Payments and Practice (SEC Report; Stevenson, 1976), also denounced the discovery of the falsification and massaging of the accounting records of several companies, often to disguise or minimize irregular transactions and illegal payments in company accounts. This finding called into question the integrity and reliability of accounting records and corporations' financial information.

In other words, the risk of questioning the foundations of companies' accountability systems to comply with federal laws was highlighted. The concern of the SEC Report can be summarized as follows: a company that alters the integrity of its accounting books poses a danger to its shareholders – and to the market in general – by failing to report the true nature of its transactions in its financial statements.

This investigation and report were the origins of what years later, in 1977, became known as the US Foreign Corrupt Practices Act (FCPA) (US Department of Justice, 2017). The FCPA is a United States federal law prohibiting US citizens and entities from bribing foreign government officials to further their business interests.

The FCPA encompasses the transactions of these entities and companies undertaken anywhere in the world and extends to companies of any nationality registered in US stock markets, including all their personnel, shareholders, and agents, as well as subsidiary companies. Since the amendments of 1998, the Act has also applied to non-US citizens and companies who, directly or through intermediaries, help facilitate or make corrupt payments.

In addition, the FCPA requires that all companies listed on the US stock market, including their subsidiaries, comply with applicable accounting regulations to ensure accurate and transparent financial records and maintain internal accounting controls.

The US entities responsible for monitoring compliance with this federal law are the Department of Justice (DOJ) and the Securities and Exchange Commission (SEC). As will be seen later, the FCPA became one of the key compliance elements because of its profound global influence from the 1990s onward.

Before that, it is worth mentioning another event in the 1970s that marked a turning point in compliance history. In 1970, the famous litigation case between the United States and Hilton Hotels Corp took place, laying the foundations for the modern notion of corporate criminal liability. It established that corporations could be held liable for the criminal activities of their employees or representatives, even when they act against corporate policies or directive instructions, provided they act within the framework of their competencies and with the partial or total aim – of benefitting the corporation for which they work or represent (United States vs. Hilton Hotel Corp., 1972).

The concept of corporate criminal liability is extremely old. It comes from Roman law under the concept of Let the Master Answer (Respondeat Superior) and is used to designate the relations between a Superior (such as an employer) and an Agent (such as an employee). In this relationship, the Superior is responsible for what the Agent does on behalf of and/or for the benefit of the Superior. This notion of joint criminal liability would become particularly important decades later when the FCPA came under the scrutiny of the DOJ and SEC.

The notion of corporate criminal liability, together with laws such as the FCPA and the creation of new public safety agencies (such as the US Environmental Protection Agency, created in 1970, and the Drug Enforcement Administration (DEA), founded in 1973) (Environmental Protection Agency, n.d.; DEA; n.d.), led to a complete overhaul of compliance.

From that decade onward, the model moved toward a proactive view of compliance in which companies were obliged to adopt internal controls and policies that ensured they complied with the regulations to which they were subject and convincingly demonstrated consistent business practices, with applicable laws and regulations in their respective industries, to the regulatory agencies. A significant transition began toward a logic of endogenization of compliance: from merely a regulatory and oversight activity to gradually becoming a fundamental aspect of the organization's health.

In other words, compliance shifted from a purely regulatory measure to a model in which it is important to ensure the legal and ethical behavior of individuals who participate in an organization. Furthermore, to a certain extent, one that defined the organizational and management logic of any organization. Then, a profound reflection began here on the critical internalization of ethical elements through compliance rather than merely regarding it as an instrument to comply with regulations.

1.2.3 1980s – Consolidation

The 1980s saw the consolidation of compliance as it is known today, giving rise to some of its most distinctive features. The corporate scandal once again triggered the creation of new regulations and various corporate practices designed to strengthen the ethical behavior of corporations, directly involving company managers and employees.

In 1981, the Ronald Reagan administration set about increasing the size and capabilities of the US armed forces. This effort led to a significant rise in purchases by the US government. However, a major scandal erupted in 1985 when the Project on Government Oversight (POGO) released a report citing purchases made by the US Department of Defense with overpriced items, including $400 hammers, $600 toilet seats, and $7,000 coffee pots.

The scandal prompted the creation of the Blue-Ribbon Commission on Defense Management, better known as the Packard Commission because it was chaired by David Packard (co-founder with Bill Hewlett of the Hewlett-Packard electronics company). This commission was mandated to review the operation of various management processes in the Department of Defense and clarify the apparent irregularities of the over-pricing detected.

In 1986, the Packard Commission released the results of its investigation. Its conclusions stated that there was no rational system governing the purchasing process of the Department of Defense and that, although no evidence of abuse or fraud was found, the cost overrun problem was explained by the rigidity and complexity of government procurement. As a result, the Packard Commission made several recommendations such as urging defense sector contractors to improve the purchasing process by reinforcing self-regulation.

In response to the recommendations of the Packard Commission, in 1986, thirty-two defense industry contractors created the Defense Industry Initiative (DII). Since then, the DII has operated as a nongovernment organization with the mission of promoting a culture of ethical behavior in companies that supply the government with goods and services. This initiative is mainly due to promoting the creation, adoption, and implementation of codes of conduct in the corporate sphere.

In the 1980s, another step in the consolidation of compliance originated in the banking and financial industry with the regulations promoted in the area of money laundering. The term "money laundering" was coined in the 1920s to describe the American mafias' practice of using laundry networks to conceal the illicit origin of the money obtained from their criminal activities (Ehrenfeld, 1994). The mechanism involved in making the profits from illicit activities appears to come from the laundry business. Given that the only payment method was cash at the time, it was difficult to distinguish which money came from extortion, arms trafficking, alcohol, or prostitution and which was obtained from legal business.

The phenomenon of money laundering was already a severe problem in the 1970s due to the strategy employed by drug gangs. Proceeds from the sale of drugs were deposited in banks with no form of control. Once the money had been introduced into official financial systems, the money obtained from an illicit activity became legitimate, enabling it to move easily through the formal, legal, financial and productive circuit. In this context, the expression "money laundering" was first used in a legal context in the United States in 1982 to refer to money from the sale of Colombian cocaine (United States vs. $4,255,625.39, 551 F. Supp. 314, 1982).

In 1986, the United States made money laundering a federal crime through the enactment of the Money Laundering Control Act (Gurule, 1995), which, together with the Bank Secrecy Act (BSA), introduced a decade earlier, formed the legal framework for banks and financial institutions to cooperate with the US government to combat financial crime and ensure that they did not enable money laundering.

The organization charged with enforcing the BSA is the Financial Crimes Enforcement Network (FinCEN), which imposes various compliance obligations on financial institutions. To meet these obligations, senior management must ensure they have a detailed understanding of the legislation. To achieve BSA compliance, financial institutions must meet regulatory requirements that focus on 1) reporting and establishing links with the authorities; and 2) creating internal controls to prevent money laundering (US Treasury/FinCEN, n.d.).

The BSA requires financial institutions to each develop an Anti-Money Laundering (AML) program. According to the guidelines issued by FinCEN in 1987, an effective BSA-AML compliance program must be tailored to the unique needs of the financial institution it serves, including the risk profile it faces. The main elements of an AML compliance program, according to FinCEN, are as follows:
-   Internal systems and controls: an AML program must be built around written policies and procedures designed to help employees detect and monitor money laundering activities and financial crimes.
-   Compliance Officer: a lead employee must be appointed to oversee the development and implementation of their institution's program. In addition to overseeing internal controls, the Compliance Officer is responsible for organizing independent audits and reviews of their institutions' AML compliance programs.
-   BSA Training: Basic BSA-AML compliance training must be provided for all employees. Those with higher levels of responsibility may need advanced training or certification.
-   Independent Audits: a regular schedule of independent audits must be established to test the continued effectiveness of an AML program. Qualified third parties must perform audits (US Treasury/FinCEN, n.d.).

These guidelines soon began to resonate in the international arena. In 1989, the United States government, through the G8, promoted the creation of the International Financial Action Task Force (FATF). As an intergovernmental institution, the purpose of the FATF is to develop policies that help combat money laundering and terrorism financing. In fact, the FATF has played a key role in disseminating protocols and standardized understandings of compliance (FATF, 2012/2022).

Hence, the 1980s culminated in the underpinning of two key elements in the compliance discourse: on the one hand, the emphasis on codes of conduct and ethics in business (as visible aspects of self-regulation) and, on the other, the creation of the position of Compliance Officer.

Indeed, the anti-money laundering regulations created in this decade led to the understanding that compliance is a central, endogenous activity essential to any organization. It is undoubtedly always driven by exogenous elements: laws, regulations, punishments, and fines. But a project is underway to reshape it as a logical, functional activity of the administrative process of an organization, not as an external obligation to fulfill but as a vital internal need. Thus, the appearance of their own compliance structures and, in particular, the management position to oversee adherence to ethical and legal practices: the Compliance Officer. From the outset, this management position was designed to serve as a guarantor of regulatory compliance in money laundering matters and the ethical behavior of financial institutions. It is, therefore, the origin of what in subsequent decades would become one of the most important positions in the corporate world: one that embodies the aspiration of any corporate compliance program. One of the critical issues will be how much this desire to internalize and make compliance endogenous has managed to ensure its adaptation and adoption in organizations, in its flow, culture, meaning, and routines.

1.2.4 1990s – Institutionalization

In the last decade of the 20th century, compliance was institutionalized as general and universal guidelines for designing and implementing its programs. As a response to the rise in corporate scandals and the perceived inconsistency of criminal sentences handed down by American federal judges, in November 1991, the US Sentencing Commission published the first Federal Sentencing Guidelines for Organizations, better known as the US Sentencing Guidelines for Organizations – the Organizational Guidelines (Ferrell, LeClair, & Ferrell, 1998).

These Organizational Guidelines were designed to address two fundamental elements in corporate criminal sentencing: just punishment and deterrence (Ferrell, LeClair, & Ferrell, 1998). Whereas just punishment seeks to reflect the degree of guilt of the offender, deterrence is used as a mechanism to provide incentives for organizations to detect and prevent bad deeds or practices that can subsequently become crimes.

In this respect, it is important to note that Organizational Guidelines are tantamount to the institutionalization, by other means, of the concept of Respondeat Superior. Although the actions of an employee may contravene company policy, the company may be held legally responsible, despite its best efforts to prevent unethical behavior by its employees. Organizational guidelines were devised to address this institutional vulnerability, encourage corporations to foster good corporate citizenship and provide a means of rehabilitating corporations that have engaged in criminal conduct.

The Guidelines are, basically, an acknowledgment of the fact that the corporate codes of conduct drawn up in the 1980s did not, on their own suffice to reduce corporate crimes (much less to internalize the ethical values of compliance in organizations).

In this respect, Organizational Guidelines recognize that an effective compliance program is necessary to prevent and deter corporate criminal activity. The Guidelines establish the minimum criteria for a corporate program in the following terms:
- Establish rules and procedures to prevent and detect crimes
- Provide oversight by high-level management, usually the board of directors
- Exercise due care in delegating substantial discretionary authority
- Establish effective communication mechanisms and training programs for all employees on business ethics
- Monitor, audit and report any suspected irregularities and periodically evaluate the effectiveness of the compliance program
- Promote and consistently enforce the corporate compliance program by encouraging the use of established mechanisms and disciplining employees who commit crimes or fail to adopt the necessary measures to prevent or detect criminal behavior
- Take reasonable steps to respond to criminal behavior once it has been detected and prevent further criminal behavior (Ferrell, LeClair, & Ferrell, 1998; Fargason, 1993)

As can be seen, compliance has historically developed within this double gripper logic. There is a first legal and oversight and punishment objective that serves, for example, to establish standards that guide the analyses and sentences of federal judges and a secondary increasingly important objective, which outlines the catalog of specific elements that the organizational programs would have to create and incorporate.

In practice, beginning in the 1990s, these programs translated into a set of standardized measures, at least initially. These measures included the endorsement and commitment of senior management, the appointment of an officer responsible for running the program (Compliance Officer), risk assessment, the implementation of policies and procedures, an ethics training program, the alignment of internal financial controls, the launching of a due diligence program, the establishment of investigation protocols, the development of a sanctions policy and the institutionalization of regular audits to evaluate the effectiveness of the compliance program (Tarantino, 2008).

From the perspective of its effects, it is essential to note that the logic of the Organizational Guidelines emphasized that adopting compliance programs would make companies eligible for more lenient sentences or more detailed, fairer legal processes. This is both because of the possibility of better defining certain responsibilities in the event of failures or crimes and because of the promise that a formal, recognized organizational process will create a discourse and image that, over time, will be able to internalize practices and processes that are not only ethical but also organizationally intelligent and effective.

A salient aspect of Organizational Guidelines is that, for a compliance program to be rated effective, it not only has to establish standards and procedures to prevent and detect criminal conduct but also must promote an organizational culture of ethical behavior and compliance with the law. This emphasis on ethical culture is a critical element in understanding the context in which another of the founding events of compliance originated in the 1990s: the global anticorruption movement.

Why did this qualitative leap become so crucial in the early 1990s? It is important to understand the profound transformation of the international order that serves as a backdrop to this process. It can safely be said that the critical date was November 9, 1989, the day the Berlin Wall fell. This was also a fundamental event in the history of compliance because it marked the start of a new way of seeing and understanding the phenomenon of corruption globally. The end of the Cold War revolutionized the process of economic interdependence. In a matter of days, companies in the capitalist world had access to markets that until then had been impossible for them to penetrate with their goods and services.

However, the economic openness of Eastern Europe did not happen in an orderly manner. Access to new markets was hampered by the corruption of local oligarchies that prevented the establishment of market rules. This was a situation that triggered a significant transformation in the way corruption was understood and justified.

During the Cold War (1945–1989), the phenomenon of corruption was not a matter of global importance. On the contrary, in academic and political discussions, corruption was not addressed; if it was considered, it was basically referred to as a domestic issue (Sissenach, 2001). Furthermore, the international policy of Western powers adopted a double standard concerning corrupt regimes. To escape the influence of the former Soviet Union, capitalist countries justified the corrupt practices of governments in peripheral countries, sometimes even supporting and financing them.

With the end of communism, however, the issue of corruption became global. Corruption affected the possibilities of transaction, negotiation, and certainty of business on a global scale. The first to raise the alarm about this problem were corporations. This was largely because global companies began to suffer firsthand the ravages of corruption when they saw market prices distorted and slower rates of return on their investments in the new Eastern European markets (Hough, 2013; United Nations, 2005).

Corporate discontent was fanned by international organizations such as the World Bank and the Organization for Economic Cooperation and Development (OECD) and the emergence of a powerful nongovernmental organization, Transparency International, which has led the global anticorruption movement since its inception

In 1993, a group of former World Bank employees founded Transparency International, led by Peter Eigen. In 1995, as part of their communication strategy, they published the first edition of the Index of Perceptions of Corruption (IPC), which by ranking countries and measuring their degree of perception of corruption, managed to place the topic of corruption on the international agenda (Andersson & Anechoic, 2019).

Thus, in 1997, the World Bank published its first anti-corruption strategy in its World Development Report. In this document, the World Bank echoed the concerns of the corporate world and declared the need to support concrete measures against corrupt practices, both nationally and internationally.

That same year, the OECD published the "Convention on Combatting Bribery of Foreign Public Officials in International Business Transactions," whereby countries that join the Convention agree to criminalize the bribery of foreign public officials in their national legislation and implement effective policies to prevent, detect, investigate, and punish foreign bribery. The OECD Anti-Bribery Convention was, in effect, the internationalization of the FCPA, which gave rise to multiple anticorruption laws and regulations in the following decades.

In short, the anticorruption movement became global in the 1990s, promoting debates and studies that would also critically affect the development of compliance. In the discourse of the time, the fight against corruption was framed as a matter of public ethics and international interest to build more equitable societies. In practice, it had much more to do with the efforts of companies to create market competition.

However, the predominant discourse from that moment onward was ethics as a priority issue in government affairs and the private sphere of organizations. Bribing a public official to obtain a private benefit has become a reprehensible, criminal matter since the modifications of the legal frameworks of the signatory countries of the OECD Anti-Bribery Convention.

The anticorruption movement and the Organizational Guidelines are the basis for understanding two key characteristics of the current understanding of compliance: its emphasis on self-regulation and its insistence on ethical conduct. These two elements act as a powerful argument for insisting that corporations must have compliance programs that allow them to detect potential violations of laws, immediately inform the corresponding authorities when they are discovered, and undertake prompt and voluntary corrective efforts.

From that moment onward, compliance was poised to be exported worldwide. With the emergence of the "global village" and the interdependence of economies, compliance became internationalized and was adopted in various countries in Europe, Asia, and Latin America.

1.2.5 2000s – Globalization

The 1990s ended on an upbeat note. The end of communism and the rise of the global anti-corruption movement led to the assumption that a new type of world order based on ethical principles would crystallize. However, the corporate scandals of the first decade of the 21st century shattered those illusions.

The Enron (2001) and WorldCom (2002) corporate fraud cases marked the start of the escalation of corporate white-collar crime scandals. Enron and WorldCom were prosecuted for manipulating their financial statements and falsifying their balance sheets to inflate their income (McLean & Elkind, 2013).

The criminal trial that followed the discovery of Enron's corporate fraud, with the complicity of the Arthur Andersen external auditing firm, had profound collateral consequences. This scandal challenged the entire corporate accountability system by demonstrating that virtually every element of control and oversight had failed. From the regulator who was unable – or unwilling – to detect the fraud scheme being developed at the time to the company's top management, passing through the external auditor and the corporate culture, nothing worked.

Consequently, the Enron case led to a momentous change in the terms in which corporate crimes are addressed. From that moment onward, attention focused on the permanent attempt to reform and strengthen corporate cultures, emphasizing the strengthening of internal controls to prevent, detect and respond to potential illicit corporate acts.

The case of Enron was the moment when the discourse of compliance became radicalized. Since that event, it has been categorically stressed that its ultimate goal is deterring unethical conduct and cleaning up possibly illegal actions that may have been committed. As a result, since then, compliance programs have been considered a fundamental part of risk management and the supervision of internal controls.

In this respect, the 2004 amendment of the Organizational Guidelines reflected the need for boards of directors of companies to demonstrate knowledge of compliance programs as evidence of their effectiveness (US Sentencing Commission, 2004). This was a meaningful reform because it spelled out the responsibility of the top management of companies for managing the internal affairs of companies, particularly as regards the legality of their business.

The real change came in 2002 from a new regulation for the corporate world: the Sarbanes-Oxley Act (commonly known as SOX), named after its sponsors, Senator Paul Sarbanes, and Congressman Michael Oxley. Through this law, the United States Congress introduced corporate compliance measures which, according to its initial considerations, would make it possible to mitigate corporate crises, such as those experienced in the Enron and WorldCom cases.

SOX was designed to protect investors from fraudulent financial reporting by the companies they invest in. SOX makes it easier for company executives to be held accountable for fraudulent reporting, as it had previously been difficult to prosecute in the event of wrongdoing. SOX also set out detailed guidelines for the internal controls (SOX controls) and audit procedures a company must incorporate to establish effective cybersecurity practices (Tarantino, 2008).

SOX requires that CEOs and CFOs accept responsibility for the accuracy, documentation, and filing of all financial reports reported to the SEC. Management is therefore responsible for the internal control of the financial records of the company and any shortcomings that may exist in its accounting and financial information (Sarbanes, 2002).

Therefore, SOX requires corporations to develop, communicate, and enforce formal data security policies that ensure the integrity of financial data stored and used in financial statements (Sarbanes, 2002). SOX also demands annual audits and requires external auditors to certify that the internal controls of the company they are auditing are appropriate (Sarbanes, 2002). Finally, SOX also stipulates that the results of annual audits and the certification of the integrity and veracity of financial information by the senior management of companies must remain available to the general public (Sarbanes, 2002).

For the purpose of this overview of the evolution of compliance, it is important to note that SOX also includes a provision to protect people who report potential wrongdoing in publicly traded companies. This provision triggered another of the contemporary, distinctive elements: ethical hotlines. This SOX provision encourages internal investigative reporting of allegations of unethical or illegal conduct that should be reported to the SEC (Tarantino, 2008).

In the following years, SOX became internationalized. While SOX does not apply to companies operating outside the United States, it strongly influenced the regulations put in place by other countries to promote diversity in the marketplace and foster investor confidence. In response to the US regulation, the European Union, for example, has established its own set of legal auditing requirements for companies operating within its borders (Tarantino, 2008).

Like SOX, the rules established by the European Union limit the nonaudit services an auditor can provide to companies. This, it is thought, strengthens the independence of auditors, and enables them to enhance investor confidence.

Realizing the value of regulations like SOX, countries around the world are adopting regulations inspired by their US counterpart. These regulations hold companies accountable for their financial reporting so that investors can feel safe and trust the companies in which they have invested money. Thus, SOX strongly contributed to the globalization of compliance, associating this concept with transparency and accountability in the corporate world.

Another key element was introduced into the discourse with SOX rules: the notion of compliance risk. This type of risk has been recognized as a distinct class of risk that requires dedicated resources, program design, and oversight by senior management (Ethics Resource Center, 2007).

In the world of organizations, the concept of risk is not new. But it was in the context of globalization that the concept of compliance risk acquired the status of a key element. It is not possible to pinpoint where and when it began to be used, but large consulting firms (such as Kroll, Control Risk, KPMG, EY, Deloitte, and PwC) were probably responsible for disseminating it and positioning it as a hinge concept between the duty of compliance and internal control (Slager, 2017).

By incorporating the concept of reputational risk into the discourse of compliance, some of the basic premises of risk management, so common in the business consulting industry, were adopted. These premises can be summarized as follows:

reputational risk events can erode the expected cash flows of a company, either due to the loss of customers or business partners, thus increasing the rate of return on business investment (Perry & de Fultonville, 2005). Given this possibility, compliance risk management can mitigate the effects of these events, either by eliminating inappropriate business practices or by improving the company's external reputation with customers, business partners, and, above all, regulators.

In 2005, the Basel Committee on Banking Supervision defined compliance risk as "the risk of legal or regulatory sanctions, material economic loss, or loss of reputation a bank may suffer as a result of a breach of laws, regulations, rules, standards, of self-regulation and codes of conduct applicable to its banking activities."

Accordingly, since 2005, global banking regulators have held that financial organizations must design effective compliance risk management programs with a risk-based approach, which incorporates controls designed to maintain compliance with regulations and standards assessed by the risk (Basel Committee on Banking Supervision, 2005).

However, the events of 2008 revealed the complexity and challenges of risk management in a globalized world. The fall of Bear Stearns and Lehman Brothers demonstrated the extent to which external risk events can create a loss of confidence of such magnitude that it results in permanent reputational damage and a collapse in the value of companies and even of an entire market system (Williams, 2010). The 2008 crisis can indeed be considered the first global crisis directly associated with the concept of compliance.

The fall of Bear Stearns and the Lehman Brothers, and the Ponzi fraud schemes uncovered in late 2008 involving Bernard Madoff and Allen Stanford, taught the world two important lessons. First, no matter how much regulation is in place or progress has been made in implementing compliance programs, the risk of deception and fraud will always be present. Second, disclosing fraudulent activities or improper business practices can permanently damage a company's reputation, alienating customers, shareholders, and strategic partners (Williams, 2010).

In this respect, the crises at the beginning of the 21st century accelerated the perspective that was dealing with corporate scandals entailed meeting the more profound challenge of establishing a global but profoundly organizational logic (and therefore a micrologic at the level of each organization) of compliance that went beyond surveillance and punishment.

1.2.6 2010s – The Scandal

In 2010, as a response to the financial crisis triggered by the bankruptcy of Bear Stearns and the Lehman Brothers, the Dodd-Frank Wall Street Reform and the Consumer Protection Act (better known as "Dodd-Frank") was enacted. The main objective of this Act was to protect the US economy from financial collapses, such as the one experienced in 2008.

Dodd-Frank is a regulation that goes beyond the SOX because it establishes significant amendments to the model of accountability and transparency in corporate accounting. In addition, it implemented improvements in corporate governance, such as establishing guidelines to regulate executive salary compensation and bonuses.

However, the aspect of Dodd-Frank that has had the most implications concerns the extension of protection for whistleblowers. These were initially created with SOX, but due to the Dodd-Frank Act, a system of "rewards" was created for potential corporate crime whistleblowers. Based on this law, the US Security Exchange Commission (SEC) and Department of Justice (DOJ) were empowered to financially reward whistleblowers who voluntarily report original and helpful information to prosecute and criminalize possible criminal acts within the corporations listed on the stock market. A whistleblower is therefore eligible to receive a reward of between 10% and 30% of the fine collected. This provision encourages whistleblowers to report possible illegal acts or fraudulent practices within companies directly to the SEC.

From a historical perspective, a strong link can be observed between SOX and Dodd-Frank, perhaps the two most important regulations in the 21st century, created in the wake of corporate scandals. The whistleblower provisions established by Dodd-Frank and the set of internal controls established by SOX shifted attention to the internal workings of an organization as essential to mitigating unethical behavior and noncompliance with regulations. Accordingly, the corporate prosecution strategy of the DOJ and the SEC shifted from punishing corporate conduct to reforming corporate cultures that can easily lead to truly corrupt organizational cultures or normalize corruption.

This is the context in which two key elements were incorporated to understand the current compliance model: corporate monitors and self-disclosure of noncompliance or potentially illegal situations (Eng & Mak, 2003).

For the DOJ, one way to assess a corporation from within is through an external corporate monitor. Typically, the external corporate monitor is a law or auditing firm that independently performs its monitoring duties, reporting its findings directly to the DOJ or SEC.

The first time the DOJ used an external corporate monitor was in 2008, in the case of the German company Siemens, which was found guilty of violating the FCPA. The DOJ and SEC use corporate monitors as part of a company's plea deals, especially when they believe its compliance system is not adequately developed or mature. In this respect, a corporate monitor is responsible for monitoring a corporation's compliance program to ensure the DOJ or SEC that the company in question has eradicated the bad practices that elicited the plea agreement.

The 2010s were also a period when several initiatives were launched to reinforce self-regulation in the corporate world. In the United States, regulatory agencies have created policies to encourage self-disclosure of violations of regulations and standards. The bases for self-disclosure require companies to have an "effective" compliance program, in other words, one that complies with the Organizational Guidelines and best industry practices. Thus, when a company finds it has engaged in any type of illegal action or noncompliance, it is expected to inform the regulatory entity of the finding and collaborate in the investigation, and the sanction imposed.

In practice, self-disclosure programs have meant a sharp increase in internal company investigations since it is always more beneficial to adhere to self-disclosure protocols than to conceal the crimes committed (Wiggin, 2002).

In this context, it is unsurprising that several guides were designed to help organizations implement these programs during this decade. In 2010, for example, the OECD published a good practice guide for establishing and ensuring the effectiveness of compliance programs and internal controls to detect and prevent bribery payments in international business transactions (OECD, 2010). The guide is, in fact, similar to the US Organizational Guidelines and "acknowledges that to be effective, such programs or measures must be interconnected with a company's overall compliance framework."

In 2012, the DOJ and the SEC issued joint guidance that clarified that prosecutors would seek to determine whether companies under investigation for alleged wrongdoing had a compliance program and whether there was a commitment on the part of the company to make effective use of this program.

The DOJ expanded this guidance in its FCPA Corporate Enforcement Policy. In that document, the DOJ states that reliably demonstrating the effectiveness of a company's compliance program can help change the structure of a resolution, moving it from a criminal charge to a deferred prosecution agreement, and reduce compliance obligations such as having to hire an external monitor.

In this respect, if a company accused of violating the FCPA can demonstrate that the violation occurred despite an effective program, possible sanctions could be significantly reduced. Needless to say, these guidelines apply to all corporate criminal conduct, not just FCPA violations.

Despite these compliance guidelines and the change in the corporate prosecution strategy of the DOJ and the SEC, the second decade of the 21st century will be remembered as one in which there have been more investigations for FCPA violations (Epstein, 2020).

The increase in the number of investigations can largely be explained by the combined effect of Dodd-Frank and the incentives that companies must make self-disclosures of acts of corruption. However, it is also important to note that during this decade, many countries enacted their anticorruption laws, which largely fostered collaboration between government agencies in various countries, partly contributing to the number of investigative actions and sanctions for corruption issues.

In this aspect, three anti-corruption laws deserve special mention because they emulate and surpass the FCPA, at least regarding its scope and sanctioning resources. These laws are the UK Bribery Act, Brazil's Anti-Corruption Law, and France's SAPIN II.

These three laws are a clear example of the process of globalization of compliance that began in the first decade of the 21st century and has increased their scope by facilitating cooperation between investigative agencies, as borne out by the highly publicized case of the Brazilian construction company, Odebrecht, in 2016, which enabled the prosecution of corrupt public servants and politicians in eight different countries. It is also important to note that the 2010s were the period when most fines were levied for corruption cases (Epstein, 2020).

As can be seen, in the second decade of the 21st century, the fines collected for violations of the FCPA exceeded one billion dollars. In addition to the number of company executives and individuals sentenced to prison terms for FCPA violations, this list of fines highlights what may be one of the last distinguishing elements: the punishment of compliance, or rather, the punishment for noncompliance.

Sanctions for regulatory noncompliance or criminal conduct are obviously extremely old elements in compliance. Since their inception in 1906, sanctions (in the form of fines or corporal punishment) have existed as a consequence of noncompliance. Nevertheless, what distinguishes the current era is the magnitude of the punishment.

Punishment has gone from being a matter of minor or small-time sanctions to events that can eventually call into question the viability of organizations found guilty of corporate crime. Fines that exceed the barrier of one billion dollars and prison sentences totaling 24 years or more speak of an issue that cannot be ignored.

From this perspective, compliance has become a matter of growing interest and corporate concern. It can be said that companies' significant impact is confirmed not only in the production of goods and services and the generation of employment but also in the political and economic destabilization that possible improper behaviors can generate. Compliance, therefore, becomes a matter of public and political interest. Crimes committed by companies or on their behalf always have a negative effect, which goes beyond the organization's borders. Society can be deeply affected by practices and routines that normalize corruption and fraud.

For example, when the Bear Stearns and Lehman Brothers banks went bankrupt due to the lack of ethics and inexperience in managing market risks, it dragged much of the world's population into an unprecedented economic recession. In this respect, it is hardly surprising that from now onward, compliance will be a key issue for understanding and debating corporate scandals and their repercussions. In other words, it is as important as a mechanism for understanding the dynamics of improper acts and their normalization as it is for the effectiveness of the instruments to prevent and deal with them. These two different organizational dynamics with repercussions, instruments and organizational techniques are sometimes not only different but also contradictory. Indeed, as discussed in the next chapter, organizational behavior, both proper and improper, is often the result of an intricate interaction process between people, groups, rules, and devices that crystallize order and organizational stability. This topic will be covered in detail in the next chapter. For the time being, it is important to identify the goal of contemporary compliance in producing effects in both logics: punishment and prevention.

This leads us to highlight one last important aspect from the 2010s regarding the evolution of compliance: the emergence of scandal as a trigger for preventive actions, but also investigations of cases of corruption, corporate fraud, and, in general, any corporate crime.

Indeed, the emergence of social networks such as Facebook, YouTube, Instagram, WhatsApp, Twitter, and Snapchat marked the start of a period of maximum publicity for the internal affairs of companies. The speed with which information is conveyed exceeds any ability to control or anticipate media crises. Moreover, in this respect, the compliance discourse has also been affected in multiple ways. For example, in the era of social networks, company compliance is constantly challenged by the reputational effect that information disclosed about them may have, mainly if it is related to a corrupt or improper practice.

Social networks already act as exogenous elements of organizational oversight. Government agencies responsible for enforcing laws and regulations have been greatly strengthened by this type of social control because news divulged on social networks can trigger internal investigation mechanisms and self-disclosure to an unprecedented degree.

1.2.7 2020s – Disruption

Compliance is therefore acquiring a distinctive feature thanks to two innovative elements: the use of data analysis and Big Data that has streamlined the way internal control is exercised to ensure the ethical behavior of employees and company decision-makers (van den Broek & van Veenstra, 2018). The second element is expanding the agenda of wrongdoing and the scope of ethical behavior beyond fraud and corruption.

Indeed, corporations are increasingly turning to internal data to oversee employees and increase the effectiveness of compliance programs. Data analytics is helping compliance officers identify patterns of unethical behavior or potential crimes (such as fraud or bribery) more effectively and subtly.

This enables better compliance risk management and a faster response to emerging compliance issues. In this regard, the compliance discourse has been fostered by the effectiveness of its programs and structures in various countries and organizations. However, data mining techniques require robust, reliable data management systems to be helpful. Furthermore, on this point, the evolution has not been homogeneous. Since not all organizations have the same level of technological advancement, the descriptive and predictive capabilities of compliance data analysis still have a way to go. However, significant progress has been made incorporating sophisticated new software.

At the same time, this new decade marks the beginning of an approach that considers not only traditional aspects of compliance programs but also aspects not previously associated with its agenda. These include sexual harassment in companies and aspects of responsibility and social welfare.

In this respect, it seems we are witnessing the start of a new cycle in the evolution of compliance. It has moved from a model focusing on punitive aspects to one centered on corporate culture and is now moving toward one whose focus is the social dimension, or so it would seem.

This latter approach requires corporations to go beyond the letter of the laws or regulations to which they are subject or actions within corporate policy and to view compliance as a benefit to society.

At this point, all that remains is to wait. The history of compliance has yet to be written, and the possibilities of its evolution are diverse. However, it is clear that various characteristics and elements have been incorporated that distinguish the current concept of compliance throughout its evolution. It is a complex, sometimes diffuse concept yet one that is crucial in the organizational world. Seen from any angle, compliance influences how business is done and changes how organizations interact with each other and their broader social contexts. The topics addressed in the next section are understanding why this is so and what it seeks.

1.3 How is Compliance Understood Today? What is its Goal?

The major corporate fraud scandals of the first decade of the 21st century and the corresponding risks of millions in fines have made compliance much more than a passing managerial fad. The cost of misconduct is so great for companies, shareholders, and the general public that organizations are now obliged to find ways to forestall crimes.

Its purpose, as discussed earlier, is to solve two management problems that are particularly important from the perspective of the adverse effects they can have on an organization. These two problems can be summarized as follows:

1. The problem of regulatory noncompliance results in economic damage in the form of fines or sanctions.
2. The problem of unethical behavior that harms the reputation of the organization and therefore causes economic losses or tarnishes the corporate image, as well as asset damage due to the misappropriation of assets or any other type of fraud committed under any scheme of deception.

In this respect, compliance is associated with two aspects. One emphasizes regulatory compliance. In other words, it is designed to serve as a management tool for ensuring that the organization complies with the laws or regulations it must obey. The other focuses on ethical behavior as a management tool to ensure that members of organizations behave ethically by adhering to the values and principles of the organization (Silverman, 2008).

These two aspects can be explained by the evolution described in previous sections. In other words, they respond to the managerial problems compliance has attempted to solve by providing practical solutions. The two aspects are interconnected, making them difficult to distinguish. In any case, what is important to highlight at this stage is that compliance currently governs two spheres: regulations and ethical behavior.

In this dual sense, it has been imposed as a management tool loosely defined as a set of supervision and control policies and procedures designed to ensure that organizations comply with regulations and that they ensure ethical behavior on the part of their participants.

In the regulatory dimension, compliance usually has a less unequivocal definition because, in principle, it involves the establishment of internal controls and procedures that ensure compliance with formal regulations that are exogenous to the organization and linked to the legal framework regulating the organization.

However, as will be seen later, this dimension is often misleading. Organizational evolution can bend compliance. Indeed, through normalized organizational routines, regulatory noncompliance can subsist – and even coexist – with close monitoring and supervision. This issue will be addressed in detail in Chapter 2 of this book, where the perils of compliance are analyzed and discussed.

In the ethical dimension, compliance is associated with the establishment of internal controls that encourage individuals to behave and make decisions following the values of the organization.

In this other dimension, it is essential to reflect on the following. According to organizational behavior theories (Simon, 1947; March & Simon, 1958; Cyert & March, 1963), we know that every organization can be described as a network of decisions. It is understood that decisions are continuously made in every organization. Decisions, therefore, become the focal point for understanding organizational dynamics in their everyday lives. In simplified terms, we can speak of two types of decision-making processes: programmed decisions and nonprogrammed decisions (Simon, 1947).

Programmed decisions refer to those made within the framework of previously established procedures. Conversely, nonprogrammed decisions refer to those that occur outside preexisting procedures, resulting in decision-making based on an evaluative framework that constrains and constitutes the decision-making act.

In this respect, when individuals make decisions, they do so based on the decision-making premises of their evaluative framework, which enables the individual not only to define what is possible but also what is desirable from the perspective of meeting their personal and group goals.

Therefore, influencing the evaluative framework of individuals becomes a key aspect in the control of organizations. The argument is simple: if it is possible to influence the evaluative framework of the individuals who participate in an organization, there is a greater likelihood that their decisions will be made under the set of values and principles that the organization defines and wishes to institutionalize.

In this respect, it is important to understand that as a management tool, compliance is mainly interested in nonprogrammed decisions because they are precisely the type of decisions that, since they lack a normative prescription, are made based on evaluative frameworks.

The ethical dimension of compliance can therefore be explained as an interest in shaping the evaluative framework of members of the organization to ensure that their behavior adheres to certain standards of ethical behavior preestablished in codes of conduct and organizational policies.

These reflections enable us to contextualize the set of distinctive elements of compliance that have been incorporated into its discourse throughout its evolution. The point is to show that compliance is a professional practice that is constantly evolving and has incorporated various recommended solutions to the management problems on which it has been focusing. Nonetheless, what are these distinctive elements? What characterizes the twofold dimension of compliance today?

Based on the historical account presented in the previous section, it is possible to identify at least sixteen distinctive features of compliance. The distinction is arbitrary and undoubtedly limited. However, these sixteen features are those which, in our view, are the most important ones for understanding the assumptions on which compliance is based to propose solutions to the problem of regulatory noncompliance and unethical behavior.

These distinctive elements were incorporated into the compliance discourse at different moments. This means that each contribution seeks to address the specific problems people have attempted to fix, overlapping and not necessarily solving the problems they sought to address. This has given rise to a complex conceptual framework of different managerial contributions that interconnect and influence each other.

In addition, each of these distinctive elements focuses particularly on one of the two dimensions to which the compliance discourse responds. Some elements were incorporated to solve regulatory compliance problems and others to address ethical behavior problems, and some even have effects on both dimensions.

As shown in Table 1.1, there are relevant changes in the distinctive elements of compliance or what can currently be understood through decades. Each element was incorporated into the discourse based on the timeline presented in the previous section, and it also states the type of problem its contribution is targeting.

Table 1.1: Distinctive elements of compliance by decade.

No.	Key elements of the compliance discourse	Period of time of its incorporation	Dimension of compliance it focuses on
1	Regulations	1900s	Regulatory
2	Government agencies	1900s	Regulatory
3	Respondeat Superior	1970s	Regulatory
4	Self-regulation	1980s	Ethics
5	Ethics codes	1980s	Ethics
6	Compliance officer	1980s	Ethics / Regulatory
7	Compliance programs	1990s	Ethics
8	Corporate culture	2000s	Ethics
9	Internal controls	2000s	Ethics / Regulatory
10	Ethical hotlines	2000s	Ethics
11	Compliance/ reputational risk	2000s	Ethics / Regulatory
12	Reward system	2010s	Ethics
13	Corporate oversight	2010s	Ethics / Regulatory
14	Self-disclosure	2010s	Ethics / Regulatory
15	Compliance guides	2010s	Ethics / Regulatory
16	Compliance punishments	2010s	Ethics / Regulatory

The first management problem compliance attempted to solve was regulatory compliance. This problem is associated with the *regulations* by which each organization must abide. In the early 20th century, the matter was framed in the form of rules and regulations which the authorities – in this case, the US government – mandated for specific industries to ensure minimum hygiene and food quality standards. That was the origin. Nowadays, the regulatory frameworks any type of organization must adhere to are complex.

Over time, compliance has incorporated various issues into its sphere of action. Today, it encompasses aspects ranging from money laundering and corruption to sexual harassment and personal data protection. In this respect, virtually every aspect implying some type of regulation for organizations can fit into the realm of compliance.

Compliance is the act of obeying. The etymology of the term "compliance" goes back to the Latin verb "*Complere*," which is also the origin of the English word "complete." In a legal context, this means obeying legal orders and abiding by the rule of law.

At the organizational level, the rule of law is applied to corporate governance to enhance business, reduce risks and increase market confidence. For example, corporations that engage in improper waste disposal, mislead consumers or ignore labor laws are subject to regulatory and market retaliation. In other words, without legal compliance, organizations cannot earn the trust of the market in which they operate. There is an inherent incentive for organizations to comply with the law. However, in any society, there are cases where organizations break the law for several reasons. At this point, compliance intervenes as the management "solution" to ensure regulatory compliance.

Effective regulation is usually associated with a *government agency* charged with monitoring and ensuring that the regulation is followed. In this respect, compliance materializes the need for the observance of regulations through the specific regulators to which they must be accountable. For example, in the case of the FCPA, the regulator is the DOJ and the SEC. Each organization responds to different rules and regulators, depending on many variables such as industry, jurisdiction, and origin. In any case, the vital thing to highlight at this stage is that these two distinctive elements, regulation, and government agencies, were perhaps the first elements incorporated into the compliance discourse because they were primarily the triggers for its creation.

Another key element in the discourse is *respondeat superior*, simply the criminal liability of organizations for the acts their members commit on their behalf or for their benefit. This element is the origin of the ethical dimension of compliance, the second management problem attempting to be solved. When organizations are considered jointly responsible for their employees and decision-makers, the management problem emerges of how to ensure that individuals make decisions following the principles and values of the organization.

In response to this problem, *self-regulation* is presented as a possible solution to the ethical dilemmas faced by the members of organizations. From this perspective, self-regulation is related to the idea that individual can constrain their behavior insofar as they internalize certain decision premises that shape their actions. In this respect, compliance includes self-regulation as part of its distinctive elements with two aims: on the one hand, to project a message of self-control toward the regulator to which it is accountable and to the market; and, on the other, to influence the evaluative framework of the members of the organization.

In this way, self-regulation is strongly associated with the emergence of *codes of ethics* because they are an explicit declaration of the values and principles the organization hopes its participants will commit and use to guide their behavior. Thus, although self-regulation is the strategic aspect, the code of ethics is the tactical aspect whereby compliance proposes to solve the problem of the possible ethical deviation of the individual.

Nevertheless, no value framework will be guaranteed if no one is directly responsible for monitoring and punishing possible behavioral deviations or noncompliance with regulations. This is where the *compliance officer* is indispensable in the compliance discourse. In practice, compliance officers play a twofold role: in the regulatory sphere, they are responsible for accountability, and in management, they are responsible for designing, implementing, and maintaining the compliance management system.

In the discourse, the compliance management system materializes in a specific program that describes all the attributes an organization must have to achieve the objectives of the compliance model. In practice, the program becomes the "navigational chart" of the compliance officer since the document justifies their raison d'être and defines much of their work as the person responsible for compliance.

Compliance officers often come from areas other than organization management. At the outset, compliance officers were corporate lawyers. Nowadays, compliance officers come from various sources such as human resources, security, operations, audit, and risks. This diversity of profiles entailed a practical problem: a lack of knowledge of designing a management model and implementing and guaranteeing it. Thus, to facilitate these tasks, *guides* emerged, which generally offer recommendations to organizations on how to set up their compliance systems. One of the consequences of these guidelines is the effect of the mimicry of organizations. Compliance management models are more similar than different, mainly due to the guidelines that have been conceived and designed to shape them.

It should be remembered that the guidelines arose as recommendations made by certain regulators (such as the DOJ and SEC), stipulating the minimum standards for a compliance program to be effective, so that when faced with the possibility of a sanction, organizations can defend themselves by alleging that the illicit or unethical conduct occurred despite the *internal controls* in place to prevent and detect compliance problems. In this respect, the discourse offers a set of internal controls designed as a solution to the problems of regulatory compliance and unethical conduct.

The repertoire of internal controls suggested in the compliance discourse is extensive. They typically include due diligence of employees, customers, and suppliers, proactive data analysis, surprise audits, and *ethics hotlines*. This last control is particularly important in the compliance discourse. First, it is a control mechanism that receives great attention in key laws in the narrative (SOX and Dodd-Frank). Secondly, empirical evidence shows that most compliance events are detected through complaints, particularly complaints made by the employees themselves (World Economic Forum, 2022; ACFE, 2021).

Moreover, ethical hotlines are a fundamental element of the *reward systems* proposed as complementary mechanisms to force organizations to self-monitor and encourage permanent oversight by employees and external parties who may become aware of situations that can be reported to the regulators. Thanks to the reward systems, a growing number of cases of FCPA violations (134 cases through 2021) have been detected through reports obtained from the DOJ and SEC reward protocols.

Another distinctive element characterizing compliance is its insistence on *corporate culture* and the efforts that must be made within organizations to reinforce the control environment. From the logic of the discourse, there is a powerful link between, on the one hand, corporate crime and lack of regulatory compliance and, on the other, corrupt corporate cultures that encourage and allow misconduct. This is a critical point in the compliance discourse because it is an attempt to explain that problems can be solved to the extent that the corporate culture is reformed, understanding corporate culture as the sum of individual behaviors (Treviño, Weaver, Gibson, & Toffler, 1999).

For the compliance discourse, corporate culture reform necessarily entails guaranteeing the organization's routines and processes through direct, independent oversight mechanisms. In this respect, another critical component of the compliance discourse is the notion of *corporate monitoring*. This is a well-known tool borrowed from the world of auditing, which attempts to ensure that decisions within the organization adhere to established policies and procedures.

Although corporate monitoring is conceived as a mechanism for ensuring efforts to reform corporate culture to transition from a corrupt to ethical culture, the ultimate test of that transition is *self-disclosure*. This would be the minimum action expected from an organization with an effective program. Given the possibility of regulatory noncompliance or ethical behavior, compliance encourages disclosure and cooperation with the regulator to resolve issues before they are detected by other means. The notion of self-control is established and reinforced in panoptic surveillance, whereby the organization serves as its own security guard.

Within this set of distinctive elements, the notion of *compliance or reputational risk* plays a vital role. The risk condition is used as a type of permanent threat, from which it is impossible to free oneself completely. Yet, it can be managed through internal controls that promote an ethical corporate culture based on self-regulation and self-monitoring.

Lastly, the other distinctive element of compliance comprises sanctions or *punishments*. If an organization fails to prevent or detect corporate wrongdoing or unethical conduct among its participants, there is a stark warning: there will be consequences. In this regard, it should be said that over the past four decades, the money obtained from legal proceedings for FCPA violations has surpassed $16.2 billion. Of this amount, the DOJ has accounted for over $9.4 billion and the SEC more than $7.2 billion. These numbers undoubtedly reinforce the compliance penalty argument because organizations can face tangible consequences.

From this point of view, these sixteen elements are a good summary of the core of the compliance discourse. Each of them is used to present various explanatory arguments and allegedly effective solutions to address the management problems in which they are interested. The contemporary compliance scheme can therefore be understood as the result of the combination of management practices used to address specific problems of organizations in terms of regulatory compliance and ethical behavior.

Discourse not only refers to rhetorical aspects. The discourse category can also be understood as the construction of shared understandings based on experiences, analyses, reports, training, and, in general, the interactions that exist in a professional field to address the problems with which compliance is concerned. Knowledge and understanding of organizations are enabled and limited by invisible power relationships embedded in how people act and interpret. In this respect, the compliance discourse is offered as an integrating conceptual category for analyzing the main components and arguments promoted by what is currently understood as compliance.

Given this inventory of distinctive elements, it is important to ask what the promises of compliance are, in other words, what it aspires to as professional practice. It is understood that it is intended to solve regulatory compliance problems and ethical behavior. However, on what assumptions does it base its recommendations? What understandings does compliance assume a priori to respond to the management problems it attempts to solve? From this point of view, these questions are essential because they enable us to adopt a critical view of the discourse.

Given that compliance has become a powerful management tool, influencing how people do business and the interactions of organizations with society and the individuals who participate in them, it seems necessary to advance a critical analysis of its postulates. This will make it possible to anticipate the unwanted consequences of compliance (which there are many) and prevent some of its limits. These assumptions are discussed in the next section.

1.4 What are the Promises of Compliance?

Compliance has been framed as a management tool defined, in general terms, as a set of control and oversight policies and procedures designed to ensure that organizations comply with the regulations they are supposed to adhere to, and which also ensure ethical behavior on the part of their members. In this respect, compliance is framed as a set of promises to protect organizations from misconduct and sanctions for regulatory misconduct.

These promises are based on an a priori understanding of the organizational phenomenon and its internal dynamics. This understanding can be summarized in five assumptions that tend to be taken for granted. The five assumptions that can be debated and dominate compliance discourse are presented and discussed:

1. *Establishing a compliance program reduces the risk that organizations will commit crimes or fail to comply with their regulatory obligations.*
This first promise is the most important one in the discourse, and this promise forms the basis for all the other explanations and solutions proposed. In other words, this promise is the leitmotif of the compliance discourse because it is often repeated in documents, studies, programs, and regulations.

The argument put forward is simple: given the management problems entailed by regulatory noncompliance and unethical behavior, it is necessary to have a program that establishes the necessary internal controls to ensure that the organization's processes and decision-making are implemented within the framework of an established order. It seeks to mitigate compliance risks, and if they occur, they can be detected in time to respond accordingly.

In this light, the promise has two critical aspects that must be discussed. On the one hand, there is the concept of a "compliance program." What does this refer to? As mentioned earlier, these programs usually become official documents that define an organization's internal controls and are the responsibility of a compliance officer charged with overseeing their adoption (Tarantino, 2008).

A typical compliance program includes the key elements mentioned by the US Government Organizational Guidelines. However, the Guidelines deliberately avoided addressing the implementation challenges of these programs. The idea was probably to give organizations the flexibility to tailor their programs to their needs and industry. This is a good point in principle. In practice, it can entail significant design and management problems, as will be discussed in the next chapter, when the perils of compliance are explored.

The other important concept in this promise to discuss is the concept of "risk mitigation." Mitigation implies reducing the criticality of the risk condition. Is this possible? The answer given by the compliance discourse is affirmative. However, it is a response determined by how risk is defined and how its risk condition is evaluated or measured. Moreover, in this respect, there does not seem to be a single criterion or methodology for measuring risks, which also poses danger for implementing compliance.

This promise assumes that the organization is aware of the compliance risks to which it is exposed, and, thus, the program adopted will be able to define the necessary controls clearly. Furthermore, the promise is based on the idea that the controls established will suffice to control the behavior of members of the organization and the decision-making processes.

This promise is based on a rationalist view of the organization, in other words, on a conception that the organization is fully aware of its risks and that the measures adopted will be mechanically implemented and executed. From this perspective, there are no scenarios of conflicts in the organization due to conflicting objectives or scarce resources. Furthermore, it would appear that organizations will be in no doubt about the kind of problems they face or how to tackle them. The question is: do organizations work like this?

2. Compliance programs can be managed in a planned manner.
The second promise can be interpreted as an extension of the first. This promise argues that compliance programs can be designed and implemented as if they were a planned, virtually instrumental, or linear project.

This means that programs follow a preestablished path of action. In general, this route can be described as follows:

i. The compliance risks to which the organization is exposed are identified and measured
ii. Existing internal controls are evaluated to determine their degree of maturity
iii. Controls or improvements are designed to mitigate the risks identified

iv. A control implementation plan is designed

v. Residual risk is evaluated, and corrective actions defined

vi. Controls are implemented

vii. Results are evaluated to recalibrate risk analysis

This promise is based on an idea deeply rooted in administrative thinking that any problem can be managed based on action plans arranged in means-ends chains. Hence, the compliance program becomes an implementation roadmap, which happens – according to the discourse – in a coordinated manner with the different areas that participate in risk identification, control evaluation, and establishment of policies, controls, and codes of ethics (Silverman, 2008).

This promise is therefore based on the assumption that there will be cooperation in the organization regarding the program. In other words, the organizational actors will come together in a coordinated way to set priorities and assign resources. This promise raises the question of whether this happens in organizations and whether it is a realistic promise.

3. *Compliance programs are justified; in other words, they are of obvious benefit to the entire organization.*

The third promise is that compliance programs do not cause conflict within organizations because the benefit obtained from having oversight and surveillance mechanisms is readily acknowledged. The corollary of this promise is that the resources (human and financial) available to promote the compliance model will be sufficient, and the political and human costs involved in its implementation and operation will be offset by the benefits the organization will obtain from having a specific program that all members of the organization willingly accept.

The argument is that the organization is a cohesive entity with no differences of opinion or competition for scarce resources. Compliance programs have an intrinsic value that helps the organization adopt the programs voluntarily, without conflict or negotiation.

At the center of this promise is the notion of "tone at the top" as a fundamental element for the organization to move cohesively toward establishing policies and controls prescribed by compliance. The concept of "tone at the top" is a term that originated in the field of accounting and is used to describe the ethical climate of an organization promoted – through leadership – by the highest governing bodies of the organization.

The compliance discourse often assumes that the tone at the top permeates the entire organization. Therefore, it is assumed that there is a consensus around the figure of the organization's leader. When this leader calls for the establishment of a program, this happens voluntarily. In this discourse, the tone at the top is set through policies, codes of ethics, a commitment to hiring competent employees, and developing incentive structures that promote proper internal controls and effective governance (Tarantino, 2008).

This promise assumes that the organization is a perfectly cohesive, monolithic entity, in which there is no discrepancy regarding the leadership and program goals will be assumed without much conflict. The idea of organizational conflict over compliance is considered unlikely because, after all, who would be against legality and ethics within the organization? One can therefore assume that these programs justify themselves.

This reasoning raises questions. Does that level of cohesion exist in organizations? Are ethics and legality sufficient elements to eliminate the possibilities of conflict in organizations?

4. *The behavior of individuals can be shaped by compliance programs, in other words, through control and supervision mechanisms.*
The fourth promise is that ethical problems within the organization are solved by modeling the value frames of individuals. In other words, the values of the people in an organization can be induced by incentives (negative and positive) and education. Furthermore, the effects of these incentives and training are uniform throughout the organization. According to the compliance discourse, this is possible through controls and supervision that influence the way individuals define their organizational reality and their relationship with this reality. In this respect, this promise assumes that it is possible to "program" the evaluative framework of individuals to ensure that their decisions are made in keeping with the values and principles of the organization.

This promise is based on the theories that explain corporate fraud. According to the "fraud triangle" theory, fraudsters engage in deception as a result of three leading causes:

i. Pressure, in other words, situations that lead individuals to perceive circumstances as overwhelming or especially stressful. These may include overly aggressive budget goals, variable compensation disproportionate to salaries, and an adverse organizational climate.

ii. Rationalization is the justifications of wrongdoing through narratives or verbalizations that help fraudsters justify their actions to themselves and others. These include expressions such as, "I'm not hurting anyone," "We've always done it that way," and "They don't appreciate my efforts."

iii. In other words, opportunities lack effective controls or perceptions that wrongdoing will not be discovered or go unpunished. These include the lack of segregation of duties, absence of review and supervision in sensitive tasks that give the individual direct access to money.

In this respect, this promise assumes that it is possible to modify, in a homogeneous and controllable way, the behavior of individuals by monitoring and controlling the pressures to which they are exposed. Furthermore, it is assumed, these changes in individuals are accumulating and fostering a global cultural change in the organization as a whole. This cultural change is similar and consistent throughout the organization and eliminates the bases of behaviors that rationalize and normalize fraud and corruption.

By this logic, the promise is that it is possible to influence the perception that individuals have of the likelihood that they will engage in inappropriate behavior, they will be detected and that, once detected, they will receive some form of punishment or negative consequence. If through this conscious, rational evaluation, the individual concludes that the consequences their action may have are greater than the possible benefits that they hope to obtain, they will limit their corrupt behavior and adhere to the rules and policies of the organization. If, on the contrary, they perceive that the profits they will obtain outweigh the possible consequences, then they will have strong incentives to commit the crime.

Explained in this way, unethical behavior can effectively be understood as the result of poor evaluative frameworks that define the perception of punishment. Accordingly, the promise of compliance is that reinforcing the control environment and strengthening the threat of punishment can shape human behavior The question, however, is does it really happen like that? If it is possible to "program" the value framework of individuals, why does corporate fraud continue to take place? Is it possible to control human behavior?

5. *Ethical organizational behavior, prescribed by compliance programs, is the result of the sum of individual behaviors.*

The fifth promise is that regulatory compliance and ethical behavior problems will be solved to the extent that coherent, homogeneous collective and organizational change is brought about by changing the behavior of individuals in an organization.

From this perspective, regulatory noncompliance or unethical behavior results from individual deviations. In this manner, rotten apples can be avoided and, at worst, removed. Thus, the organization can reverse bad practices as the compliance program matures and is internalized within the organization.

This promise assumes that organizational logic is defined solely by the sum of the behaviors of individuals. Nevertheless, if an organization is more than the sum of its parts, changes in people can lead to organizational changes of quite distinct kinds and with different effects. Collective and organizational behavior results from interrelationships, contexts, and concrete situations. People do not act in a vacuum and instead create frameworks of interdependencies. People in an organization create groups, coalitions, group norms, and subcultures. All these elements, which are often overlooked in compliance programs, can have a final critical effect on the type of actions and processes that end up being produced.

In light of these assumptions, one wonders: can organizational action be expected not to have its own dynamic beyond the sum of its parts?

These five promises constitute the most important goals of the compliance discourse. Judging by the empirical evidence, one can infer that something is wrong with these promises. Corporate crime and regulatory compliance failures have not decreased. On the contrary, increasing numbers of organizations are being investigated and fined for this failure. Compliance is obviously not to blame for the lack of ethics in organizations. But 50 years after compliance was institutionalized; one might expect better results.

Before concluding this chapter, it is necessary to undertake a final analysis of the compliance discourse. It involves the discussion that has to do with the type of rhetoric it uses. As noted earlier, it is important to understand why a professional practice that has proven to be not just a fad yet has not done away with the problems that gave rise to it, is in such good health in terms of popularity. What makes the compliance discourse so appealing in the world of organizations? The following section addresses this matter.

1.5 Why is the Compliance Discourse So Appealing?

The promises of the discourse are embedded in a rhetoric that must be analyzed to understand the success of this professional practice fully. As mentioned throughout this chapter, compliance did not emerge as a theory or a single programmatic proposal. What we currently know as compliance is the result of a long history of ideas, practices, and collective understandings that have been added and overlapped with each other.

Compliance emerged as the response to two specific managerial problems: the problem of regulatory compliance and the problem of ethical behavior. In this respect, the professional practice has been built on the fly: it has evolved in the face of different situations and needs or new corruption or corporate fraud scandals under conditions created by globalization. Along the way, shared understandings have been developed of what apparently works and what does not to tackle the management problems with which is concerned.

In this respect, it is imperative to identify the characteristics of the discourse that make it so popular. Today we can say that there is a veritable compliance industry. Books, courses, conferences, professional organizations, and academic programs, not to mention the enormous number of job offers created daily to join compliance teams in the corporate world, speak of a growing industry.

Some data can put this popularity in perspective. The Society for Corporate Compliance and Ethics (SCCE) was established in 2004 to provide compliance professionals with networking, training opportunities, and other resources for professional development. Since its inception, the SCCE has mushroomed into an organization with over 5,000 members (Society of Corporate Compliance and Ethics (SCCE), 2015).

Perhaps the clearest sign of the maturation of the compliance industry has been the development of an entire industry of consultants and experts on the subject. Large consulting firms, such as Kroll and KPMG, offer compliance and risk management services, touting their ability to help companies navigate a changing regulatory environment and develop strong compliance departments. Based on its state-of-the-art surveys, PwC predicts that by 2025, Chief Compliance Officer will be the most highly sought-after corporate position.

Another key aspect reflecting the level of importance the compliance industry has acquired is the multidisciplinarity that can already be observed today in the various areas responsible for the issue in companies. Given the diversity of issues addressed, such as cybersecurity, other skills and experiences will become increasingly valued.

In this context, it is particularly important to ask what characterizes the discourse of compliance that makes it so seductive. Its popularity cannot necessarily be attributed to its achievements. Corporate fraud, the growing number of corruption investigations, and scandals due to regulatory noncompliance do not allow us to conclude that compliance has already managed to resolve the problems that have given rise to it. So, what makes it so attractive? How has compliance been positioned despite its questionable results?

Three key characteristics usually distinguish the compliance discourse:

1. It is *Prescriptive*. In other words, the discourse establishes a series of measures that, if implemented, predict that the behavior of individuals and the organization will behave in a certain way. This assumes that the behavior of individuals and organizations is comparable and equivalent, regardless of their local specificities.

2. It is *Reductive*. In other words, the discourse reduces organizational complexity to a series of measures (policies, procedures, and controls) that enable human behavior to be shaped and ensure compliance with rules and regulations. The same is true of establishing a controlled environment that can be monitored and supervised to detect deviations.

3. It is essentially *Decisive*. In other words, discourse provides solutions for management problems, solving the problematization of complex events with practical solutions, which minimize or omit possible limitations in the design, implementation, and management of compliance programs. For example, the discourse lacks a solid reflection on issues related to organizational conflict. It is assumed that the organization is a monolith, which flies in the face of the piles of empirical evidence accumulated over a hundred years in disciplines such as organization theory. Compliance is practically sold and accepted as a prescriptive and universal management tool for a homogeneous, monolithic phenomenon that is unlikely to exist. (Koo, 2008)

These three characteristics make the compliance discourse particularly appealing among professional management and administration communities because it establishes an understandable, simple, and reassuring frame of reference (because of its promise that management is in control). This reassuring frame of reference, however, does not necessarily tally with the empirical evidence accumulated over decades that organizations are not monoliths in which conflict, power, and dynamic interaction between people, groups, and coalitions are critical elements of the everyday life of any organization (Poole & Van de Ven, 2004).

This type of simplistic discourse entails various risks, failing to fulfill the promises made by compliance and making mistakes, and producing administrative shortcomings due to failing to grasp organizational reality. Implementation errors in compliance programs are already generating inflated costs for companies in the form of reprocessing, investments in wasted equipment and technology, high-cost specialized consultancies, and, of course, million-dollar fines for not having an effective program.

It is clear that compliance is in excellent health as a professional practice. It is therefore not foreseeable that it will soon disappear. On the contrary, everything suggests that compliance is here to stay in organizational management. It is even more important to look critically at its discourse's perils. This critical analysis could explain some of its methodological and practical shortcomings and limits. This discussion is presented in the following chapter.

References

ACFE. (2021). *2020 ACFE Report to the Nations: Insights and Lessons on Occupational Fraud*. Retrieved from https://www.withum.com/resources/2020-report-to-the-nations-insights-and-lessons-on-occupational-fraud/ (accessed March 18, 2022).

Andersson, S., & Anechiarico, F. (2019). *Corruption and Corruption Control*. New York: Routledge.

Basel Committee on Banking Supervision (2005). *Compliance and the compliance function in banks*. Bank for International Settlement. https://www.bis.org/publ/bcbs113.pdf (accessed March 18, 2022).

Church Committee. (1976). *The Select Committee to Study Governmental Operations with Respect to Intelligence Activities, Foreign and Military Intelligence*. Church Committee report, no. 94–755, 94th Cong., 2d Sess. Washington, DC: US Congress, p. 392.

Cyert, R. M., & March, J. G. (1963). *A Behavioral Theory of the Firm*. Malden, MA: Prentice Hall/Pearson Education.

DEA. (n.d.). *Our history*. Retrieved April 18, 2022, from https://www.dea.gov/about/history (accessed March 18, 2022).

Ehrenfeld, R. (1994). *Evil Money: The Inside Story of Money Laundering & Corruption in Government, Banks and Business*. New York, NY: S.P.I. Books.

Eng, L. L., & Mak, Y. T. (2003). Corporate Governance and Voluntary Disclosure. *Journal of Accounting and Public Policy*, 22(4), 325–345.

Environmental Protection Agency. (n.d.). *EPA*. Retrieved from https://www.epa.gov/history/origins-epa (accessed March 18, 2022).

Epstein, E. (2020). *La Ley de Prácticas Corruptas en el Extranjero (FCPA) en América Latina (2019)*. Medium. Retrieved from https://evan-epstein.medium.com/la-ley-de-pr%C3%A1cticas-

corruptas-en-el-extranjero-fcpa-en-am%C3%A9rica-latina-2019-243428663b1e
(accessed March 18, 2022).

Ethics Resource Center (ERC). (2007). *Leading Corporate Integrity: Defining the Role of the Chief Ethics & Compliance Officer (CECO). Chief Ethics & compliance Officer (CECO) Definition Working Group*. Ethics Resource Center.

Fargason, J. S. (1993). *Legal Compliance Auditing and the Federal Sentencing Guidelines*. Altamonte Springs, FL: The Institute of Internal Auditors.

Ferrell, O. C., LeClair, D. T., & Ferrell, L. (1998). The Federal Sentencing Guidelines for Organizations: A Framework for Ethical Compliance. *Journal of Business Ethics*, 17(4), 353–363. http://www.jstor.org/stable/25073086

Financial Action Task Force (FATF). (2012/2022). *International Standards on Combating Money Laundering and the Financing of Terrorism & Proliferation*. FATF: Paris, Retrieved from www.fatf-gafi.org/recommendations.html

Greeley, A. (1907). *The Food and Drugs Act, June 30, 1906: A Study with Text of the Act, Annotated, the Rules and Regulations for the Enforcement of the Act, Food Inspection, Decisions and Official Food Standards*. Washington, DC: J. Byrne & Company.

Gurule, J. (1995). The Money Laundering Control Act of 1986: Creating a New Federal Offense or Merely Affording Federal Prosecutors an Alternative Means of Punishing Specified Unlawful Activity? 32 *American Criminal Law Review*, 823.

Hough, D. (2013). *Corruption, Anti-corruption and Governance*. Hampshire, UK: Plagrave MacMillan.

Koo, J. (2008). What to Look for in Enterprise Content Management for compliance. In Tarantino, A. (ed.), *Governance, Risk and Compliance Handbook. Technology, Finance, Environmental, and International Guidance and Best Practices*. New Jersey: John Wiley & Sons, pp. 259–266.

March, J. G., & Simon, H. A. (1958) *Organizations*. New York: Wiley.

McLean, B., & Elkind, P. (2013). *The Smartest Guys in the Room the Amazing Rise and Scandalous Fall of Enron*. New York: Penguin.

Naciones Unidas. (2005). *Acción mundial contra la corrupción. Los documentos de Mérida*. Naciones Unidas: Viena. Retrieved from https://www.unodc.org/pdf/corruption/publications_merida_s.pdf

Organization of Economic and Cooperation Development. (2010). *Good practice guidance on internal controls, ethics, and compliance*. OECD. Retrieved from https://www.oecd.org/daf/anti-bribery/44884389.pdf (accessed March 18, 2022).

Perry, J., & de Fontnouvelle, P. (2005). *Measuring Reputational Risk: The Market Reaction to Operational Loss Announcements*. https://ssrn.com/abstract=861364 or http://dx.doi.org/10.2139/ssrn.861364

Poole, M., & A. Van de Ven. (2004). *Handbook of Organizational Change and Innovations*. Oxford: Oxford University Press.

Sarbanes, P. (2002, July). *Sarbanes-Oxley Act of 2002*. In The Public Company Accounting Reform and Investor Protection Act. Washington DC: US Congress (Vol. 55).

Silverman, M. (2008). *Compliance Management for Public, Private, or Nonprofit Organizations*. New York: McGraw Hill.

Simon, H. A. (1947). *Administrative Behavior: A Study of Decision-Making Processes in Administrative Organization*. New York: Macmillan.

Sinclair, U. (1906/1985). *The Jungle*. New York: Penguin Books.

Sissenich, B. (2001). Corruption as Domestic and International Concern: An Overview of Causes, Consequences, and Reform Efforts. *SEER-South-East Europe Review for Labour and Social Affairs*, (02), 9–21.

Slager, R. (2017). The Discursive Construction of Corruption Risk. *Journal of Management Inquiry*, 26(4), 366–382. https://doi.org/10.1177/1056492616686839

Society of Corporate Compliance and Ethics (SCCE). (2015). Compliance and ethics profession continues its dynamic expansion as SCCE reaches 5,000 members. *Cision PR Newswire*. Retrieved from https://www.prnewswire.com/news-releases/compliance-and-ethics-profession-continues-its-dynamic-expansion-as-scce-reaches-5000-members-300068061.html (accessed March 18, 2022).

Stevenson, R. B. (1976). The SEC and Foreign Bribery. *The Business Lawyer*, 32(1), 53–73. http://www.jstor.org/stable/40685743

Tarantino, A. (ed.). (2008). *Governance, Risk, and Compliance Handbook. Technology, Finance, Environmental, and International Guidance and Best Practices*. New Jersey: John Wiley & Sons.

Treviño, L. K., Weaver, G. R., Gibson, D. G., & Toffler, B. L. (1999). Managing Ethics and Legal Compliance: What Works and What Hurts. *California Management Review*, 41(2), 131–151. https://doi.org/10.2307/41165990

US Department of Justice. (2017). *Foreign Corrupt Practices Act*. US Department of Justice. Retrieved from https://www.justice.gov/criminal-fraud/foreign-corrupt-practices-act (accessed March 18, 2022).

US Sentencing Commission. (2004). *Commission tightens requirements for corporate compliance and ethics programs*. US Sentencing Commission. Retrieved from https://www.ussc.gov/about/news/press-releases/may-3-2004 (accessed March 18, 2022).

US Treasury/FinCEN. (n.d.). *Appendix A: BSA Laws and Regulations*. FFIEC Bank Secrecy Act/Anti-Money Laundering InfoBase. Retrieved from https://bsaaml.ffiec.gov/manual/Appendices/02 (accessed March 18, 2022).

US Treasury/FinCEN. (n.d.). *Assessing The BSA/AML Compliance Program*. Bank Secrecy Act/Anti-Money Laundering InfoBase. Retrieved from https://bsaaml.ffiec.gov/manual/AssessingTheBSAAMLComplianceProgram/01 (accessed March 18, 2022).

United States v. $4,255,625.39, 551 F. Supp. 314. (1982). Retrieved May 17, 2022.

United States v. Hilton Hotels Corp. – 467 F.2d 1000 (1972). Retrieved April 19, 2022, from https://www.lexisnexis.com/community/casebrief/p/casebrief-united-states-v-hilton-hotels-corp (accessed March 18, 2022).

van den Broek, T., & van Veenstra, A. F. (2018). Governance of Big Data Collaborations: How to Balance Regulatory Compliance and Disruptive Innovation. *Technological Forecasting and Social Change*, 129, 330–338.

Wiggin. (2002). SEC Reveals Key Considerations in Self-Disclosure Actions. *White Collar Crime Reporter*, Volume 16, Number 1, Retrieved from https://www.wiggin.com/publication/sec-reveals-key-considerations-in-self-disclosure-actions/ (accessed March 18, 2022).

Williams, M. (2010). *Uncontrolled Risk*. New York: McGraw-Hill Education.

Chapter 2
Compliance Programs and the Perils of Organizational Misconduct

2.1 Introduction

In Chapter 1, we briefly outlined the recent history and the hopes and assumptions that have shaped compliance as it is known today. It was observed, among other issues, that the general view of compliance is based on a series of assumptions. A key one is that by changing the people's behaviors in an organization, it is possible to transform the values of both the people and the organizations themselves. In other words, implementing a series of measures such as changes in the organizational structure, new oversight systems, robust spaces for compliance within the organization, updated codes of conduct and stricter controls, will mean there is a good chance of endogenizing the values of honesty and thereby reducing misconduct (and its attendant legal risks). Although these basic assumptions (among others described in the previous chapter) are consistent and normatively desirable, they face a critical dilemma: organizations are not homogeneous monoliths or collective robots. They are composed of people in various environments, confronting uncertainties from vastly different logics and organizational spaces. Thus, organizations are intricate arenas full of actors, games, contingencies, values, and norms. Under this realistic vision of organizations, traditional compliance projects fall short of coping with an entirely different organizational reality that is much richer, more dynamic, and alive.

Hence, this chapter lays the groundwork for an organizational analysis of compliance under different assumptions than those traditionally found in the field. The main arguments are examined in this chapter. The first section (2.2) argues that organizations are not monoliths and instead comprised of people behaving based on diverse and often contradictory interests. Rather than a conviction or consensus based on unique values, the main glue binding people together in an organization is something quite different: interdependence. In other words, the organization is made by teams, groups, coalitions, and people built and sustained to give life to the organization within a dynamic interplay of interdependencies. The second (Section 2.3) is that, on the one hand, these collective dynamics of interdependence stabilize and allow certainty and, on the other, become rigid and create equilibriums that are difficult to change. Organizations institutionalize behaviors, constructing arguments and sagas that rationalize decisions.

Furthermore, organizations socialize people into understood values and practices. The third section (2.4) is that various organizational equilibriums can be perverse. In other words, they may involve routines and practices that facilitate or encourage normalizing acts and actions that lead to error and even justify and

https://doi.org/10.1515/9783110749113-002

rationalize improper acts. These elements make it easier to understand the paradoxes of the organizational disaster created by improper or unethical acts, yet ones that can be rationalized and institutionalized. Section 2.5 reviews infamous cases of organizational disasters in which the stabilizing dynamics of an organization as an arena played a key role. Finally, Section 2.6 summarizes the challenges of compliance in a complex reality vastly different from the assumption of an organization as a monolith and instead involves the internal dynamics of organizations as arenas.

In the real world of organizations, compliance faces multiple challenges since its success depends on the ability to modify these equilibriums in an organizational arena where people not only act based on individual incentives (both positive and negative) but within a dynamic context of interaction, interdependence, hierarchies, symbols, and culture. Examples from various organizations are used to highlight these points. The chapter ends with a summary of the profiles that organizational dynamics create for any compliance program wishing to be successful.

2.2 Organizations: Obedient Machines or Human Constructs? The Metaphor of the Monolith Versus the Arena

2.2.1 The Monolithic Organization

As mentioned in previous chapters, compliance is an organizational tool that seeks to modify the behavior of the people comprising a company, government agency, or nonprofit. It seeks, in short, to create the conditions for common action based on the ethics and logic of what is correct. For an organization to implement a solid logic of compliance, it will first be necessary to affect people's behavior individually. Changing people's perspectives and behavior is hoped that, in some way (which is not always clear), will change their behavior. In this way, it will transform the group logic, both formal and informal. In other words, it is assumed that if one or more people change their behavior, the group or even organizational effect will be consistent with these changes in people's behavior. The causal chain does not end here. It is assumed that if individuals change their behavior, this will bring changes in the logic of groups and coalitions, which, in turn, will positively affect the performance of the organization as a whole.

Therefore, the causal chain assumes that after these individual and group changes, the organization, seen as a whole, will regard itself as being inserted in a homogeneous logic of compliance and honesty. In other words, all the people, groups, and coalitions will share the same way of understanding and viewing the organization's compliance regime means and does.

Moreover, something extraordinarily ambitious and critical is expected: compliance will be reproduced continuously and stably as a natural part of the organizational culture. It would not be of much use if a certain logic of compliance had a short life. It is expected to become structural and be reproduced and accepted in a relatively automatic, disciplined way by people in the organization over time.

This brief description of the logic of compliance has a characteristic that is generally overlooked and ignored in the discussions and texts on the subject: it is based on the assumption that is not always made explicit. In other words, its causal logic (from the change induced in the individual, to the modification of group practices, to the systemic change of the organization as a whole) is based on a highly specific vision of what an organization is. This view, which we will call the monolithic organization, is a view or metaphor (following Morgan's concept, 1996) that has proved extremely useful and productive. It is also a simplifying view and understandable, simple, and easy to accept. The monolithic organization is usually the dominant metaphor in the world of those who study organizations. It is also helpful to those who direct, inhabit, and regulate them through laws or regulations. Customers, consumers, and citizens often require a convenient simplification for understanding their relationships with companies or government organizations.

The view of the monolithic organization is predicated on a simplification: that an organization is, literally, a single actor, a "body" that acts and decides as a whole. This has been called a unified rational actor (Allison & Zelikow, 1999). Although organizations comprise people or individuals, an aggregation process occurs almost automatically: people build groups, groups that cooperate and coordinate to engage in collective acts which, together, seek to achieve the objectives of an overarching collective subject: the organization. Thus, through the combination and aggregation of individual and group acts, people, individually and in groups, achieve the objectives of the collective person representing the organization.

As one can see, this metaphor achieves a gross transmutation: the organization exists as an actor who thinks and has goals and values (Coleman, XX). An organization has a mind of its own with identifiable goals that can be rationally pursued. Understanding the organization as a monolith assumes that it can establish the goal to be achieved and the values, expectations, and beliefs supporting that goal. It also assumes it can identify affordable, logical means of achieving them.

If organizations are a monolith, a collective actor, and a Leviathan, how are decisions made in an organization? Who sets the goals? How are these goals constructed in the mind of the collective actor called an organization? Once the objective or goal has been set, who compares the values sought, calculates the appropriate means, and implements the appropriate actions? The answer to all these questions is people, identifiable individuals. The monolithic organization is a metaphor: in practice, it is impossible to find the organization's mental or decision center. Certain people and groups will always be identified as those who decide and act, often on behalf of "the organization."

An additional assumption underpins the metaphor of the monolithic organization: the people who comprise it have somehow decided to subsume their individual goals and objectives under the goals of the organization (Barnard, 1938). From the simplest view of the economy, where people decide to cooperate to achieve ends they would otherwise be unable to (Arrow, 1974), to more detailed, complete views such as the one known as Simon's "decision to participate" (1965), the idea is clear: organizations transmute people so that rather than acting as individuals in pursuit of their objectives, they act in pursuit of the organization's objectives. How is this transmutation achieved? In organizational studies, this logic of aggregation of individual objectives that lead to collectives has been extensively studied to understand how an organization can get people to subsume their own objectives to pursue a homogeneous whole with rational goals and decision-making capabilities. The argumentative circle of the monolithic organization is ultimately contradictory: it is people who decide, calculate and act, but at some point, they do so in pursuit of an organizational objective that someone must establish at some point. That someone must be a specific member or group of the organization.

In any case, the metaphor of the monolithic organization has helped to create instruments and mechanisms for organizational change and improvement. Examples of valuable instruments created in a certain way under the metaphor of the monolithic organization include strategic planning (Ackoff, 1991), process reengineering (Mohapatra, 2015), and the balance score card (Kaplan & Norton, 1996), among many others.

The argumentative base, the history or narrative of the monolithic organization, is attractive but can be broken down to shed light on its assumptions and causal chain. These assumptions, incidentally, are rarely discussed in the field of compliance:

1. Although organizations comprise people, they have subsumed their goals and interests, at least to some degree, under the goals and interests of the organization.
2. The organization can be considered a whole, with a general logic above the interests and logic of those who comprise it.
3. Any reform or change project can reasonably hope that this general view of the organization is understandable to people and legitimate. In other words, the purpose of a reform or improvement project, if it seeks to achieve the organization's objectives, is legitimate as a project, meaning that the people in an organization can agree to follow and obey the premises of this project.
4. Suppose people are convinced of the legitimacy of a change project. In that case, they will have the will, strength, and ability to change or modify their behavior (in a rational, calculated way) to achieve the objectives of any organizational reform or improvement project.
5. By changing their behavior and accepting the premises of a given project, people can achieve the expected general change in the organization, seen as a whole.

This summary of the argumentative chain is assumed in the metaphor of the monolithic organization. It is a direct chain: every change or improvement project begins with the hope of being understood homogeneously by those who comprise the organization. People will adopt the new premises of action or decision if they consider them legitimate and if they have the appropriate incentives to initiate and sustain the behavioral change expected of them. All this is part of the expectation that people intend to prioritize the pursuit of the organizational objective.

The metaphor of the monolithic organization assumes a highly rational process, as can be seen. People are essentially utility maximizers entities. First, they can identify their interests, and second, they can thoughtfully subsume them under the organization. This implies that they can reasonably understand and make sense of the organization's objectives and, therefore, can intelligently calculate the means to achieve them. Given the enormous capacity of people to understand their goals and those of the organization, managing and reforming an organization cannot be anything other than a highly rational act. Organizational change or improvement projects, such as compliance projects, therefore, focus on providing new and better rationales to make everything work better. People agree to change their behavior. First, it should be observed that people are assumed to have the power, willpower, and the ability to modify their behavior intentionally. Second, it should be mentioned that this change is not only intentional but rational: it is known relatively accurately what the specified behavior change will achieve.

Then, a compliance project under the metaphor of the monolithic organization can be described in a detailed flowchart of action: rational, transparent, and legitimate objectives are established, the goals and processes to be implemented are communicated, and structures, norms, and rules are created so that they are observed and implemented by people, and positive and negative incentives are established for them to comply, and the results are evaluated (Silverman, 2008). Monolithic organizations facilitate the view of a unified rational actor that operates like a Leviathan as a relatively harmonious whole. The Leviathan has goals he can define and pursue appropriately and rationally. Furthermore, when something needs to be changed, it is again just a matter of introducing rational processes for its various parts to adapt and adjust. In this case, its parts are obviously people. Moreover, it is people who achieve everything the organization does through their actions and behavior. However, here is a critical assumption: people are rational and have rationally subsumed their goals and interests under those of the organization.

The organizational metaphor of the monolith is a powerful form of explanation (Morgan, 2006; Mintzberg, 1992). As one can see, organizational metaphors are more than just a play on words. Metaphors lend meaning (Weick, 2001) to people. Organizational sense gives people, inside and outside the organization, a perspective and logic to act. What is the organization looking for? What obstacles and uncertainties does it face? How does it successfully communicate and create cooperation between different and often distant people? How are the various problems dealt with, who is responsible, and to what extent? Which steps have been successful, and which have failed over time? Why should other people be obeyed and why should leadership and subordination be expected? How are negative incentives (punishments, sanctions, and reprimands) and positive incentives (prizes, recognition, and promotions) distributed and provided? Answering all these questions (and many others) involves an effort of understanding and acceptance on the part of the specific people comprising each organization in their reality and context. The ultimate aim is to act, decide and participate in collective action with logic and direction. Organizational sensemaking is crucial to this: a firefighting organization makes sense of its rules, expertise, and group action in the event of a fire. This is different from a financial organization that acquires a sense of risk management and technical expertise to understand the movements of the context, firms, and governments.

So, a metaphor is usually more than a play on words. In organizational dynamics, metaphors help with sensemaking so that people have a guide, an educated intuition, of what is correct, what is rational, how, and when to cooperate, and how and when to act.

Like any metaphor, that of the monolithic organization is a group of assumptions that lend meaning to people's actions and decisions. A compliance project will then be created, designed, interpreted, and implemented according to the metaphor that ends up being valuable and functional. According to the logic of the argumentative chain that was previously defined for the monolith organization, we would have:

1. A compliance program can expect people to change their behavior by substantively thinking about the organization's goal (their own goals are subsumed).
2. A compliance program may expect that a change in people's behavior will in itself imply a change in the behavior of the organization as a whole.
3. If a compliance program is successful, it is because of its ability to create rules, structures, and incentives that encourage or induce people to change their behavior.
4. Since they are rational, people require adequate incentives and rules. An effective compliance program is primarily a program of incentives and adequate structures to shift people's behavior.
5. Suppose the incentives, structures, and rules are appropriate. In that case, since they are rational, people will modify their behavior, and by changing it relatively automatically, the organization will achieve better results or performance. A compliance program modifies people's behavior through rules and incentives and thereby expects general results.

Logically, metaphors are simplifying versions. Without simplification, meaning and action would be highly complicated. A person or a group can barely act without lending meaning to reality. Additionally, all meaning is ultimately a simplification: a route, path, or perspective that enables action to happen, even if the uncertainties are vast and permanent. A group of firefighters knows that every fire they encounter is different regarding its strength, context, size, and the specific people involved. However, the organization gives firefighters meaning through processes, training, socialization, structure, rules, and esprit de corps. The metaphor of the monolithic organization is a powerful means of sensemaking and of creating those structures, rules, and incentives.

However, like all metaphors, this metaphor has its limitations, particularly since the monolithic organization has proven to be largely inadequate in the face of the influential contemporary, globalizing dynamics filled with changes, challenges, and risks.

2.2.2 The Problems of the Monolithic Organization

What factors are generally posited as the source of organizational failure? From the perspective of the monolithic organization, a permanent contradiction usually appears as resistance to change. In other words, conflict emerges as a critical destroyer of cooperation, coordination, and organizational harmony. It is important to remember that part of the argument of a monolithic organization is that harmony is rational because people have subsumed their own goals under the organizational goal.

Indeed, under this logic, organizations experience problems because people deviate from organizational goals. The natural state of people and organizations is harmony and cooperation since both results from rationality. Therefore, whether out of ignorance, incapacity, or malice, when the assumption that the goals and objectives of people are subordinate to the general objectives of the organization is destroyed, conflict emerges, and the monolith cracks.

In the case of compliance, it is relatively easy to find this assumption in various classic texts: misconduct is a distortion of what an organization should be and the behavior of the people comprising it (Taylor, 1997; Fayol, 2013; Roethlisberger, 2018; Drucker, 2008). Inappropriate behavior is ultimately a violation, first of the pact of the monolithic organization. A person who engages in illicit activity or questionable behavior is probably putting their interests or those of their group above organizational ones. It is quickly assumed that improper behavior is a disease that harms the organization and society, and it is a profoundly irrational act, even socially speaking.

Indeed, the monolithic organization and its assumptions are often transferred to the social sphere. The administrative tradition that transfers these assumptions from the administrative to the social realm is extensive: Saint Simon (Pullinger, 2015), Elton Mayo (2014), and Braverman (1998) are just some examples of analysts who have discussed, in different ways and under different assumptions and ideologies, the image that the organizational order is intimately related to the social order in some way. It can often be assumed, reasonably quickly, that since organizing is a natural act, conflict must therefore be an anti-social act. Indeed, conflict or acts deviating from the norm are events that disrupt order, both organizationally and socially. People must then realize rationally and clearly that their private entity must be separated and controlled from their collective duties (in both an organization and a society). Conflict and deviance can emerge when people allow their private beings to invade collective spaces. Therefore, chaos. It does not matter that the opposite is precisely what is most evident to people: that the public or the collective is something abstract. People experience intensely the sphere of their person, family, and those close to them. Although the private sphere is intense and immediate for people, it must be controlled and limited for the social, the collective, and the organizational to emerge.

The monolithic organization is a powerful metaphor that is necessary in many forms. It allows us to think that social order is possible, provided people are capable and legitimize a belief: that it is possible and appropriate to separate the private and public spheres and individual and collective interests. If individual, personal interest unduly interferes in the order of the collective and organizational interest, for example, misconduct occurs. The rule seems specific: what is inappropriate is primarily individual interference in the collective interest. Compliance is implemented to restore the equilibrium: to avoid violating the assumption that people can clearly differentiate collective, organizational objectives from individual ones.

Given that it is based on the legitimacy of the existence per se of these general or organizational objectives, the question is why people are specifically driven or encouraged to seek individual or group objectives that destroy the harmony of organizational goals.

From the perspective of the monolithic organization, there is little chance of answering this question beyond a moralistic position: misconduct should not happen simply. Unless one believes in human malice or that people are pathologically criminal by nature, the explanation must be more practical. Inappropriate behavior should not exist, given human rationality and the advisability of separating the collective from the individual. Nevertheless, it does happen, and therein lies the dilemma. Two explanations appear to prevail from the perspective of the monolithic organization. First, it may then be that harmony is destroyed by ignorance or miscommunication. If people are rational, with reliable information and adequate leadership, they will return to the logic of harmony. The conflict then is due to the lack of information. A second possibility is that, as rational people, for a compelling reason, they first seek to satisfy their individual or group rationality over that of the organization. For example, they calculate that the chances of being caught committing an inappropriate act are lower than the benefits of committing it (Eriksson, 2011). These two logics (lack of communication or leadership and selfish yet rational calculation of wrongdoing) form the basis of many contemporary compliance programs.

The dilemma of the monolithic organization is that these two explanations speak of accidents: improper behaviors are specific, punctual, discrete failures. However, the evidence itself shows that, on the contrary, improper behaviors have always existed and are universal across political borders, social regimes, times, and eras. Moreover, they are becoming more sophisticated and can even be organized and relatively stable. So, flaws and misconduct as a kind of pathology would not appear to be a sufficient, credible explanation. If people can rationally calculate that it is in their interest to misbehave, then the pathology of inappropriate behavior does not exist.

The fact that there are people who, through misinformation or rational selfishness, can act in a way that is not subordinate to organizational objectives is a challenge to the vision of the monolithic organization. The contradiction is intense because the monolith is not as spontaneous or natural as it might initially seem. In other words, it is not entirely natural for people to subsume their goals under the organizational goal. After all, who embodies and defines organizational interest? People are the logical answer. Not all the people in an organization, then, deal with the order to subsume their goals under organizational ones in the same way.

Scholars understood this contradiction decades ago: March (1994), Cyert and March (1963), March and Simon (1993), and Crozier (1964), to mention just a few. Through these and other studies, the enormous limitations of the monolithic metaphor were documented. If people are the ones with goals and interests if people are the ones who decide and act, the metaphor of the acting rational organization is inaccurate. Organizations do not act or decide. People act and decide. Moreover, in an organization, they decide collectively or instead in collectives. Groups, for example, exist in any formal or informal organization. Do groups, then, decide? How are collective decisions made if the people who make them are the ones who have interests and objectives? Can groups in an organization, for example, have their own goals and interests? How are the various goals and ends aligned, discussed, debated, and fought to create organizational goals? The monolithic organization usually begins with an axiom, that is, from an unspoken assumption: that organizational goals and objectives are given and exist from the start. On the contrary, asking how organizational goals are built, who set them, and how they emerge is the first step toward watching the metaphor of the monolith organization crack and collapse.

Organizational objectives must be built, created, and legitimized. Suppose organizations are filled with people with interests who decide and act individually and in groups. In that case, they propose and defend diverse objectives, which may contradict each other. Every organization has a story, which is told through the actions and decisions of individuals and groups. Given this logic, the idea of the monolith ceases to be explanatory.

The limits of the logic of the monolithic organization have a powerful impact on perspectives such as compliance. Any program will be interpreted and analyzed by the various groups and coalitions within an organization. The goals of a compliance program are bound to the goals of an organization, while the goals of an organization are in turn bound to the decision process of people in various positions with a range of powers and levels of authority. These people are part of groups and coalitions, both formal and informal, who usually defend different perspectives of what organizational goals are or should be. Organizations barely exist without their groups, whether formal or informal, defending, debating, and promoting their own visions of what the organization is and should be. When the monolith is destroyed, the organization becomes something else in practice. Consequently, a compliance program will have to be seen innovatively.

2.2.3 Changing the Metaphor: The Organization as a (Political) Arena

In the same way, as we explored the monolithic organization, we can understand the organization as an arena. Its initial premise can be understood as follows: an organization only exists because of the specific people comprising it. Moreover, people relate to each other and come together in relatively identifiable groups or coalitions to create, defend, and promote their beliefs and interests.

Thus, people in groups attempt to add and align their particular perspectives, values, beliefs, and interests. Groups and coalitions with various levels of power and hierarchy, obviously: some groups may control the resources or critical elements of the organization while others may only be employees, for example. An organization is the result of the interaction (whether harmonious or conflictive) between separate groups and coalitions. It is important to recall that these groups are neither necessarily equal nor balanced, and not only because of the apparent difference in the specific people comprising them. Interaction implies that groups have different powers and start and act from different positions of authority and power. These may be formal hierarchical positions but also informal positions due to agreements, negotiations, and contextual situations.

As can be seen, the metaphor of the organizational arena provides a different view of what an organization is. Rather than being a monolith, an organization obtains cooperation and coordination through the interaction between groups and people in positions of power and authority. Hence, the idea that it is an arena (or a field): there are specific formal and informal rules that form the basis on which people and groups act and bond. An organization is not, therefore, a monolith that exists prior to people: it ends up being a result of the interaction between people and groups in an arena comprising rules, norms, practices, routines, and decisions. An organization is a product that is permanently under construction. If necessary, it is constantly validated, reproduced, and reinvented (Brunsson & Olsen, 1998). Although it does not do so according to a linear pattern, a master plan is followed perfectly from start to finish. An organization is continuously being organized. It is an action composed of interactions. Interactions can create interdependencies that may be conflicting and cooperative, stable but constantly changing. The arena is experienced as a game: certain rules are followed, and events that happen in the arena ultimately determine what an organization does or does not do, including the possibility of changing the game's rules.

The image of the arena organization is much more intricate and dynamic, and it is undoubtedly more challenging to grasp. One of the advantages of the monolith metaphor is its simplicity bordering on simplism. Although complexity is the hallmark of the arena organization, this does not mean stability. A vital element of any organization is lost. Merely the question is substantive rather than the assumption accepted as a given: how are agreements about organizational ends reached to allow for coordination and cooperation? The agreement that creates the organizational glue is never fully finished: it is an agreement that is built and under constant discussion, negotiation, and testing through the constant interaction and interdependencies comprising the organization.

The idea of organizational change concerning the causal chain, mentioned earlier in this chapter through the metaphor of the monolith, changes with this perspective of the arena. Let us take a closer look:

1. Organizations comprise people and groups who, in their constant interaction, create and recreate organizational goals. Organizations are made up of multiple interests that have achieved stability through the interaction and interdependence generated there.

2. An organization is the result of interaction: stability is agreed upon and negotiated through the interaction between groups, dependent on and influenced by the positions, powers, and capacities of the groups. The arena is neither fair nor equitable. Changing an organization means affecting the balance achieved over time through the continuous negotiation between groups and coalitions.

3. Any reform or change project attempts to strike a balance obtained by interaction, reproduced by the interdependencies that have crystallized and stabilized between the various groups and coalitions. Change requires building new stability and a new agreement. But this does not suffice. The new agreement will have to be tested in action (instituted and enacted), creating new interdependencies and new balances of power. That is why change generates so much uncertainty: It is not that there is "resistance to change" as if this were an irrational, conservative act by people. Resistance to change is more intricate since the new equilibrium is not created as if it were a blueprint for a building but is played out in an arena of interaction. The enactment of reform or change is not only achieved formally or normatively; an enactment is a political act, but it can only be achieved in day-to-day interaction, which creates new interdependencies that are stabilized.

4. Changing people's behavior is not just an individual decision. A change in a person's behavior can only be measured by modifying the interactions with others. In other words, a person's behavior is also the result of interaction and the collective logic this interaction produces. The sum of the parts does not make the system, nor does it create the equilibrium in the interaction. Changing behaviors is still crucial, but the key is what balances and interdependencies are created through those changes.

As one can see, the arena organization places great importance on interaction. The organization is not a given: it is constantly produced and reproduced. Its stability is not the result of a master plan. It is actually the byproduct of interactions, events, situations, and of people and groups who defend spaces of power and authority. They play in an arena with certain cards and established rules, which can be modified and remade. Not automatically or completely rationally, although this is possible.

As can be inferred from this metaphor of the arena, the logic of organizational change, such as compliance, is presented very differently, based on a range of assumptions and needs. Let us take a closer look.

1. A compliance program attempts to change the behavior of people to transform organizational balances that may be opening the door to inappropriate normalized behavior.
2. A compliance program cannot expect a change in people's behavior to involve a transformation of the organization's behavior as a whole or the effects an organization ultimately achieves.
3. A compliance program cannot be successful solely because of its ability to create rules, structures, and incentives that encourage or induce people to change their behavior. It requires creating the conditions for compliance to be organizationally enacted through acceptance and negotiation, and bargaining between groups in the organization to change, break and create new interactions and interdependencies.
4. Incentives do not suffice. People acting in an arena are perfectly capable of creating normalization processes for inappropriate behavior. People's rationality is limited, and they face not only interaction with groups and people but also cognitive and psychological limitations and biases (such as reducing cognitive dissonance, cognitive biases, and wishful thinking).
5. Compliance is a project that must be enacted politically and organizationally. It also requires understanding that the compliance structure, whatever it may be, will inevitably be embedded in the organizational arena, and it will form part, eventually, of the organizational arena. For better or worse, the people, structures, and processes responsible for compliance will eventually become another player in the organizational arena.

The metaphor of the arena allows us to see that the key to compliance is to be able to play from within the organizational game, first to change it structurally and stably, and second for it to be endogenously adopted in the organizational dynamics. It is not enough to appeal to the abstract need for a compliance program and structure. It is necessary to draw up a roadmap and a strategy that will make it possible to achieve the acceptance of a program and its enactment. Furthermore, regarding an organization as an arena implies that it is reasonable to expect the organization, its groups, and its individuals to resist change initially. Not as pathological resistance that is merely resolved through common sense and by appealing to people's cooperation or good faith. It will be a form of resistance resulting from deep action and practices enacted in an organization, from the agreements and balances that have crystallized between groups and coalitions. This does not mean that these equilibriums are healthy or pertinent, or at least not all of them. Understandably, many de facto enacted balances and practices can, without fundamental contradictions, form the basis of a series of behaviors and practices that allow or encourage inappropriate practices in a structural, stable manner.

Through the metaphor of the arena, it will be much more logical to understand that compliance will be successful because it engages in the organizational game to generate (and subsequently enact) a new game successfully. Compliance will be adapted before it is adopted, and it is important and logical to expect groups and individuals to attempt to boycott it if necessary. Any program will face these resistances and adaptations, which, at one extreme, will lead it to be an innocuous or merely formal proposal without bringing about genuine changes in the behavior, routines, and dynamics of real people.

2.3 The Challenge of Compliance: Organizational Stability and its Equilibriums

An organization is a network of people behaving and creating an arena. People cope with uncertain, dynamic day-to-day situations through rules, routines, agreements, and negotiations. People in an organization face constant uncertainties: in the behavior of others (both inside and outside the organization) and the effects of their decisions and actions. They face uncertainty about how an organization can achieve in a changing context. Organizations are highly effective in enabling people to cope with all these uncertainties with a certain degree of confidence in their success (Simon, 1965; Weick, 2001; Crozier & Friedberg, 1980; Brunsson, 1985).

The structures and hierarchies, rules, routines, and organizational norms create stability. Stability is checked and renewed daily in the dozens of interactions in which people engage, with some regularity and following certain guidelines. Stability makes organizations, and this stability is somehow agreed upon, which lends meaning to the arena itself. Any change from this stability requires careful consideration: change is not bad; it merely involves risks. Every change is a threat and an opportunity.

Therefore, the metaphor of the arena allows us to understand a substantive paradox: acts such as fraud or corruption, or other inappropriate behavior in an organization result from these processes of stabilization and agreement between people and groups. Moreover, it is highly likely that the practices, routines, and agreements that enable an organization to function in different ways at the same time also allow the stabilization of fraud and corruption. Indeed, fraud and corruption are not accidents, strange pathologies, or exceptions that run parallel to organizational dynamics. This strong paradox makes it possible to explain the surprising phenomena of systemic corruption. Likewise, of course, the proven persistence of fraud (ACFE, 2020). Corruption exists in every country and government at various levels and shapes, and it is a phenomenon embedded in profound cultural and social logic (such as exchanging favors) (Arellano-Gault, 2020). Fraud, as defined by ACFE, leads us to ask questions not about whether there are fraudulent practices in an organization, but what type, what degree of damage they produce, and how these practices are embedded in the dynamics of the people, groups, and structures of an organization.

How can this paradox be explained? The fact that the practices and routines that create the capacity for cooperation and coordination that make an organization work are the same as those which, under certain circumstances, stabilize improper acts and practices is one of the critical elements to advancing a compelling compliance logic.

By using the image of an organization as an arena, it is possible to resolve the paradox. Organizations are made up of human beings who establish a sense of what they do through constant negotiations and bargaining. The battle for organizational ends is the battle between groups and coalitions. It involves reaching agreements through practices, routines, forms of governance (decision-making), and actions that make sense and lend certain stability to the interactions and interdependencies that make the organization exist. Organizations are intricate, effective forms of machinery that create a stable psychological environment (Simon, 1965) to allow interaction and agreement between people and their coalitions. This psychological environment is critical: acts and decisions can be normalized and rationalized. Under a broader lens, these acts and decisions can be considered improper or unethical. However, from the scaffold of the established organizational vision, they can be seen as different and rational.

At least three organizational dynamics are critical to enabling members of an organization to decide and act within the logic of the organization as an arena: institutionalization, rationalization, and socialization (Ashforth & Anand, 2003; Ashforth, Gioia, Robinson, & Treviño, 2008). Moreover, it is these three logics that, at the same time, build the stability of fraudulent and corrupt practices and behaviors.

2.3.1 Institutionalization

To be effective, organizational behavior requires providing certainty. People in an organization expect certain behaviors and reactions to be stable and repetitive. And by extension, legitimate. This is essential for people to have a degree of certainty about what to expect when certain actions or behaviors are or are not performed. It is unnecessary to reinvent organizational relationships every day, which would be a nightmare. Relationships are stable because they are assumed to be repetitive, and that repetition is expected to be stable. Institutionalization implies that the ordinary activities of an organization are stable and enacted by various members of the organization and their groups without their having to be thought of in terms of utility, ownership, or nature (Ashforth & Anand, 2003; Greenwood & Hinings, 1988; Olivier de Sardan, 1999).

The logic of institutionalization enacts practices and routines. Among them, it is possible to institutionalize, for example, assumptions such as the fact that an order from a superior is always obeyed. Alternatively, it is not acceptable to doubt the vertical decision-making culture of a group or that the moral value of a group in the organization is unquestionable and far superior to that of any other group. These three institutionalization examples can help build stable dynamics of fraud or corruption. If the decisions of a person in a certain position cannot be challenged, then their subordinates are trapped, with no scope for maneuver in response to acts or decisions that may be questionable. Suppose a culture of decision involves little debate or deliberation, the search for more evidence, or the reasonable search for flaws or mistakes being made. In that case, the chances of falling into groupthink are high (Janis, 1972). Groupthink can appear when there is an excessive search for group cohesion. Indeed, every group needs significant levels of cohesion to arrive at agreed, legitimate decisions. However, the need for consensus is exaggerated. In that case, it can fall to an extreme where consensus is forced, doubts or opposition are hidden, and the need to seek better alternatives and more information is denied. All this helps the group to be blinded to reality and the possible mistakes being made in any decision and action process. Under the dynamics of groupthink, accepting errors begins to be avoided, internal or external criticism of the decisions made is underestimated, and collective veils are created that prevent people from seeking more evidence and data to make decisions or correct course. A logic of institutionalization that eases groupthink; paradoxically opens the door to normalizing fraud or corruption. What a group does can be regarded as unquestionable, even if it is improper or on the verge of being illegal (since they are a select group, everything they do is justified).

Organizational institutionalization processes can be described in three phases (Ashford & Anan, 2003: 5): openness, embedding, and routinization. A practice or decision is initiated, experienced, or evaluated in the opening phase. That practice can, for example, involve bending a rule. A manager or leader minimizes not following a regulatory procedure conscientiously, based on the view that it is exceptional and saves time. So that exception is accepted without much discussion, and repeating it becomes acceptable. In the embedding phase, certain rules' practices, exceptions, or bending are transmitted and stabilized. Exceptions are becoming routines, and bending the rule is becoming a widespread practice that is rarely questioned. The control process, which, for exceptional reasons, was ignored, is now constantly ignored without being discussed or regarded as odd. This practice then becomes routinized and goes from being an exception to a known route, shared and accepted by various members or groups in the organization.

2.3.2 Rationalization

Rationalizing is a fundamental human psychological process. Human beings interpret reality and make sense of it (Weick, 1979). What do the organizations face, what is reality like, and how should the members act? These critical elements are designed to provide meaning, without which acting or deciding in the real and concrete world would be extremely difficult and even more distressing.

To rationalize is to impose a determined logic. A logic that gives the people meaning. Not only in terms of instrumental-rational causes, in other words, thinking that reality was merely the result of a chain of causes and effects in the sense of "If you do X, you get Y." In addition to this rational logic of means and ends, causes and effects, people rationalize to understand and test their beliefs and values. Dealing with reality is not only a matter of instrumental calculation but also of acceptance, emotion, and learning. When an action leads to failure, people's beliefs can be challenged, together with their core values.

For this reason, rationalizing has been an object of study in psychology in both the psychoanalytic branch and social psychology. In the case of the former, rationalization is essential in certain situations to protect a person from the distress and pain of being wrong, of having done something wrong, and not having the intelligence to succeed, for example. Social psychology has studied the strength of cognitive dissonance reduction: when a person maintains two psychologically inconsistent cognitions, a solution is required (Festinger, 1957); or if the behavior is incompatible with a belief, in both cases, the person experiences dissonance and discomfort, so the person needs to resolve that dissonance. Sometimes that dissonance is resolved directly: the belief was wrong, and the person changes their belief. However, this is not that simple: it can be painful or inconvenient for the specific circumstance of the person in question. Instead, it is possible to reduce cognitive dissonance by creating a veil of self-delusion: the belief remains intact, and the person reinterprets what is happening in reality, adjusting reality to belief (even if it involves deceiving themselves).

As one can see, rationalization is often both an individual and a group or social process. Still, it involves the construction of an acceptable, reassuring, explanatory argument that makes reality intelligible to people. Rationalizing allows understanding but does not necessarily create an accurate vision of reality, at least not entirely. Indeed, reducing cognitive dissonance is a fundamental socioindividual mechanism for human beings to make sense of their actions, interpret reality and, above all, endure the perennial uncertainty reality imposes on everyone. However, the key is understanding that this mechanism can create various levels of self-deception. Rationalizing involves creating, and that creation sometimes implies using certain veils to avoid seeing. Those veils can be of great assistance, enabling people to trust, for example. Ultimately, trusting a person involves accepting many things that are not observable about them. People present themselves to others in a chiaroscuro of essence and appearance (Goffman, 1959). They want to seek others to see certain things but also not to observe certain other things.

Additionally, those veils are critical for cooperation to exist and for communication to take place. The secret (Simmel, 1906) has been widely studied regarding its negative side and its necessity for human relations, communication, and organizational work. Goffman extensively studied how acting and deciding behind the scenes, as a working team, is essential for group action: some things are said within the group that would not be said outside it.

Thus, rationalizing is a double act involving transparency and concealment. The problem is when the veil created by rationalizing leads to extremes. Just as rationalization makes it possible to interpret and lend stability to an organization, it also allows the normalization of improper acts and routines to become a reality. People do not enjoy feeling that they are stupid, corrupt, or unethical. Faced with the institutionalization of practices, as seen before, it is preferable to rationalize that certain exceptions or attitudes are justifiable because of the circumstances and the situations. One concept related to rationalization is that of neutralization: people use this cognitive device as a defense to neutralize negative emotions associated with inappropriate behavior (Skyes & Matza, 1957). In other words, people see themselves as decent and sound, so when they are faced with possible or obvious wrongdoing, they tend to protect themselves with a linguistic mechanism that protects their self-image and reputation.

Several types of neutralization have been studied in cases of fraud and organizational corruption (Anand, Ashforth, & Joshi, 2005; Hauser, Simonyan, & Werner, 2020):

1. *Denial of responsibility.* People claim or justify themselves by saying that they had no choice but to engage in inappropriate activity. They rationalize, for example, that they were following orders they could not avoid.
2. *Denial of damage.* People are convinced no one was harmed or significantly affected by the actions undertaken, even arguing that, for this reason, it should not be considered an improper or corrupt act. For example, they allege that damage would have occurred if the action had not been taken.
3. *Denial of victims.* People avoid feeling guilty over their actions because the affected person, group, or organization deserved what happened to them. The classic example is to think that a fraud was committed against an organization that harms others.
4. *Denial of weighting.* People assume other people commit the worst acts, and it is rationalized that, for example, there are always those who do more damage and go unpunished.
5. *Appeal to higher loyalties.* People argue that they violated rules or processes to achieve a greater good or higher value. For example, acts of bribery are committed, and it is claimed that otherwise, the goods or services would not have been delivered.

6. *Ledger metaphor.* People rationalize that they have a right to engage in inappropriate behavior, given that they are owed payments or rewards for past acts. They argue that they work hard or overtime, yet unfairly, these efforts are not rewarded. It is argued then that the wrongdoing evened out the situation.

Rationalizing allows people to find arguments and justifications, both for their inner self and to explain the reason for their behavior to other people. It is difficult for people to accept, for example, that they have engaged in improper, corrupt, or fraudulent acts. Rationalizations reassure and balance the image a person accused of wrongdoing has of themselves ("I know I am not that bad") and allow them to give other people reasons that justify what was done ("See, I am not really a bad person").

The psychological process of neutralization and normalization can therefore involve complex mental and linguistic operations, such as the following:

1. *Acquittal of personal accountability.* The illusion that blaming others for events frees one from responsibility.
2. *Consequentialist redemption.* The delusion is created by the idea that there is no substantial harm caused by what was done.
3. Deontological redemption or self-delusion that the fact that a person did not violate a law or rule makes them less guilty.
4. A narcissistic indemnity or the creation of a fantasy that a person's self-assigned moral greatness entitles them to certain liberties.
5. A sacrosanct indemnity or the fantasy that because a person's cause is so special and unique, it gives them a special protected position.
6. An intentional indemnity or the creation of fallacies to justify themselves (De Klerk, 2017).

It is essential to emphasize the double logic of rationalization: psychological for the person and at the social and group level (Zyglidopoulos, Fleming, & Rothberg, 2009). In other words, people develop rationalizations but share in groups or socially. For this reason, they not only exist ex-post, that is, after the act or when the person has been observed and accused. Rationalizations work ex-ante, stabilizing practices and routines, forms of work, and communication. Rationalizations are critical elements of organizational stability, for good and wrongdoing. Rationalizations are perfectly understandable in an arena-type organizational logic: the games and balances between the groups and coalitions feed and produce rationalizations that become acceptable and legitimate.

People are essential in an organization viewed as an arena. Moreover, people have cognitive biases and engage in group and social processes involving rationalizing and normalizing acts in their constant interaction. These acts and behaviors can be political, rational, and improper or unethical. A compliance logic that loses sight of these elements is likely to have a limited capacity to bring about the substantial changes that will move an organization toward its own compliance objectives.

2.3.3 Socialization

Finally, socialization implies the process of communication and legitimation of practices: people discover the organization through other people, their groups, languages, and routines. Doing something or failing to do something not only implies knowing and calculating the formal rules that define the organization to which they belong. Above all, it involves knowing and being accepted as a person in both formal and informal structures. Belonging to an organization involves acting like the other people in the organization, knowing the jargon, the language, the rules of etiquette, the values, and practices, and doing what others do and regarding it as legitimate. This happens at the organization's level and that of groups and coalitions (some practices and values may vary within these groups).

Moreover, belonging involves conceding. It involves not failing the group, not creating conflicts and unnecessary doubts, and using facts to show that the beliefs and fundamentals that define the group and the organization are accepted. Failing the team can involve, for example, questioning a leader or not following a hierarchical order. Failing can entail raising doubts about the decisions or practices that have been agreed upon by the majority or by tradition (however questionable they may be) (Van Maanen, 1983).

Socialization is, once again, an individual social force. Likewise, it is a force that enables the stability of organizational dynamics for due and wrongful acts. Indeed, an illegal practice that is institutionalized and rationalized will be strengthened by socialization processes. For example, in an organization Greil and Rudy (1984) called "social cocoons" are created: people experience a process of gradual encapsulation within the dynamics of groups, their rules, and routines. If a person begins to have second thoughts about such a practice, for example and fails to do what is expected of him, he can be informed that if one cog in the machine fails, then the other parts will suffer. Failing as a person has social implications that other members of the organization will let you know of in several ways: from direct disapproval to the softer strategy of proposing moral blackmail. The glue of the organization is definitely its social relations. Social relations communicate, but even more relevant, they bind people: they unite and link them. That a person refuses to act or decides to act is not only a calculation that considers individual elements of this person: it also involves calculations regarding how those decisions, actions, or inactions affect the social relationships in which the person is embedded. Refusing to commit a certain act or engage in a particular practice will have repercussions on relationships between people and groups: relationships that are not only instrumental but also emotional and linked to belonging or even friendship. Socialization is a potent glue that organizations generate and use to sustain themselves, for better or worse.

All change processes, including compliance projects, face the challenge of being adapted and adopted by these different balances. Compliance projects are played out in the organizational arena. They are translated and interpreted and will require modifying or adapting these balancing processes through new selection, socialization, and rationalization forms.

2.4 A Short, Disturbing, and Much-debated Example: Positive Deviant Behaviors and Rule-bending

The behavior of people in an organization, seen through the metaphor of an arena, is dynamic and relational. In other words, it is affected by psychological issues in an environment of a relationship with other people participating and socializing by separate groups within a diverse and rich organizational setting.

People gather in an organization to decide and act. Also, they must interpret every situation they experience, encounter, and exchange with other people and give it meaning. Always, in a day-to-day dynamic, a situational dynamic. Organizational behavior involves the behavior of people in constant exchange that is tested with each situation that must be faced.

From this perspective, it is worth asking about behavior within what has been called the organization as an arena: what then is normal behavior? What is appropriate behavior?

People constantly need to interpret the situation in which they find themselves. Formal written rules, norms, and laws are undoubtedly a reference. But rarely a perfect, complete reference. Every situation involves details, variations, and novelties. In an organization as an arena, it is impossible to act mechanically. People who interpret are expected to act with caution. In other words, they are expected to use their judgment to cope with the contradictions they must resolve. For example, an urgent purchase must be made. Formal rules would involve slowing down the process. There are no clear rules about exceptions either. So, someone must decide to bend the rules a little to achieve the goal. Bending the rules is more common than one would think. First, rules are not always complete since they cannot foresee all the specific situations. Second, rules usually establish a general framework of action for diverse processes implemented by different people in different organizational spheres. An organization may have different rules and regulations distributed through the network of offices and departments. Rules and norms must be interpreted and communicated. There is obviously no time to communicate or explain interpretations in emergencies or when time is short. Still, even in nonemergency situations, communication between people about how to interpret a given situation may not be perfect. It will depend on the practices and customs of the groups, the resources to communicate, and the skill in doing so.

A clear example of this process is work-to-rule. Employees refuse to do anything more than the minimum established in their contract as a protest. No more decisions are made, and rules are not interpreted in such a way as to make the continued action of the organization viable, effectively paralyzing it.

The problem caused by these dynamics is obvious: where does one draw the line between bending and breaking the rules? Moreover, is bending the rules an act of deviance that can be acceptable and positive? (Sekerka & Zolin, 2007; Veiga, Golden, & Dechant, 2004; Larson & Melville, 1980)

Skerka and Zolin (2007: 230) even argue that bending the rules involves the exercise of prudence. In the classical sense, prudence is a cognitive ability people can develop to deal with ambiguous situations or fall into gray areas in practice. In response to ethical dilemmas such as having to choose the lesser of two evils, prudence is a form of practical reasoning, which then attempts to consider the consequences of a decision on other people or the situation in general. Understanding the rule-bending defense argument, thus we can return to the earlier rationalization discussion: how does legitimate rule-bending differ from the rationalization of wrongdoing?

The concept of rule-bending is also related to "positive deviance." Deviance, as a word, can immediately attract normative judgments: deviance from what is expected and, therefore bad. Though, deviance can occur concerning what is expected in statistical terms, for example. Is it possible to speak of positively deviant organizational behavior? For example, a voluntary act of departing from certain formal norms for a good reason. Whistleblowing, for example: pointing out that others are engaging in possibly illicit acts implies, to a certain extent, breaking the codes of fellowship or camaraderie. If a hierarchical superior is accused, a rule of loyalty or obedience may be broken (Spreitzer & Sonenshein, 2004).

In a way, organizational behavior is not just a matter of norms and rules but instead of social or group expectations. That is why people's specific situation in deciding what to do matters so much. Ultimately, people must make their calculations and interpretations in a social and organizational context, crystallized by expectations of what is "correct" or "normal" or "reasonable" (Dodge, 1985). It remains difficult to draw the line: a particular behavior may be deviant, reasonable, or necessary for some, and it may be consciously or unconsciously deviant (Robinson & Bennett, 1995).

Nevertheless, for some people, it can be regarded as overt wrongdoing rather than deviant. The same act, under different circumstances or situations, may vary in this respect when it is measured against expectations. Even in novel situations, there may be debate over expectations in a group or organization. Deviance is not simply a matter of black or white: it is affected by expectations, situations, practices, rules, and norms, all in motion.

When we talk about compliance, we are talking about an effort that is not linear: order, rules, and obedience. It is a process of constructing and accepting the porous lines between bending and breaking the rules, and positive or negative deviant behavior (Ben-Yehuda, 1990; Heckert, 1989). The best compliance effort requires addressing this reality when there is no clear line and probably never will be.

Speaking of legitimate or necessary rule-bending or positive deviation is extremely difficult. Although behaviors are complex in the actual practice of organizations, must cope with various situations, and are constructed in a social and group context, it will always seem necessary to continue thinking about and insisting on establishing clear boundaries and definitions of proper behaviors, precisely to avoid the problem of rationalization, for example.

That is why, although it seems necessary to better understand organizational behavior in its actual, day-to-day dynamics through concepts such as positive deviance, not all the consequences seem acceptable, at least for some analysts. Indeed, Goode (1991) argues against the concept of positive deviance. He posits that this concept must address the question of control in practice. Defining rules and the problems of breaking or deviating from them is a matter of control: the point is to control people's behavior. However, the question remains: Who creates the line establishing the need for control? Not a machine, but human beings in organizational positions coping with situations.

In any case, under the idea of the metaphor of the organization as an arena, it remains a challenge to define a world that is precisely the opposite of reality without deviant or rule-bending behavior. What is perfectly appropriate or "healthy" behavior? Perfectly healthy is impossible to establish in biological matters (entropy, for example, which is inevitable in any system) and social issues (every normative concept can be discussed from different values held by people). Denying the existence of ambiguous behavioral strategies such as bending the rules or prudent or positive deviance means closing one's eyes to an important phenomenon (Sagarin, 1985).

Improper or unethical behavior implies the existence of harmful behavior toward other people or groups, which is illegal and unacceptable to a given community (Brass, Butterfield, & Skaggs, 1998). There is, therefore, no single path for drawing that complicated line between what is right and wrong. Every compliance program has to live with this uncertainty and ambiguity. Even, be able to get the best out of them.

In any case, this is one of the significant challenges of compliance: dealing with the organizational behavior of flesh and blood people coping with different situations and attempting to observe and make sense of the different expectations placed on them. Attempting to solve the dilemma by thinking that a direct control mechanism can be established without ambiguities and directing people's behavior as if they did not have to cope with ambiguous and uncertain situations would appear to be a recipe for failure. It overlooks the ambiguity, uncertainty, and social and psychological capacity of human beings to interpret and lend meaning, rationalizing and using prudence to bend the rules, and making mistakes are inevitable and a critical element to consider. All this is compounded by the endless possibility of malice, unbridled ambition, and the tendency to engage in fraudulent behavior.

2.5 The Organizational Slide to Disaster

As we have seen in previous sections, there is a key phenomenon typical of organizational dynamics: the quest for stability and certainty required to create the interactions and interdependencies that will provide the minimum necessary coordination and co-operation between people and groups creates balances that can be perverse. They are perverse because they normalize inappropriate acts based on institutionalization, rationalization, and socialization logic. They do this either by avoiding responsibilities or justifying practices and routines that lend meaning to acts that prove to be small or big steps that protect and even encourage fraud.

A compliance program can be hijacked by these perverse equilibriums, effectively concealing the existence of practices and routines that put the organization, its staff, clients, and citizens (in the case of government companies) at risk.

How does this process of constructing perverse balances operate? Why are they so stable and not only hard to identify but also to destroy?

The answer lies in the rich social and group dynamics characteristic of organizations. In other words, they are balances built gradually, like the way one goes down a slide, gradually picking up speed. The slide metaphor also implies that the further it goes down, the more difficult it is to stop and correct course. Sunk costs, the sedimentation of practices, and the strength of groupthink or self-imposed veils solidify to such an extent that it becomes more challenging to correct course and avoid a downward plunge, even though the signs of problems are already evident.

To illustrate this dynamic, we analyze three well-known organizational cases in which the organizational slide to disaster, the normalization of fraud, and risky decision-making can be observed and studied: the Ford Pinto, Challenger, and NASA, and the Enron debacle. The point is to see how the decision-making process and risky or improper practices gradually crystallized into a slide that stabilized the use of these practices.

2.5.1 The Case of the Ford Pinto

In 1972, a woman and her son were traveling in America's second best-selling compact car, the Ford Pinto. Unfortunately, it was rear-ended by a car traveling about thirty miles an hour. Although the crash should not have caused more than a dent and a scare, a fire quickly broke out. Studies revealed defects in the Pinto's fuel tank design, which released fuel vapors into the vehicle. Any spark would therefore have been capable of creating a ball of flame that would have exploded inside the car. The 1972 accident caused the death of the driver and severe burns to her son, who had to undergo multiple operations.

Given the accident's circumstances, the Elkart County, Indiana's prosecutor charged Ford Motor Company with reckless homicide. An investigation revealed that the company had been aware of the design defect and its risk. According to the investigation, an explicit decision was made by Ford not to recall the car to correct and update the fuel system design, despite 500 similar incidents with Ford Pintos catching fire as a result of the faulty fuel tank design (Dowie, 1977).

Nevertheless, how could a multinational company have made this decision? Answering this question requires an understanding of the organizational processes that occurred within Ford and legal and regulatory contextual factors dating back to the 1950s.

The first relevant event in the history of the Ford Pinto was the naming of Lee Iacocca as vice president of Ford. He promoted new objectives, as well as a new organizational culture to deal with the context the company was facing. Iacocca's strategies included manufacturing a compact car to compete with Volkswagen, which dominated that market in the United States in the late 1960s and early 1970s. The Pinto became "Lee's car," a company's flagship project, which was expected to be presented for its immediate sale in 1971. The design and production process of the Pinto was rushed. Typically, this takes 43 months for a new car, whereas in the case of the Pinto, it was reduced to just 25 months (Legget, 1999).

Also, during the testing phase, Iacocca established "the limit's 2000" for the Pinto, meaning that the new car should not exceed $2,000 in price or 2,000 pounds in weight (Legget, 1999). Engineers faced the challenge of remaining within the established limits and were forced to find a design that primarily met that financial goal (Goia, 1992). In a series of interviews with various people involved in design and production within Ford, Dowie (1977) reports that there was a feeling that "[t]his company is run by salespeople, not engineers; and that the priority is style, not safety." Even in the process of testing during production, when the problem with the gas tank was discovered, Iaccoca was not informed since, according to an engineer who worked on the Pinto project:

> [t]hat person would have been fired. Safety wasn't a popular subject around Ford in those days. With Lee it was taboo. Whenever a problem arose that meant a delay with the Pinto, Lee would chomp on his cigar, look out the window, and say, 'Read the product objectives again and get back to work.' (Dowie, 1977)

Despite the problems encountered with the fuel tank systems, the organization promoted a series of goals in the organization where the priority was to boost sales and cut costs to achieve competitive prices. Thus, although the firm had a patent for a safer fuel tank system, the costs involved exceeded the rigid limits previously set on price and weight. A Ford employee reported that:

> [T]he people shopping for subcompacts are watching every dollar. You have to realize that the price elasticity of these cars is extremely tight. Adding $25 to production costs can put a model out of business. (Dowie, 1977)

A design change in a compact car has little scope for maneuver: upgrading the fuel system meant reducing the boot space, which in commercial terms, it was argued, would make the model less attractive than other cars in a side-by-side comparison. Another Ford employee noted the following:

[About the space that the safer tank system would take up by reducing the boot space] That's true. But you're completely missing the point . . . safety is not an issue; boot space is. You have no idea how stiff the competition is in boot space. Do you realize that if we put a Capri-type tank [the safest tank system] in the Pinto, you would only be able to fit a set of golf clubs in the boot? (Dowie, 1977)

Given the rigid specifications imposed by organizational sensemaking focused on price and competition, the next step in the slide to normalizing a decision that minimizes safety is surprising. It is because the organization took steps to justify and rationalize the decision to prioritize financial over safety considerations. The decision was based on a cost-benefit maximization analysis approved by the National Highway Traffic Safety Administration (NHTSA). A cost-benefit analysis means that a company must make decisions based on its actions' financial and social costs. The method enables it to estimate prices and costs for factors such as life, safety, and social benefits. Ford used this method to weigh the cost of human life or suffering in monetary terms. In other words, if private cost A is more than social cost B, then A>B, it is unnecessary to modify the good because it is less efficient. Conversely, if the private cost had been less than the social cost, A<B, Ford would have decided it was more efficient to change the Ford Pinto fuel system.

Thus, Ford's analysis posed an ethical dilemma because it was necessary to rate elements such as life, which are considered invaluable, in monetary terms (Birsh & Fielder, 1994). Ford estimated that the compensation cost was $200,000 per death, $67,000 per injury, and $700 per vehicle per year. It predicted that 180 incidents would occur and 2,100 vehicles would burn, so the cost was estimated to be around $49.5 million (Legget, 1999). At the same time, Ford submitted a cost report, stating that changing the system would cost $11 per vehicle for 11 million cars and 1.5 million trucks, making a total of $137 million. Based on this analysis, Ford decided that it was more practical not to modify the fuel tank because it was less efficient according to this interpretation of the cost-benefit analysis. The organization raised the decision as legal and legitimate since it adhered to the established legal parameters. It was therefore rationalized that the right thing was being done in light of a method that was regarded as legitimate and valid.

However, according to Dowie (1977) and Legget (1999), the cost-benefit analysis undertaken by Ford was skewed because it failed to include critical information, meaning that actual costs were not considered, and the cost of other factors such as changing the fuel system was inflated. Ford had previously launched an advertising campaign on safety, which backfired, so they decided it was not a major factor in car sales. Although withdrawing the Pinto model for safety reasons would have been a severe advertising and commercial blow, this unquantifiable factor was not included in the cost-benefit analysis (Legget, 1999). Dowie (1977) reported that the actual cost of modifying the fuel system would not have been $11 per car but just $5.08, and the social cost would have been $63.5 million rather than $137 million. Therefore,

Ford's analysis was skewed, pursuing stated goals in which profits were prioritized over consumer safety.

This case shows how organizational sensemaking that has been institutionalized and socialized makes it possible to normalize an extreme prioritization of criteria: financial and market over safety factors. It is then rationalized through instruments such as a cost-benefit analysis, which is valid in certain circumstances. In this case, the instrument was used to normalize a financial perspective on human life and safety. The ethical discussion would not have been easy to resolve, especially not using a technique or instrument such as a cost-benefit analysis. Not to mention the fact that the calculations were probably skewed.

2.5.2 The Case of Challenger

On January 28, 1986, NASA's space shuttle Challenger was launched to great fanfare. A few seconds after liftoff, one of the solid rocket boosters (SRB) failed, causing the spaceship to explode and plummet to the ground, together with the seven crew members. This event is still remembered as one of the greatest aeronautical tragedies in living memory. It also seriously damaged NASA's prestige, which had already come under scrutiny. In the wake of this event, a Presidential Commission was set up to determine the causes of the accident. What was it that led to Challenger's failure? Was it a technical error? Were any external factors that caused the accident identified? Or was the accident due to the organizational logic and how members made certain critical decisions?

Over time, investigations by various disciplines have attempted to clarify the situation that led to the disaster. The analyses are based on different premises and yield various findings. For this book, the results of the investigation conducted by the Rogers Commission are described. This commission provided one of the best-known explanations, which researcher Diane Vaughan used to undertake an organizational study. Vaughan conducted an ethnographic and historical analysis, focusing on the prevailing organizational decisions, dynamics, practices, and cultures at NASA. This perspective from within the organization shows how the organization made decisions that normalized certain practices and values, which resulted in poor decisions. Vaughan's study details at least three factors that contributed to the Challenger incident: technical, contextual, and organizational mistakes.

In the literature, the disaster is thought to have been caused by a technical failure. The fault lay in the O-rings designed to seal the gap caused by the ignition of solid rocket boosters. The problem is that the strength of the O-rings was affected by the unusually cold conditions on the morning of the launch. When the thrusters were fired, this affected the O-rings, first the one in the right SRB, then the one in the external tank containing liquid hydrogen and oxygen, which caused the explosion. However, there had been long outstanding problems with the O-rings that had failed to be addressed, mainly for budgetary reasons. In the 1970s and 1980s, NASA had undergone significant financial and personnel cuts. Within NASA, it was believed that they should compete for resources since the international prestige of space research had diminished.

NASA gradually shifted its priority activities to securing funding, mainly by placing satellites in orbit for private companies and partnering with the military sector to maintain its reputation as a strategic sector. This entailed two major problems that were part of those identified by the Commission. Poor selection of contractors, for example. For the O-rings, Thiokol company was selected on the basis of financial criteria: its bid was almost $100 million lower than that of the other bidders in the tender. This was decisive, even though it was not a leading company in the field.

The second problem was that very tight launch windows had been established as part of a cost reduction strategy. In the case of Challenger, liftoff had been postponed four times, creating pressure to avoid a further delay. However, Vaughan (1996) doubts that this was decisive because despite the existing schedules, for NASA's senior managers, safety has always been paramount, meaning that delaying the mission would have been expensive but not that serious.

There had been warnings about faulty O-rings with resistance problems (Isikoff & Fishman, 1986). The night before liftoff, members of NASA and Thiokol identified problems with the O-rings. Therefore, they held meetings to discuss the severity of the damage, as well as possible scenarios and solutions. At this point, a key event occurred. Members of Thiokol suggested that given how compromised the O-rings were, it would be better to postpone liftoff. NASA's middle managers were unsure. Opinions were divided since technical assessments showed a significant risk that the O-rings would be unable to withstand liftoff. In the end, members of the engineering area decided to continue with the launch. When the Commission investigated this situation, it found that senior managers had been unaware of the board's problems and even unaware that postponement of liftoff had been considered.

This reflected communication problems within the organization and the fact that it violated established protocols (Hall, 2003). The established information flows had not been followed, so the Commission declared that the decision-making process was flawed. According to the Commission's report, competition, resource scarcity, and production pressure from the national and international political environment were among the structural conditions that led to the disaster. These challenges permeated the entire NASA organization, affecting decision-making on the eve of the launch. The decision-makers were not incompetent and fully understood the situation and the technical and administrative risks. NASA administrators, in other words, took a risk: there is never a 100% safe launch. There are risks. Although the risks of failure of the O-rings had been acknowledged, they were thought to be within an acceptable range (Harvey, 2016).

The problem was ultimately not whether risks were taken; risks are always taken with space flight. The point is whether the organizational processes for determining these risks were reasonably followed, and the consensus is that they were not (Vaughan, 1990). Furthermore, Vaughan (1996) collected criticisms of NASA management, such as the fact that a risky decision was made without sufficiently considering the dangers to human lives.

However, Vaughan (1996) offers an alternative, more detailed explanation of what happened on an organizational scale from another perspective, known as "the sociology of error." Contrary to what is argued, NASA managers did not engage in intentional administrative irregularities, violate the rules, or commit acts of conspiracy. The cause of disaster for Vaughan (1996; 1990) then was a structural error, a web of issues embedded in organizational dynamics and facilitated by an environment of scarcity and competition. An organization that is forced to cope with risks, and complex technologies that interact in uncertain ways, must be an organization that learns and makes various decisions incrementally, creating stable patterns of information, routines, and an organizational culture capable of dealing with these dynamics as far as possible.

Vaughan (1999) explains that the pre-launch situation was not an extraordinary event but the norm. Likewise, proceeding with liftoff despite questions about the O-rings was not an unprecedented event: risk is treated as a significant variable that is quantified and normalized. In other words, if the risk is always greater than zero, how much is considered an acceptable risk? Making this cold, calculating reflection is part of the routines and beliefs of the organization. In this case, a technical conclusion was reached that the SRB O-rings were an acceptable risk and that it was safe enough to take off. Long before the Challenger launch, the cultural construction of the working group on risks, including the problem of the O-rings, had been institutionalized (Vaughan, 1996). Despite disagreement about what should be done about the problem, there was a consensus that it was safe to fly.

In the case of the boosters, this normalization of technical deviance was probably reinforced by the various budgetary situations and pressure on NASA. In other words, the organizational process created and institutionalized to deal with risk by calculating and recalculating it to internalize it was complicated by the context and situation of NASA, especially at a time of politically motivated cutbacks and attacks. The normalization of the ever-existing possibilities of technical failures was embedded in the decision structures and the organizational culture, creating various tools that make it possible to calculate and assess risk and live with it (Vaughan, 1990). How much risk is acceptable? The key, in this case, is that the O-ring defects had been known and calculated for years and that the organization and its decision-making mechanisms had created the conditions for these defects, despite the constant signs, to be interpreted as normal and acceptable. The normalization and even trivialization of the defects combined with the particular situation the organization was experiencing due to pressures and budgetary factors. Thus, when a critical climate situation occurred that might increase the likelihood of failure of the Challenger O-rings, the organization was so wrapped up in its routines and decision-making processes that the means of calculating risk were not altered or modified. Also, the acceptable decisions that made this risk had been building up for years. Regardless of whether they were functional, the forms of communication and hierarchy between the parts of the organization prevailed despite the contextual signals that might have called for a reconsideration of the methods that had worked in the past. As a result, the risk was defined as tolerable, and the decision to launch Challenger was upheld.

2.5.3 The Case of Enron

In December 2001, Enron Corporation, one of the wealthiest, most awarded companies in recent years, announced it was going bankrupt. Enron was founded in 1985 by Kenneth Lay, president of what had formerly been Houston Natural Gas. At its inception, the company focused on the administration of gas pipelines. However, it later expanded toward managing futures contracts in producing natural gas derivatives and gas pipeline construction and operation in Europe. Enron grew exponentially through the construction of gas pipelines, branching into areas such as electricity transmission, taking advantage of the aggressive deregulation of this sector. The company's diversification was such that, in the 1990s, it was difficult to understand in what Enron was explicitly engaged.

Enron also successfully positioned itself in its discourse as an endlessly innovative and successful company. Within Enron, a culture of ostentatiousness prevailed, fostering a culture of aggressive executives and macho leadership. They almost implemented this as a policy through attitudes and actions that emphasized the virtually infallible nature of the company. McLean and Elkind (2013) state, "Enron's aura had been such that no-one had bothered to look at the infighting, the macho posturing, the unbridled greed . . . ." The fact is that, due to this unrestrained, pretentious, and exultant culture of the aggressive pursuit of unbridled profit as a virtue, Enron gradually built its legend, which in turn allowed it to legitimize its voraciousness. The specialized press, investors, and analysts of the financial sector supported this image that rewarded arrogance and profit at all costs by making Enron a success story of the new American companies. Various agents and organizations harbored suspicions about how the company had achieved the profits it boasted of, as well as the transparency of its reported numbers and the legitimacy of its operations.

In October 2001, it was revealed that Enron executives had systematically committed fraud. How did it take so long for the truth that people had suspected for years to come to light? Jeffrey Skilling, president of Enron at the time, and CFO Andrew Fastow, instructed those responsible for financial reports to hide billions of dollars in debt and increase dividends to encourage stock purchases by investors who saw the company as a unique opportunity. Skilling and Fastow misled many people and institutions, including Enron's board of directors, investors, and audit committee. In addition, they forced members of Arthur Andersen, one of the largest accounting firms in the United States, to modify their reports on the practices engaged in by Enron and support its dubious accounting practices rather than reporting them as possible indications of fraud.

The company reported that it invoiced at least $100 billion annually. The point is that accounting engineering made these data possible, as the practices of altering the books to report debts as earnings and even massaging the figures are known. In 2000, Enron shares were worth $90, whereas after the fraudulent scheme was discovered, they barely traded at $1. In this way, more than $10 billion in share values were lost, affecting millions of investors.

Why did this happen? The main answer is that these accounting practices, with certain limits, had been normalized in the financial sector, and Enron used them since its inception. In 1987, Davi Woytek, head of Enron's internal audit department, received a call about a bank account that was not on the books. The account had been opened by Tom Mastroeni, treasurer of Enron Oil at the time. Bank transfers for more than five million dollars had been made from that account, as well as another two million that had funneled to another account in the name of Mastroeni (McLean & Elkind, 2013). Mastroeni defended his actions, claiming he had done so for the good of the company to achieve the financial objectives, which Enron accepted. This case resolves that Mastroeni conducted unusual transactions without any sanctions being imposed or any legal or administrative action being implemented. All this took place despite the fact that Arthur Andersen's internal and external auditors had pointed out the irregularities yet neglected to delve further into the scope and problems arising from these transactions.

Until it was discovered that Mastroeni had also embezzled Enron, which triggered a series of legal disputes. Enron then modified its position, calling the unusual transactions "false transactions," in one of the most obvious rhetorical forms of what is now known as post-truth. Defense attorneys for other companies argued that Enron had been aware of these transactions without doing anything to stop them until it had ended up being affected by them. One of the attorneys stated that "[Any honest, competent management, confronted with Mastroeni's conduct, as revealed to Enron's senior management in January 1987, would have fired that gentleman without delay" (McLean & Elkind, 2013).

Likewise, in the scheme led by Skilling, the company's accounting department was presumably aware of the fraudulent practices since the area director ordered the numbers to be altered. The justification was to maintain Enron's image in order to achieve success. Moreover, top executives continued to believe that the situation would improve and that the company would pay off its debts, blinding themselves to the vicious circle in which it found itself.

This shows that irregular, dishonest practices within Enron had been institutionalized. The logic within the company was that they should lie, divert funds, and alter the books to maintain the illusion they had built of a successful company. The same executives who knew about Enron's practices were openly lying to the media, investors, and the board of directors, challenging criticism and dismissing doubts raised during the process. In that respect, Skilling, president of Enron, declared that what had happened to the company was "part of the brutal cycle of business life . . . . Enron was a victim [of the system]. This reflects the fact that high-risk accounting practices were widespread in the financial sector" (MacLennan, 2005). However, the Enron case is paradigmatic because it reveals extreme abuse and fraud.

As mentioned,, Enron executives like Skilling sought to make their company "the biggest company in the world" by promoting arrogance, squandering, and insensitivity, exalting macho culture in the business sector, which rewarded those able to secure the best deals no matter how this was done. Dividends accrued to those who were successful, regardless of how they were obtained. MacLennan (2005) argues that the Enron case was treated as exceptional, although corrupt practices by business leaders are the rule rather than the exception.

In this respect, Enron represents a symbol: in a context where people were fighting for deregulation, leaving the behavior of companies to the free forces of competition, what was consolidated was the institutionalization of unscrupulous behavior. Total deregulation in a complex economy is an oxymoron. Without laws, the rule of law, courts, audits, and free competition would be an illusion. The deregulation argument was achieved precisely to allow the internalization, in various companies, of bullying as a business style. And the resulting institutionalization and subsequent normalization of fraud as a way of life.

2.5.4 Compliance in the Real World of Organizations

Organizations can slide toward normalizing fraud and wrongdoing. They can create mechanisms to justify such acts, to normalize and rationalize them not because people are bad or naturally "bad" (as the rotten apple metaphor has attempted to claim). People do not always act according to rational, conscious guidelines, and the abilities and skills to do so are quite limited, with various unconscious forces coming into play (Bargh & Chartrand, 1999). In addition, in an organization, they are hardly in a bubble: they coexist, interact, and engage in the dynamics of interdependence with other people, groups, and coalitions. Moreover, in these relationships, people can manage how they present themselves, communicate, and what they allow others to see (and prevent others from seeing), including deception and diversion tactics (Goffman, 1959; Vaughan, 1999: 282). Last but not least, organizational structures, routines, and practices stabilize, crystallize, and are not easy to change because organizations are more of an arena than a homogeneous, monolithic entity.

The challenge is interesting, exciting, and enthralling. Compliance can be a highly influential tool and organizational process for coping with dilemmas such as those shown in the cases reviewed. However, any compliance project must be responsible for the organizational dynamics of institutionalization, socialization, and rationalization. The response of any organization to a compliance program may, in the first instance, be contradictory and paradoxical: improper behaviors or the practices and meanings that allow them can form part of the organizational equilibrium. Indeed, the processes of institutionalization, selection, socialization, and rationalization, as a whole and in interaction, create equilibrium. They contribute to the normalization of behavior and social relationships, which, despite being dubious or bordering on illegality, are considered, in practice, legitimate, logical, and indispensable on a day-to-day basis. These same forces and processes paradoxically stabilize the behaviors, routines, rules, and practices which, knowingly or unknowingly, create the dynamics of fraud, corruption, and deception.

Indeed, paradoxical though it may sound, improper behavior and the dynamics of fraud and corruption may well be a stable part of the organizational arena. Perverse equilibriums, the processes of institutionalization, socialization, and rationalization which, on the one hand, produce accepted behaviors and routines, are the same as those that normalize behaviors and routines that are inappropriate or illegal. And changing them can prove extremely difficult, precisely because they have been normalized. Identifying them, for example, can be a lengthy, complex process.

As Vaughan (1996) points out, organizational successes and failures are interconnected by environment, organization, cognition, and decision. Attempting to solve every problem through rules or the creation of structures has limits. People matter, and the relationships people build matter. Also, people fail cognitively and logically. Isolating these elements as pathologies or exceptions is usually a significant error in prescriptive theories and proposals for change and better organization. And compliance. For people to accept that certain dynamics, beliefs, and routines must be denormalized is no simple task: breaking inertia, removing the veils that blind, and identifying the arguments they wield or rationalize not to change and to defend equilibriums. Lastly, it is not an act directed exclusively at individuals: denormalizing these equilibriums is a group, collective and political act. It is a group activity because normalization is a blinding veil as it is built on day-to-day interaction. It is a collective one because various rationalizations are shared between groups between hierarchical levels, fed by the organization's own culture. Finally, it is political since the participation of the upper echelons of the hierarchy in the rationalization processes is a constant. Furthermore, this broadly defines not only the correlation of forces but also the actual types of interaction between directions, groups, and coalitions within the organization.

A large part of the success of a compliance project will therefore lie in its ability to dismantle these perverse equilibriums strategically. It will need to destroy the veils of self-deception that have allowed the rationalization and normalization of routines, norms, rules, and behaviors that enable and sustain inappropriate dynamics because they are interlinked.

2.6 Organizational Dynamics and the Challenges of Compliance Programs

A program cannot be exclusively seen as a formal act, a document to communicate, or a structure to impose on an organization. At least not if the goal is to fulfill the ambitious promise of compliance: for an organization to endogenously and properly conduct ethical and legal action permanently, at all levels. As has been discussed in this chapter, a program will be interpreted, adapted, and adopted by people, groups, and structures, in the dynamic organizational arena. This implies, for example, that people in an organization can use and justify a compliance program in different ways. They can adapt and adopt it as an instrument to create a persecutory environment against groups or individuals for failing to comply with rules or codes. They can assimilate the activity into the form, pretending that routines have been radically changed, even though they are still doing the same as before. They can turn compliance into an appendix: a space that has not been fully incorporated into the organization yet allows it to show the outside world that something is being done. Likewise, they can find new elements to rationalize and justify the belief that their actions are not wrong. Alternatively, even lie to themselves about the inappropriateness of their actions. In addition, compliance will be viewed differently by each level of organizational authority, with varying degrees of power to help and hinder the implementation of a program of this nature (Jávor & Jancsics, 2016).

Compliance is ultimately both an administrative and legal project, as well as a political one. It is political because, to be effective, it requires creating the conditions for leadership, communication, negotiation, implementation, and evaluation. It is administrative because it must be implemented not only as a process but as a structure that is exogenously embedded in the dynamics and flow of the organization on a day-to-day basis. The administrative aspect involves a strategy for its endogenous incorporation into the day-to-day flows of the organization. The process itself does not ensure compliance. Following the regulatory steps defined in the formal documents of an organization is not compliance. Compliance implies embedding change in an organization, constructing a new institutionalized equilibrium capable of creating an acceptable, legitimate normalization so that the common behaviors of the organization draw closer to each other and are constructed based on the law, the norm, and ethics.

From an organizational point of view then, a series of compliance risks can be broken down and seen as a change project involving the following:

1. *Leadership.* Framing compliance as a procedural, normative program required by the context eliminates its potential to be a transformative mechanism from the outset. Leadership that sees compliance in this way will end up positioning this activity as a parallel structure that the organization must "endure" as a burden. This vision will then institutionalize adaptation mechanisms rather than the adoption of compliance. As a result, the organization will probably trigger socialization mechanisms,

for example, to evade compliance and even rationalize acting (in other words, it will pretend to comply with its processes, but only formally). Conversely, leadership plays a key role in preventing this risk by understanding the importance of participation and agreement with the different organizational leaderships (both formal and coalitions) for the program to be successful. Understanding the costs and effects that the changes and transformations of rules and behaviors will entail for effective practices, routines and values understood in the organization is a key aspect of leadership. Without costs or the energy and vitality to dare to change and denormalize statutory, stabilized practices and beliefs, there can be no compliance.

2. *Communication.* Establishing compliance as an exogenous process is one of the most common risks. In other words, the compliance program becomes a parallel path, an instance that runs parallel to the substantive processes of the organization. The compliance program does not become endogenous. It will always be exogenous, a burden that must be carried. Communicating compliance in this way reduces it to an external imposition that must be endured or tolerated rather than incorporated and embedded in the actual dynamics of the organization. It will be destined to be a parallel rather than a substantive activity. Depicting it as a strategic part of an endogenous change, with costs and benefits, can create a more consistent image of the need for transformations within the organization. This will make it possible to communicate the costs and benefits to be obtained in the short and long term. Compliance requires a constant, broad, and clearly explained commitment from the organization's top hierarchy and its most influential groups. This will not only lend the program legitimacy but also enable it to obtain realistic, relevant information about what works and what doesn't; information on the obstacles and opportunities being identified and developed along the implementation path.

3. *Negotiation.* The risk of seeing a compliance program as a block of rules and structures designed by the top of the corporate structure without considering the actual dynamics of the organization is widespread. If compliance is not intended to be an exogenous or imposed activity and instead attempts to embed itself in the normalized routines and practices of the organization, the strategic goal would be to create a new normalization. This will not be achieved without participating and negotiating between groups and key organizational actors. A program will inevitably experience obstacles and boycotts imposed by the people themselves, even in the organization's upper echelons. This is because the way people usually understand their activity, which has become legitimate and stable in the organization, will be affected. There will therefore be resistance. It is logical to expect this, and it is not worth simply accusing people of "resistance to change." Changing the normality of an organization is a serious matter that requires legitimizing and sustaining the advantages and viability of a new normalization. Reducing the doubts and insecurities that will be created with a compliance program will prevent it from becoming trapped in the current rationalization of the organization. In other words, although the organization has a

compliance program, few things will have changed. That is why there is talk of a constant process of negotiation and bargaining. The expectations of a program are directly associated with the scope, support, and commitment of the various parts of the organization. Logically, there should be two dynamics in any compliance program: the public and the strategic. The public one is the version that is widely and openly communicated. The strategic one is far more discreet and constructed based on the language and political mechanisms within the organization. The ultimate success of a compliance program is largely dependent on understanding how to combine these two phases to create the specific viability of achieving the expected changes.

4. *Implementation.* As hinted in the previous challenge, a compliance program has two facets. The first is substantive and transformative, the second formal and rhetorical. Some companies and organizations may prefer to remain in the second: it is less expensive, less problematic, and makes it possible to project a social image of responsibility, at least formally. A program that also attempts to transform an organization substantively entails significant efforts, risks, and costs. Therefore, a lengthy, detailed implementation process is required to deal with the changes and accidents that will usually be generated and coped with during implementing and operationalizing changes. A compliance program is not a straight, linear journey: it is more like a minefield. It is a process full of details, changes, contingencies, and accidents. A roadmap with phases, timing, logistics, and constant adaptability is required. Its implementation must, paradoxically, be prepared to cope with unforeseen events.

5. *Evaluation.* A compliance program is a living, dynamic process. The risk is that, in the end, efforts will focus on setting up specific steps or processes rather than creating the new normalization of organizational behaviors and routines. The goal of a compliance program is to create a transformation that will endogenously institutionalize and socialize a series of dynamics in the organization's life. Creating new normality is the substantial effect of a change process. This is not achieved in one fell swoop but through a series of phases. Each phase has its strategic and tactical logic, affecting and socializing practices and routines, showing real organizational changes. Evaluation cannot be a purely formal act performed on a single occasion. Evaluation is the constant monitoring of progress and setbacks during the various stages of the process. All this is done to constantly adjust the implementation process and redesign new mechanisms that will endogenously induce and sustain compliance.

The next chapter will explore the construction of compliance programs and the challenge of their endogenous embedding in the intricate institutionalized processes in organizations.

References

ACFE. (2020). *Report to the Nations. Global Study on Occupational Fraud and Abuse*. Austin: ACFE.

Ackoff, R. (1991). *Creating the Corporate Future*. New York: Wiley.

Allison, G., & Zelikow, P. (1999). *Essence of Decision: Explaining the Cuban Missile Crisis*. New York: Pearson.

Anand, V., Ashforth, B., & Joshi, M. (2005). Business as Usual: The Acceptance and Perpetuation of Corruption in Organizations. *Academy of Management Executive*, 19(4), 9–23.

Arellano-Gault, D. (2020). *Corruption in Latin America*. New York: Routledge.

Arrow, K. (1974). *The Limits of the Organization*. New York. W.W. Norton and Company.

Ashforth, B., & Anand, V. (2003). The Normalization of Corruption in Organizations. *Research in Organizational Behavior*, 25, 1–52.

Ashforth, B., Gioia, D., Robinson, S., & Treviño, L. (2008). Re-viewing Organizational Corruption. *Academy of Management Review*, 33(3), 670–684.

Bargh, J., & Chartrand, T. (1999). The Unbearable Automaticity of Being. *American Psychologist*, 54(7), 462–479.

Barnard, C. (1938). *The Functions of the Executive*. Cambridge: Harvard University Press.

Ben-Yehuda, N. (1990). Positive and Negative Deviance: More Fuel for a Controversy. *Deviant Behavior*, 11(3), 221–243.

Birsch, D., & Fielder, J. H. (eds.). (1994). *The Ford Pinto Case: A Study in Applied Ethics, Business and Technology*. Albany, NY: State University of New York Press.

Brass, D., Kenneth, B., & Skaggs, B. (1998). Relationships and Unethical Behavior: A Social Network Perspective. *The Academy of Management Review*, 23 (1), 14–31.

Braverman, H. (1998). *Labor and Monopoly Capital*. New York: Monthly Review Press.

Brunsson, N., & Olsen, J. (1998). *Organizing Organizations*. Copenhagen: Copenhagen Business School.

Brunsson, N. (1985). *The Irrational Organization*. Chichester: John Wiley & Sons.

Crozier, M., & Friedberg, F. (1980). *Actors and the Systems: The Politics of Collective Action*. Chicago: University of Chicago Press.

Crozier, M. (1964). *The Phenomenon Bureaucratic*. Chicago: Chicago University Press.

Cyert, R. M., & March, J. G. (1963). *A Behavioral Theory of the Firm*. Malden, Massachusetts: Prentice Hall/Pearson Education.

De Klerk, J. (2017). "The Devil Made Me Do it!" An inquiry into de Unconscious "Devils Within" of Rationalized Corruption. *Journal of Management Inquiry*, 26 (3), 254–269.

Dodge, D. (1985). The Over-negativized Conceptualization of Deviance: A Programmatic Exploration. *Deviant Behavior*, 6(1), 17–37.

Dowie, M. (1977). Pinto Madness. *Mother Jones*. https://www.motherjones.com/politics/1977/09/pinto-madness/ (accessed March 20, 2022)

Drucker, P. (2008). *The Essential Drucker*. New York: Harper Collins.

Eriksson, L. (2011). *Rational Choice Theory*. New York: Red Global Press.

Fayol, H. (2013). *General and Industrial Management*. New York: Martino Fines Books.

Festinger, L. (1957). *A Theory of Cognitive Dissonance*. Stanford: Stanford University Press.

Gioia, D. (1992). Pinto Fires and Personal Ethics: A Script Analysis of Missed Opportunities. *Journal of Business Ethics*, 11(5/6), 379–389.

Goffman, E. (1959). *The Presentation of Self in Everyday Life*. Edinburgh: Doubleday.

Goode, E. (1991). Positive Deviance: A Viable Concept? *Deviant Behavior*, 12 (3), 289–309.

Greenwood, R.; and Hinings, C.R. (1988). Organizational design types of strategic change. *Organization Studies*, 9(3), 293–316.

Greil, A., & Rudy, D. (1984). Social Cocoons: Encapsulation and Identity Transformation Organizations. *Sociological Inquiry*, 54, 260–278.

Hall, J. L. (2003). Columbia and Challenger: Organizational Failure at NASA. *Space Policy*, 19(4), 239–247.

Harvey, T. (2016). Utah engineers' warning was ignored before Challenger explosion 30 years ago. *The Tribune*. Retrieved from https://archive.sltrib.com/article.php?id=3464503&itype=CMSID (accessed March 20, 2022)

Hauser, C., Simonyan, A., & Werner, A. (2020). Condoning Corrupt Behavior at Work: What Roles do Machiavellianism, On-the-job Experience, and Neutralization Play? *Business & Society*, 1–39. doi:10.1177/0007650319898474

Heckert, M. (1989). The Relativity of Positive Deviance: The Case of French Impressionists. *Deviant Behavior*, 10(2), 131–144.

Isikoff, M., & Fishman, C. (1986). NASA Hit on O-Ring Warnings. *The Washington Post*. Retrieved from https://www.washingtonpost.com/archive/politics/1986/05/11/nasa-hit-on-o-ring-warnings/ee639319-bab1-4fd0-82a7-8e276d894550/ (accessed March 20, 2022).

Janis, I. (1972). *Victims of Groupthink*. Boston: Houghton Mifflin Company.

Jávor, I., & Jancsics, D. (2016). The Role of Power in Organizational Corruption: An Empirical Study. *Administration & Society*, 48(5), 527–558.

Kaplan, R., & Norton, D. (1996). *The Balanced Scorecard*. Cambridge: Harvard Business Review Press.

Larson, C., & Melville, S. (1980). How Far Can a Rule be Bend? *Supervisory Management*, 25, 11–14.

Leggett, C. (1999). *The Ford Pinto case: the valuation of life as it applies to the negligence-efficiency argument*. http://www.wfu.edu/~palmitar/Law&Valuation/Papers/1999/Leggett pinto.html (accesed March, 20, 2022)

MacLennan, C. (2005). Corruption in Corporate America: Enron – Before and After. In Haller, D., Shore, C. (eds.), *Corruption: Anthropological Perspectives*. London: Pluto Press, pp. 156–171.

March, J., & Simon, H. (1993). *Organizations*. New York: Wiley-Blackwell.

March, J. (1994). *A Primer on Decision Making*. New York: Free Press.

Mayo, E. (2014). *The Social Problems of an Industrial Civilization*. London: Routledge.

McLean, B., & Elkind, P. (2013). *The Smartest Guys in the Room*. Penguin Books.

Mintzberg, H. (1992). *Structure in Fives. Designing Effective Organizations*. New York: Pearson.

Mohapatra, S. (2015). *Business Process Reengineering*. New York: Springer.

Morgan, G. (2006). *Images of the Organization*. London: Sage.

Olivier de Sardan, J. (1999). A Moral Economy of Corruption? *The Journal of Modern African Studies*, 37(1), 25–52.

Pullinger, J. (2015). *Prophets of Progress. Saint Simon, Comte & Spencer*. Liverpool: Liverpool Academic Press.

Robinson, S., & Bennett, R. (1995). A Typology of Deviant Workplace Behaviors: A Multidimensional Scaling Study. *Academy of Management Journal*, 38(2), 555–572.

Roethlisberger, F. (2018). *Management and the Worker*. New York. Forgotten Books.

Sagarin, E. (1985). Positive deviance: an oxymoron. *Deviant behavior: An Interdisciplinary Journal*. 6, 169–181.

Sekerka, L., & Zolin, R. (2007). Rule Bending, Can Prudential Judgement Affect Rule Compliance and Values in the Workplace? *Public Integrity*, 9(3), 225–243.

Silverman, M. (2008). *Compliance Management for Public, Private, or Nonprofit Organizations*. New York: McGraw Hill.

Simmel, G. (1906) The Sociology of Secrecy and Secret Societies. *American Journal of Sociology*, 11(4), 441–498.

Simon, H. (1965). *Administrative Behavior*. New York: Free Press.

Spreitzer, G-, & Sonenshein, S. (2004). Toward the Construct Definition of Positive Deviance. *American Behavioral Scientists*, 47 (6), 828–847.

Sykes, G., & Matza, D. (1957). Techniques of Neutralization: A Theory of Delinquency. *American Sociological Review*, 22 (6), 664–670.

Taylor, F. (1997). *The Principles of Scientific Management*. London: Dover Publications.

Van Maanen, J. (1983). Breaking in: Socialization to Work. In Dubin, R. (ed.), *Handbook of Work, Organization and Society* (67–130). Chicago: Rand McNally.

Vaughan, D. (1990). Autonomy, Interdependence, and Social Control: NASA and the Space Shuttle Challenger. *Administrative Science Quarterly*, 225–257.

Vaughan, D. (1996). *The Challenger Launch Decision: Risky Technology, Culture, and Deviance at NASA*. Chicago & London: University of Chicago Press.

Vaughan, D. (1999). The Dark Side of Organizations: Mistake, Misconduct, and Disaster. *Annual Review Sociology*, 25, 271–305.

Veiga, J., Golden, T., & Dechant, K. (2004). Why Managers Bend Company Rules. *Academy of Management Executive*, 18(2), 84–90.

Weick, K. (1979). *The Social Psychology of Organizing*. New York: McGraw Hill.

Weick, K. (2001). *Making Sense of the Organization*. Chichester: Wiley.

Zyglidopoulos, S., Fleming, P., & Rothenberg, S. (2009). Rationalization, Overcompensation, and the Escalation of Corruption in Organizations. *Journal of Business Ethics*, 84(1), 65–73.

Chapter 3
The Long, Winding Road to Drawing Up a Compliance Program

3.1 Introduction

Compliance programs have occupied a prominent place in the corporate world. Increasingly, boards of directors frequently discuss and resolve compliance-related issues because of the increased scrutiny corporate behavior is under from governments, regulators, investors, employees, customers, and the public.

The central promise of the compliance discourse, as discussed in the previous two chapters, is that a properly designed and implemented compliance program provides crucial assurance to all stakeholders that an organization's personnel comply with all the applicable regulations, internal ethical principles, codes of conduct, and other guidelines governing their actions.

However, experience has shown that compliance programs encounter numerous pitfalls in their design and implementation that make it challenging to achieve their stated goal. Many compliance programs fail to forestall the misconduct they were intended to prevent. On the surface, a compliance program may provide systems for identifying and mitigating risks such as fraud, bribery and corruption, sexual harassment, cyberattacks, and many other concerns. However, the reality can be very different.

Obstacles in the design, implementation, and execution of compliance programs may hinder their effectiveness. This is a significant hazard because months or even years can elapse between the occurrence of an incident and its detection. Compliance programs often appear to be working, even when they are not. An organization can have all the pieces in place to demonstrate an effective compliance policy and controls until a serious crime or reputational scandal occurs. Only then will the organization discover that its compliance program was not as robust as it was thought.

This gap between the reality and perception of effectiveness is closely linked to the organizational dynamics with which a compliance program is created and implemented. These action plans do not occur in a vacuum or as a result of spontaneous generation; they are made up of specific actors acting in specific organizational contexts. It is therefore essential to discuss the organizational factors that determine the effectiveness of compliance programs.

The purpose of this chapter is to explain how compliance programs are actually developed and implemented. The key aspects that must be considered when discussing their real-world effectiveness are discussed. Compliance has yet to resolve the administrative problems that gave rise to it. This chapter describes and analyzes aspects of the design, implementation, and execution of compliance plans that can help one understand their limitations and insufficiencies.

https://doi.org/10.1515/9783110749113-003

To this end, this chapter discusses how compliance programs are designed and what they really are. The origin of this action plan and its purpose within the compliance discourse have already been explained in previous chapters. This chapter addresses the most practical aspects of its design and formal, explicit purposes, as well as practices that are usually not spelled out yet, which significantly impact how organizations construct their compliance models.

The following section outlines the challenges organizations often encounter in implementing compliance plans. Implementing compliance policies, procedures, and controls usually deal with obstacles such as organizational resistance, budget limits, and functional rearrangements. All this leads to unexpected or unwanted consequences that must also be discussed.

The obstacles faced in the compliance plans implemented are addressed in the following section. Experience has shown that programs are often distorted when they are implemented. This is because action plans occur in a specific organizational context, with their own dynamics and conflicting agendas that compete for the same resources. In this respect, the implementation imposes another type of limitation on the compliance plan's strategic and tactical objectives.

Finally, the last section of this chapter explains what, in our view, are the results that are actually obtained when the effectiveness of compliance programs is evaluated. Thus, considering the design, implementation, and execution obstacles, the results will be expected to differ from the original promises of the proposed discourse or plan described in Chapter 1, Section 1.4. It is assumed that this set of reflections will permit a more realistic view of what compliance programs are and are not beyond the discourse.

3.2 What are Compliance Programs, and How are They Designed?

The development process is complex and vague for organizations seeking to construct a compliance program. First, there is no single benchmark program, although handbooks indicate the aspects compliance programs must consider. Organizations end up basing their programs on general regulatory guidelines and what they consider "best practices" under their own criteria or with the help of a consultant. This implies significant biases and shortcomings in the design of compliance models that must be considered.

As already pointed out in previous chapters, compliance programs occupy a crucial position in the reform and change discourse of organizations attempting to prove that they have specific mechanisms for addressing unethical behavior by their members. These programs represent the most concrete aspect in which compliance materializes because they are usually formal documents describing the policies, controls, and procedures that the organization incorporates to mitigate the risk of regulatory noncompliance and inhibit unethical conduct.

The origin of compliance programs can be found in the Organizational Guidelines published by the US Sentencing Commission (US Sentencing Commission, 1991) in November 1991. In addition to serving as standards to govern the sentences judges can hand down for crimes committed by companies, these Guidelines also specify the essential characteristics these programs need to have. These characteristics can be summarized as follows:

- Establish rules and procedures to prevent and detect crimes.
- Provide oversight by senior management, usually the board of directors.
- Exercise due care in delegating substantial discretionary authority.
- Establish effective communication mechanisms and training programs in business ethics for all employees.
- Monitor, audit, and report any suspected irregularities and periodically evaluate the compliance program's effectiveness.
- Promote and consistently enforce the corporate compliance program by encouraging the use of established mechanisms and disciplining employees who commit crimes or fail to adopt the necessary measures to prevent and detect criminal conduct.
- Take reasonable steps to respond to criminal conduct once it has been detected and prevent further criminal conduct.

In practice, compliance programs have translated into a set of standard measures that have been incorporated into organizations, which have made inconsistent efforts to adapt them to the specific characteristics of each organization.

In a key document released in 2017, the DOJ published the aspects prosecutors must consider when determining whether a compliance program meets the minimum requirements established by the Organizational Guidelines. This is a key point because these considerations can be used to mitigate sentences for companies found guilty of corporate crimes. In this respect, this document, entitled *Evaluation of Corporate Compliance Programs* (US Department of Justice, 2020; O'Shea, Bourtin, Lewis, 2020; Grubman, & Tanner, 2018), has become a benchmark for considering the elements a program should include.

According to the DOJ document (2020), programs are expected to include at least six attributes or characteristics. These elements are given in Table 3.1.

Organizations are incorporating these attributes differently in practice because neither the Organizational Guidelines nor the DOJ document set out specific procedures or criteria for designing or implementing compliance programs. This is because the aim is to give organizations the flexibility to design their own programs according to their particular needs and industry.

Companies usually design their programs with a certain margin of discretion (Chen & Soltes, 2018). However, regardless of what company it is or what type of organization we are talking about, in the end, compliance programs usually incorporate the vast majority – if not all – of the attributes prescribed by the DOJ.

Table 3.1: Elements included in a compliance program according to DOJ.

No.	Elements that should be included in a Compliance Program according to DOJ
1	Risk analysis
2	Policies and procedures
3	Training and communication
4	Anonymous reporting mechanism and investigation protocols
5	Due diligence processes
6	Protocols for mergers and acquisitions

Source: US Department of Justice, 2020.

We will now briefly describe each of these attributes to detail the criteria that should be considered in the design of each compliance control. This description also allows us to comment on the limitations or shortcomings usually observed in the design of each of these attributes.

1. Risk Analysis

According to the DOJ (2020), the starting point for an organization to declare that it has a well-designed compliance program is to identify, evaluate, and define its risk profile. In other words, the program is designed to detect the particular types of misconduct or regulatory noncompliance most likely to occur in the line of business in which it operates.

For example, it is essential to consider whether the company has analyzed and addressed the risks incurred by factors such as the location of its operations, the industrial sector, market competitiveness, the regulatory framework, type of customers and business partners, transactions with governments, payments to public officials, use of third parties, gifts, travel and entertainment expenses, and donations.

In this respect, the design of a program will be expected to be a "risk map" exercise that will help the organization identify what risk situations it faces in its lines of business and establish priority criteria for distinguishing between critical, moderate, and low risks.

The DOJ suggests evaluating the risk analysis of a compliance program based on three criteria:
- Risk management process: What methodology has the organization used to identify, analyze, and address the risks it faces? What information or metrics has the organization used to identify the type of misconduct to which it is exposed?
- Risk-adapted resource allocation: Does the organization spend sufficient time and resources monitoring high-risk areas? Does the organization scrutinize high-risk

transactions (such as a large contract with a government agency in a high-risk country) more than more modest, routine expenses?
- Updates and revisions: Is the risk assessment up to date and subject to periodic review? Have any policies and procedures been updated in light of lessons learned? Do these updates consider risks discovered from misconduct or other issues identified through the compliance program? (US Department of Justice, 2020: 3)

In practice, risk analysis is one of the most critical aspects when designing a compliance program. Assuming that what cannot be measured cannot be controlled, the facts show that organizations tend to fail in this requirement of "effectiveness" in their programs. Although several factors account for these shortcomings, two main ones will be analyzed here:

First, there is a limit on completeness. Organizational reality will always be much more complex than the ability to diagnose risks (Makkai & Braithwaite, 1993). An organization will be unlikely to be able to identify each of the risks it faces, be it regulatory noncompliance or ethical behavior. Organizational dynamics go beyond the capacity for rational control and supervision (understood as means-end chains). Risk maps tend to be somewhat limited diagnoses of what is considered a compliance risk in a specific situation and in the eyes of those who perform the exercise.

Second, there is a limit on risk measurement. There is no clear consensus on the criteria or methods for measuring the criticality of compliance risks. Risk weighting will always be contingent on subjective considerations, which are methodologically argued, yet ultimately subjective. Consequently, there may be – and in fact there are – discrepancies between members of an organization and regulators about what constitutes a critical, moderate, and low critical risk. The solution is not easy and often leads to differences of opinion on how risk is defined and how risk should be addressed. Moreover, that assessment always entails a large component of conflict between the parts of the organization.

2. Policies and Procedures

For the DOJ, any well-designed compliance program also implies policies and procedures that lend content and effect to ethical standards and reduce the risks identified by the organization as part of its risk assessment.

Therefore, for the compliance discourse, an important aspect to consider is whether the organization has a code of ethics that establishes, among other things, the organization's commitment to complying with the regulations and laws that apply to it, which is accessible and applicable to all the employees in the organization. Additionally, the design of a program must contemplate establishing policies and procedures that incorporate compliance controls into its daily operations.

In this respect, the design of a compliance program is expected to include a normative framework for self-regulation, which formally defines the margins of organizational action and the ethical principles under which, in principle, the organization must act.

The DOJ suggests evaluating a program's policies and procedures based on the following criteria:

- Design: What is the organization's process for designing and implementing new policies and procedures? Has that process changed over time? Who has been involved in the design of policies and procedures? Have business units been consulted before they are implemented?
- Comprehension: What efforts has the company made to monitor and implement policies and procedures that reflect and address the risks it faces, including changes in the legal and regulatory landscape?
- Accessibility: How has the company communicated its policies and procedures to all employees and relevant third parties? If the organization has overseas subsidiaries, are there any language or other types of barriers to access for foreign employees?
- Responsibility: Who has been responsible for the incorporation of policies and procedures? Have they been implemented to ensure that employees understand the policies? How are compliance policies and procedures enforced through the organization's internal control systems?
- Gatekeepers: What training has been provided for critical gatekeepers in the control and supervision processes? Do they know what misconduct to look? Do they know when and how to scale possible findings? (US Department of Justice, 2020: 4)

In practice, the elaboration of policies, procedures and, above all, the code of ethics, is regarded as an effective control mechanism. Many organizations naively assume that because they have a code, members will act ethically and under the policies and norms of the organization. The reality is very different. Individuals tend to behave ambiguously. The fact that there is a code of ethics does not guarantee that the decisions of the Board of Directors or that the business practices of the commercial area will adhere to those principles. In fact, the vast majority of recent corporate scandals have occurred in organizations with well-developed, self-regulatory frameworks. This apparent paradox can be explained by several factors, the most important of which is that the way organizations work is often unknown. Some ideas will help explain this argument:

First, it is important to understand that an organization is, at the same time, actors and structures (Crozier & Friedberg, 1980). Actors are the people who participate in an organization and interact with each other in multiple ways. The structure is the spaces of interaction defined by the policies and procedures which, in principle, tell actors what to do, when to do it, and whom to report. In other words, they define the rules of their possible interactions. Human behavior occurs in extremely varied ways, beyond the possibilities of regulating policies, procedures, and ethics codes.

Therefore, a code of ethics is not a foolproof guarantee to prevent misconduct or regulatory breaches. Codes are merely expressions of intent, of values indicated as guiding principles of behavior. However, they are not at any time capable of prescribing the conduct of individuals with absolute certainty.

Does this suggest that organizations should not invest time and resources in developing policies and codes of ethics? Not at all. Organizations must develop policies and procedures because they are how they institutionalize the routines and procedures required to achieve their objectives. Codes also serve as a frame of reference for evaluating the appropriateness of certain behaviors. In other words, policies and codes help the organization to have a management framework within which the interactions of individuals take place, and which makes it possible to distinguish, at a given moment, what is correct from what is incorrect.

Nevertheless, this does not mean that codes or procedures, in themselves, define organizational behavior. Since compliance discourse does not usually point this out, several organizations misunderstand the purpose and scope of these attributes of the program. A much more honest and, therefore, more effective attitude is to design policies, procedures, and codes of ethics as elements that contribute to the definition of what is appropriate within the organization. Yet, which must also be complemented by training and communication programs that reinforce this understanding of appropriacy (March & Olsen, 1996; 1998).

In fact, decisions and organizational behavior are derived from the rules defined for a given role or function. These rules are institutionalized in organizational practices and maintained over time through learning. People adhere to them because they are natural, legitimate, and expected. In other words, based on a logic of what is appropriate, strengthened through communication and learning programs, actors will be able to decide based on what the organizational norms consider correct rather than cost-benefit calculations, which is usually the prevailing logic in a person who commits a corporate crime (such as financial fraud or the payment of bribes to secure a contract).

3. Training and Communication

For the DOJ, another hallmark of a well-designed compliance program is the training and organizational communication model to ensure the procedures and controls are designed in the context of the compliance program.

The discourse expects organizations to have specific procedures in place to ensure that compliance policies and procedures have been embedded in the organization through regular training or certification for all the relevant directors, officers, employees, and, where applicable, agents and business partners.

In this respect, communication programs are expected to be designed so that the information is tailored to the audience's size, sophistication, and experience to which it is transmitted.

In short, a program design evaluation examines whether the compliance program is being disseminated and understood by employees in practice. To this end, the DOJ suggests considering the following criteria to analyze the training in and communication of a compliance program:

- Risk-Based Training: What training have employees received in relevant control functions? Has the company provided personalized training for control clerks in high-risk areas? Have supervisory employees received different or additional training? What analysis has the company conducted to determine who should be trained and on what issues?
- Form/Content/Efficacy of Training: Has the training been delivered in the appropriate form and language for the audience? Is the training provided online or in-person (or both), and what is the company's justification for its choice? Did the training address lessons learn from previous compliance incidents? How has the company measured training effectiveness? Have employees been evaluated on what they have learned? How has the company dealt with employees who do not pass all or part of the tests?
- Communication Regarding Misconduct: What has senior management done to make employees aware of the company's position on misconduct? What communication has there usually been when an employee is fired or otherwise disciplined for failing to comply with company policies, procedures, and controls?
- Guidance Availability: What resources have been available to employees to provide guidance related to compliance policies? How has the company determined whether its employees know when to seek advice and whether they would be willing to do so? (US Department of Justice, 2020: 5–6)

In practice, training and communication programs are usually the weakest links in the chain of integrity compliance programs aspire to create. Whoever designs a program usually has limited knowledge of suitable teaching methods to effectively transmit the minimum, critical messages to management and members of the organization (all of whom are in different spheres of responsibility and functions). Additionally, the resources available for developing a communication and training program tend to be limited.

Consequently, apprenticeship programs are often poorly designed. A study conducted by Kroll in 2021 yielded an essential piece of information in this regard: boards of directors usually spend less than 5% of their annual time on the discussion, review, or evaluation of compliance communication and training programs (Kroll, 2021). The study is based on a sample of large companies, some public, so one can assume that in other types of organizations, communication and compliance training programs receive scant attention, despite their enormous importance.

Can organizations really develop a logic of appropriateness without a communication and training program? That is unlikely. Organizational learning is an ongoing process; moreover, learning happens in multiple ways, using various communication channels. Understanding this point is essential because when the issue of organizational learning is addressed in the compliance discourse, it is often overlooked that what is learned in organizations is not only what is transmitted through formal channels, such as training and official announcements.

Learning also occurs informally, over coffee, during chance meetings in the corridors, or discussing goals while waiting for a plane. In this respect, communication and compliance training programs start with a major disadvantage. The time and means available to formally transmit a set of compliance instructions are infinitely less than informal means. That is why the learning and reinforcement of corrupt or unethical practices and routines (in other words, those that contradict the program) are difficult to eliminate because these practices are usually transmitted in informal communication processes, with a far more effective instructive effect.

The design of communication and training programs tends to overlook this aspect of informality in organizations. Whoever designs compliance programs should contemplate differentiated communication strategies, supported by strategic use of symbols, rituals, and other forms of nonformal, subconscious communication to reinforce the understanding of appropriacy they wish to convey. Otherwise, compliance messages will invariably always be at a disadvantage compared to other day-to-day organizational priorities.

Another key aspect limiting the design of compliance communication and training programs involves the cultural diversity within organizations. Programs tend to be designed using a centralized approach, and someone within the organization or assisted by a consultant designs the program from a particular standpoint. However, organizations are often characterized by having multiple forms of cultural aggregation, which is true even for companies that are not necessarily transnational. Within a single organization, cultural and social diversity may influence how individuals interpret and assimilate compliance messages.

Considering local realities in the design of communication programs and compliance training becomes a critical issue for establishing the logic of what is appropriate within an organization. In its ethical dimension, compliance aspires to create behaviors with the same understanding of what is appropriate. Achieving this consensus goes beyond merely translating company policies and codes of ethics into different languages. Establishing shared understandings involves the acknowledgment and proper use of distinct cognitive processes. Unfortunately, these efforts are rarely seen in the design of compliance communication and training programs.

4. Anonymous Reporting Mechanism and Investigation Protocols

Another distinctive element of a compliance program for the DOJ is a mechanism whereby employees can anonymously or confidentially report noncompliance with the organization's code of ethics or policies. This mechanism is commonly referred to as the Ethics Hotline. With this attribute, organizations are expected to have a complaint handling process, including proactive measures to create a work environment free of fear of retaliation and processes to protect whistleblowers.

The development of a program will also be expected to include the design of processes to investigate the complaints received, including protocols to involve the appropriate personnel in the investigation and procedures to ensure the completion of the investigations and follow-up on the corrective measures adopted.

In this respect, it is important to note that complaint mechanisms and investigation protocols are usually presented as sufficient evidence to prove that an organization has established robust corporate governance mechanisms. Consequently, in the compliance discourse, a great deal of emphasis is usually placed on Ethics Hotlines, creating the illusion that the mere existence of this type of mechanism improves the capacity to detect and respond to potential unethical acts or regulatory noncompliance situations.

Recent empirical evidence shows that up to 53% of corporate fraud is detected through reports received by Ethics Hotlines (ACFE, 2021). However, this statistic does not provide any information on the key design aspects that Ethics Hotlines and research protocols must have to be effective. In our experience, enabling a telephone number or email to receive complaints is not enough, and more sophisticated design criteria must be considered.

For example, the DOJ suggests evaluating a program's anonymous reporting mechanisms and investigation protocols based on the following criteria:

- Effectiveness of the complaint mechanism: Does the organization have an anonymous reporting mechanism, and if not, why not? How is the reporting mechanism disclosed to employees of the organization? Has it been used? How does the company assess the seriousness of the complaints it has received? Has the compliance function had full access to the investigation reports?
- Investigations with the appropriate scope by qualified personnel: How does the organization determine which complaints or red flags warrant further investigation? How does the organization ensure that investigations have the proper scope? What steps does the organization take to ensure that investigations are independent, objective, properly conducted, and documented? How does the organization decide who should investigate and who makes that decision?
- Response to the investigation: Does the company use time metrics to guarantee responsiveness? Does the company have a process for monitoring the outcome of investigations and ensuring accountability for the findings or recommendations of the investigation?

- Resources and results-based monitoring: Are information and investigation mechanisms sufficiently financed? How has the organization collected, tracked, analyzed, and used information from its reporting mechanisms? Does the organization regularly review reports or investigation results for patterns of misconduct or other red flags of compliance issues? (US Department of Justice, 2020: 6–7)

In practice, however, the design of Ethics Hotlines tends to pay little or no attention to three factors that are usually present when a person chooses not to report the facts of which they may be aware.

First, is fear of retaliation. This may be the main factor hindering the use of Ethics Hotlines. Its design must adopt protocols that guarantee safeguards to protect the whistleblower's identity and physical and psychological integrity. One way to overcome this obstacle is by having an independent third party to manage the Ethics Hotline. However, this measure will not solve the problem unless the independent third party has acceptable protocols for dealing with complaints and avoiding leaking information.

The second obstacle to using Ethics Hotlines is the perception that nothing will happen when a complaint is made. When a person decides to file a complaint, and nothing happens, in other words, the organization makes no effort to follow up on the events reported, there is a danger of sending a message of pretense and apathy. In this situation, members of an organization may quickly stop believing in the compliance discourse, leading to attitudes and behaviors that will undermine confidence in the reform efforts the program is attempting to promote.

The third major obstacle to using the Ethics Hotlines is the lack of knowledge about the complaint mechanism if there is no effective communication campaign. Establishing an Ethics Hotline and failing to make people aware of it (as often happens) will condemn this detection mechanism to failure. Therefore, it is essential to have specific procedures to explain how it works and where it can be accessed in the design of an Ethics Hotline.

One interesting fact should be noted. Companies often say they rely on whistleblower information as one of the key fraud detection methods. This is borne out by studies reporting that a high percentage (between 45% and 55%) of frauds were identified by an internal whistleblower (ACFE, 2021; Kroll, 2017; KPMG, 2022). However, it is surprising that a relatively large number of respondents with whistleblowing programs already in place (36%) do not intend to review, modify, or expand them (Kroll, 2017). This is striking because it suggests that organizations do not consider self-assessment and correction mechanisms in designing their Ethics Hotlines. Why don't organizations improve a mechanism that has proven to be effective? What stops organizations from adapting their Ethics Hotlines? There is no easy answer, but it probably has a lot to do with the internal political cost for organizations of reviewing and changing something that has proven effective.

As for investigation protocols, they design compliance programs that face other challenges. Undertaking an internal investigation of possible corporate crimes or regulatory noncompliance is no easy task. Depending on the facts reported, the organization must design its investigation strategy. In practice, companies have different types of capacities for conducting internal investigations on their own. An investigation sometimes requires special protocols to obtain, protect and analyze vital information to search for evidence. Organizations tend to have limited resources and experience to conduct this investigation.

However, the main obstacle faced in the design of investigation protocols is the complexity of organizations. It is impossible to predict what kind of investigation will need to be conducted. As a result, protocols are too general to be practical. Protocols are a list of steps to follow which, in the best of cases, will guide decision-making on how and when to investigate certain facts. However, in practice, organizations are plagued by doubt when it comes to filing a complaint. In addition, the design of a protocol does not guarantee that decision-making will be done orderly considering the specific situation faced in a specific reality. This creates biases and shortcomings when internal investigations are conducted (Magallanes & Sierra, 2020).

5. Due Diligence Process

According to the DOJ, another critical element in the design of a compliance program is the due diligence process, which is used to assess the risk that their relationship with third parties implies for organizations, in other words, commercial representatives, consultants, distributors, managers, suppliers, and customers.

Due diligence is a control mechanism that was quickly incorporated into the compliance discourse. This mechanism was institutionalized in the 1970s due to antimoney laundering regulations. Since then, organizations have designed and adopted procedures that enable them to assess the reputation and business practices used by the third parties with whom they deal.

There is no single due diligence approach or procedure. In this respect, those who design compliance programs face the dilemma of which procedure to follow. Organizations at this point typically have several questions: how should risk be assessed? When and how should due diligence be conducted? what should be done with the findings? The answers to these questions are not easy because they largely depend on the type of organization, the market in which it operates, its regulations, and its risk appetite. In any case, what is evident is that nowadays, organizations are expected to have due diligence procedures that go beyond the bureaucratic corroboration of specific documents. In principle, due diligence must be based on an investigative approach, which genuinely helps the organization assess the risk of engaging with a specific third party.

In this respect, an organization that adopts a compliance program is expected to know what kind of relationships it has with third parties and why it has these relationships. Furthermore, organizations are expected to continuously monitor third-party relationships through updated due diligence, training, audits, and/or annual third-party compliance certifications.

The DOJ suggests evaluating a program's policies and procedures based on the following criteria:

- *Integrated and Risk-Based Processes*: How has the organization's third-party management process matched the nature and level of risk identified by the organization? How has this process been incorporated into the relevant procurement and supplier management processes?
- *Appropriate Controls*: How does the organization ensure that there is an adequate business justification for the use of third parties? If third parties were involved in the misconduct detected, what was the business reason for using those third parties? What mechanisms are in place to ensure that the terms of the contract specifically describe the services to be performed, that payment terms are appropriate, that the contractual work described is performed, and that compensation is proportionate to the services provided?
- *Relationship Management*: How has the organization considered and analyzed compensation structures and third-party incentives against compliance risks? How does the organization monitor its third parties? Does the organization have audit rights to review the books and accounts of third parties, and has the company exercised these rights in the past? How does the organization provide training for its relationship with third parties? How does the company encourage third-party compliance and ethical behavior?
- *Real Actions and Consequences*: Does the company track red flags identified through third-party due diligence, and how are those red flags addressed? Does the organization keep track of third parties that do not pass due diligence? Does the organization take steps to ensure that these third parties are not hired or rehired at a later stage? If third parties were involved in the compliance issue detected, were any red flags identified from due diligence or after the third party was engaged, and how were they resolved? Has a similar third party been suspended, terminated, or audited as a result of compliance issues? (US Department of Justice, 2020: 7–8)

Understanding whom one is doing business with is not only good business practice but also a legal requirement. Organizations are responsible for the actions of their business partners and suppliers. Legislation such as the FCPA in the United States (US Congress, 1977), the UK Bribery Act in the United Kingdom (Bribery Act, 2010), and the Dodd-Frank Act (US Congress, 2010) places special emphasis on risk management in the relationship with third parties.

Third parties are a critical component in the operations of many companies. They perform myriad functions, from providing cloud data storage to outsourcing construction projects. Third parties can help mitigate operating risks, reduce costs, and provide gateways to new markets, among many other functions. As a result, third parties have become critical to the success of organizations.

However, employing a third party creates compliance risks for an organization, particularly in emerging markets where companies are more likely to face legal, ethical, and reputational challenges from using third parties. Issues such as business integrity, product safety, intellectual property, licensing, and human rights violations can jeopardize a company's reputation and profitability.

In light of these dangers, compliance discourse emphasizes that companies must take steps to protect themselves. By understanding the methods and ethics of their third parties, companies can avoid the potential imposition of fines and penalties. From this point of view, designing a third-party due diligence program is key. However, as already mentioned, the process of designing a due diligence procedure is not without problems. From the designer's perspective, certain minimum definitions must be considered when designing the due diligence process. For example:

1. In what processes or in what type of activities will due diligence evaluations be conducted? Every organization has limited resources, and the actual possibilities of evaluating each possible business association could be challenging. It is necessary to have a clear definition in this regard, to avoid the risk of excessive budgets or unachievable goals.

2. Who undertakes the due diligence process, and with what tools? Due diligence functions may be performed in various areas of the organization, such as purchasing, contracting, relations with third parties, and compliance. It is usually a function that may compete with many of those departments. Therefore, the functional location in which these tasks are performed weighs heavily on their design. There is also the issue of what tools to use, what methodologies to follow, and how to report findings. These issues are critical because they can influence the effectiveness of the due diligence procedure. Not having the right tools or not knowing how to conduct investigative due diligence can lead to false expectations of control and the pretense of reputational risk management.

Who decides what to do with a due diligence report? The principal goal of the due diligence process is to produce information for decision-making in evaluating compliance risks. Unless the report issued is taken seriously, the control effort will be of little use. In organizations, the logic of business and profitability is usually imposed to the detriment of risk management. In this respect, the precise definition of a diligence report triggers decision-making processes, which is vital for the process to make sense.

The definition of these critical points should facilitate designing the due diligence process. However, none of these will work if companies fail to conduct due diligence in a coordinated manner. Too often, the third-party due diligence is carried out in a piecemeal, ad hoc manner due to flaws in the design of the procedure to be followed. Companies can overfocus on performance management and overlook risk management and compliance. As a result, they may fail to identify potential ethical issues, security breaches, bribery, money laundering, and regulatory violations, for example.

Every company is different and will have different risk profiles and appetites. As such, there is no plan to manage third-party risks. However, to take just one example, the enforcement and ruling guidelines surrounding the FCPA make it clear that companies must know who their third parties are and with whom they do business. It is no longer possible for organizations to turn a blind eye to the actions of their business partners. Third-party due diligence cannot be a box-checking exercise. Companies must take a holistic view if they genuinely wish to understand the array of risks posed by their third parties. The challenge is to design a transparent, due diligence process that is consistent with the resources and nature of the organization's business.

6. Due Diligence for Mergers and Acquisitions (M&A)

Finally, for the DOJ, another important element to consider in the design of a compliance program is the due diligence process for mergers and acquisitions or M&A. Why is due diligence for M&A so crucial in the context of compliance? Because through an acquisition or merger, the acquiring party not only assumes the assets and operations of the acquired or target company ("Target"). The buyer also assumes the liabilities and criminal liability of the company acquired. This process is called successor liability.

The concept of successor liability is fundamental when dealing with liabilities associated with regulatory compliance obligations. In these cases, the buyer absorbs the responsibility for any regulatory transgression of the target company, such as responsibilities for violations of anti-bribery and corruption ("ABC") or anti-money laundering ("AML") regulations, becoming responsible for the sanctions that may be imposed, even if the crime occurred before the acquisition or merger. It should be noted that regulatory sanctions may involve substantial fines and imprisonment for this type of issue. These types of sanctions usually generate reactions in the market, which can cause negative consequences for corporate reputation, damage the brand of the acquiring organization, and cause a drop in sales and share prices.

In this respect, due diligence for M&A should be designed to allow acquiring organizations to assess any compliance risk the asset may have.

The DOJ suggests evaluating a program's policies and procedures based on the following criteria:

- Due diligence process: What due diligence process is in place to assess M&A targets? Was misconduct or risk of misconduct identified during due diligence? Who conducted the risk review for the acquired/merged entities, and how was this done?
- Integration of the M&A process: How has the due diligence process been integrated into the remaining evaluations for mergers or acquisitions?
- The process that connects due diligence with implementation: What has been the company's process for tracking and remedying the misconduct or risks of misconduct identified during the due diligence process at a target? What has the company's process been for implementing compliance policies and procedures in the new entities? (US Department of Justice, 2020: 9)

Although the DOJ's emphasis on due diligence processes for M&A is apparent and the negative consequences of failing to conduct a detailed review of a Target are particularly harmful, organizations experience problems designing this type of procedure. The main problems can be divided into two main issues:

1. Problems designing due diligence protocols in functions and acquisitions that place equal emphasis on compliance risks and other types of considerations, such as financial, operational, and legal due diligence.
2. Flaws in designing protocols that will allow a comprehensive analysis of compliance risks (either due to lack of tools or sufficient time). (Davis, 2009)

These two deficiencies at the design stage can be detrimental if not adequately addressed. In practice, much of the due diligence efforts in functions and acquisitions processes fall to external consultants who assist the organization. This does not necessarily solve the problem. On the contrary, it could aggravate it if there is a lack of expertise and care to properly link the external consultant's due diligence efforts with the organization's decision-making. This is a common problem in acquisitions and mergers.

Conducting extensive due diligence with integrity is often even more critical when the target firm is in a foreign country, as available data sources can vary widely. In Latin America, for example, where intermediaries such as agents and managers are commonly used, information on private companies can be surprisingly incomplete (compared to that available in the United States or Europe) and challenging to obtain because the information is not digitized. Identifying a problem before an acquisition or with time limits often affects the quality of a review of a Target.

Furthermore, verifying the information received from a Target can also be a troublesome issue. The starting point for due diligence may include what is known as aggregate databases, which can compile hundreds of sanctions and watchlists from around the world, as well as a list of politically exposed persons, also known as PEPs. These searches are supplemented by additional media searches such as unfavorable reports on a target or its key executives and personnel in both English and local languages.

These sources are useful but may not be as complete as they seem, and they may overlook an anonymous beneficiary owner of a company with political or government ties. Additionally, it will probably fail to yield information on lower-level managers who may be engaging in dubious transactions. The due diligence process should therefore encompass more sources. The problem becomes critical when the due diligence procedures for M&A fail to contemplate these information gaps or complications in their execution.

These considerations are intended to point out some of the biases and limitations often faced in the design of the components of compliance programs. Far from the rationalist vision, which prescribes an ideal design process, in practice, designing compliance plans encounters challenges in each of its components. This is not to say that reform and compliance efforts are impossible or irrelevant. Designing a compliance program is essential and necessary to instituting measures in the organization that will help prevent, detect, and respond to risks.

What must be emphasized, however, is that the design process does not happen automatically. Whoever designs a program faces multiple methodological and resource challenges that necessarily influence how compliance controls, policies, and procedures end up being designed. In this respect, the idealized vision of the compliance discourse must be nuanced so that it is realistic and, above all, that the final result is functional and serves the purpose for which it was designed.

Each of the limits discussed in this section imposes biases and constraints on a program's actual performance. This is no minor issue, particularly if one considers the central promise of compliance discourse, which tends to minimize the fact that the adaptation and adoption of a program will take place within a process of competition, interpretation, and battle between groups and coalitions in an organization regarded more as an arena than as a monolith (as explained in the two preceding chapters). Hence, the rhetorical promise of compliance programs depends on a range of variables that affect how, by whom, and with what resources these programs are designed and adapted to organizational dynamics.

3.3 How are Compliance Programs being Implemented?

The compliance discourse acknowledges that even a well-designed compliance program may not succeed in practice if the implementation is lax or ineffective. The key issue is to understand that even in the most advantageous situation if the program has been designed with the utmost care and detail, implementation will never go smoothly. Every implementation process faces several uncontrollable or unpredictable conditions that influence the result. In other words: between the program that is designed and the one that is implemented, there will invariably be gaps, some that can be anticipated while many others will be fortuitous. In this respect, although it sounds contradictory, it is better to be prepared for the unexpected (Weick & Sutcliffe, 2007).

It will be advisable first to review the problems anticipated in the compliance discourse itself in the implementation process to complement or qualify the arguments. The DOJ warns of three critical elements that can hinder implementing a compliance program. These potential obstacles are:

1. Lack of commitment on the part of senior management and middle managers
2. Lack or insufficiency of resources and autonomy for implementation
3. How the company encourages third-party compliance and ethical behavior (US Department of Justice, 2020: 10–14)

To address these implementation pitfalls, DOJ recommends the following criteria to determine the effectiveness of the implementation of a program.

a) Lack of Commitment on the Part of Senior Management and Middle Managers

For the DOJ, the prominent leaders of the company, in other words, the board of directors and senior management set the pattern of behavior for the rest of the organization. Therefore, the analysis of an implementation process must review the extent to which senior management has clearly articulated the company's ethical standards, transmitted and disseminated them in clear, unequivocal terms, and demonstrated rigorous compliance by example.

It is also necessary to examine how middle managers, in turn, have enforced these standards and encouraged employees to adhere to them. The specific criteria suggested by the DOJ to analyze the commitment of senior management and middle managers in the implementation of a program are:

- Tone at the top: How do senior leaders encourage or discourage compliance through their words and deeds? What concrete actions have they taken to demonstrate leadership in the company's compliance and remediation efforts? How have they modeled appropriate behavior to subordinates? Have managers tolerated higher compliance risks in pursuit of new business or higher revenue? Have managers encouraged employees to act unethically to achieve a business objective or prevented compliance staff from effectively performing their roles?
- Middle management commitment: What actions have senior leaders and middle management stakeholders (such as business and operational managers, finance, procurement, legal and human resources) taken to prove their commitment to compliance or compliance staff, including their remediation efforts? Have they maintained that commitment in the face of conflicting commercial interests or goals?

– Supervision: What compliance experience has been available on the board of directors? Have the board of directors and/or the external auditors held executive or private sessions with the compliance and control functions? What type of information has the board of directors and senior management reviewed in their oversight exercise in the area where the misconduct occurred? (US Department of Justice, 2020: 10–11)

Undoubtedly, implementing a compliance program requires the support and commitment of Senior Management and the participation of middle managers, especially those responsible for implementing, supervising, and ensuring compliance controls (the first, second, and third line of defense, to borrow a concept from the auditing world).

However, what exactly is meant by "tone at the top" and "middle management commitment"? Why do they appear at the center of the implementation discussion? These are terms that have acquired very different meanings, so it is necessary to remember their origins because they are concepts that are indeed important for understanding the compliance implementation process, yet paradoxically for reasons contrary to those usually referred.

The concept of "tone at the top" originated in the accounting field to refer to the attitude of an organization's senior leaders toward internal financial controls. The concept was popularized in the wake of the corporate accounting scandals at Enron and WorldCom and subsequently institutionalized by the Sarbanes-Oxley Act (2002), which established the "tone at the top" as an essential requirement for corporate fraud prevention and detection. Nowadays, the term is used broadly to describe an aspect of corporate culture associated with the integrity of an organization's leadership.

However, the notion of "tone at the top" is essential, but for a different reason than the alleged integrity of the leadership, which is more of an a priori value judgment than an objective management condition. The tone at the top is important because the purpose of management is to modify and influence behaviors so that things happen, either to solve problems or to stabilize and lend continuity to what is done within an organization (Barnard, 1938). In this respect, the tone at the top matters because it is a resource available to management to promote cooperation within the organization, despite the conflict and competition between agendas that invariably exist, from which compliance is not exempt.

In this respect, the "tone at the top" is relevant in the process of implementing a program because senior management, taking advantage of its position of power, can create the necessary real and symbolic conditions that promote identity and sufficient cohesion among rival groups, to cooperate in adopting the program. From this perspective, it is understood that implementing a compliance program will be the result of political negotiations within the organization rather than a mystical call to ethical behavior.

The origin of the notion of "middle management commitment" is somewhat vaguer. It is unclear who was the first to use this concept or in what context. However, this term designates the prevailing conditions among those who execute, control and supervise the organization's tasks. The middle managers of an organization are a critical link in the process of implementing a compliance program since they are the ones who make things happen, and their position is critical in the segregation of duties. Although only in some cases do they make the big decisions, middle managers are responsible for planning, executing, and controlling work teams.

In this respect, middle managers occupy a key position in the implementation of the programs because the organization's vision and compliance strategy are channeled through them. They negotiate the program's objectives and – through their negotiations – make teams perform assigned tasks. Ultimately, they are the linchpins of the program's performance.

One unavoidable aspect in organizations is that most of their participants tend to have limited or partial knowledge of compliance when implementing a program of this nature. Lack of experience and, in some cases, minimal knowledge of crucial aspects of regulatory compliance and ethical behavior cause unexpected effects when a program is implemented. This results in half-baked plans, unplanned adjustments, and budget restrictions that affect the achievement of the formal objectives of compliance programs. The supervision that can be achieved during the reform process to implement a program will therefore be contingent on experience in managing this type of program.

Many organizations meet this challenge by relying on consultants or independent third parties to guide them through the implementation process. Experience shows that, in these cases, no matter how much effort the consultant makes, day-to-day implementation falls to the organization. Therefore, even when professional support is available, there will always be a gray area of ignorance, improvisation, and pretense in compliance change processes.

b) Autonomy and Resources

For a compliance program to succeed, those responsible for the daily supervision of the program must act with the necessary authority and resources; otherwise, the reform process will be even more complicated to implement.

In this regard, the DOJ suggests that the areas responsible for compliance be examined on the basis of three essential points to determine how well a program is being implemented:

1. Sufficient seniority within the organization, that is, the personnel in charge will have the necessary experience and knowledge to understand and monitor the nature of the organization's business

2. Sufficient resources, that is, trained personnel to effectively undertake compliance functions
3. Sufficient management autonomy, that is, with direct access to the board of directors or the audit committee (US Department of Justice, 2020: 11)

The specific criteria recommended by the DOJ to analyze the autonomy and sufficiency of resources in the implementation of a program are as follows:

- Structure: Where in the organization is the compliance function located? To whom does the compliance function report? Is the compliance function led by a designated chief compliance officer or another executive within the company, and does that person have other functions? Is the compliance staff dedicated to compliance responsibilities, or does it have other noncompliance responsibilities within the company? Why has the company chosen the compliance structure it has?
- Seniority and authority: How does the compliance function compare with other strategic company functions regarding status, compensation levels, rank/title, hierarchical structure, resources, and access to key decision-makers? What has been the staff turnover rate of the relevant compliance and control function? What role has compliance played in the company's strategic and operational decisions? How has the company responded to specific instances in which compliance raised concerns? Were there any transactions or deals that were halted, modified, or further scrutinized as a result of compliance issues?
- Experience and qualifications: Do compliance and control personnel have the appropriate experience and qualifications for their roles and responsibilities? Has the level of experience and qualifications in these roles changed over time? Who reviews the performance of the compliance function, and what is the review process?
- Financing and resources: Have there been sufficient staffing for compliance staff to effectively audit, document, analyze, and act on the results of compliance efforts? Has the company allocated sufficient funds for the latter? Have there been occasions when requests for resources have been denied by compliance and control functions and, if so, for what reason?
- Autonomy: Do the relevant compliance and control functions have direct reporting lines to someone on the board of directors and/or the audit committee? How often do they meet with the directors? Are members of senior management present at these meetings? How does the company ensure the independence of compliance and control personnel?
- Outsourced compliance functions: Has the company outsourced all or part of its compliance functions to an outside firm or consultant? If so, who is responsible for supervising or liaising with the outside firm or consultant and why? What level of access does the firm or external consultant have to the company's information? How has the effectiveness of the outsourced process been evaluated? (US Department of Justice, 2020: 11–13)

The implementation of a program, like almost any other change process, is faced with the reality of scarce resources and divergent interests, making it impossible for the reform process to happen without conflict. In this respect, it is essential to recognize that compliance programs compete for the same resources other programs or areas of the organization wish to have.

Experience has taught us that three critical resources in any compliance process determine the degree of success of its implementation:

1. Human resources. Programs require sufficient trained staff. Even in world-class organizations, that is, with large budgets, there are human resource constraints. It is still common to find small compliance areas (three or four professionals) supervising programs in companies with several thousand or hundreds of thousands of employees. From that perspective, implementation is necessarily limited by a lack of personnel who can ensure that the components of a program are implemented according to the reform design or plan. In addition to the problem of the number of professionals, there is the problem of sufficient capacity or experience to supervise the programs with a certain level of confidence. The experience referred to does not only involve knowledge of compliance, and the experience required is also responsible for process management and experience like the organization's business. Both experiences are essential if supervision is to be implemented with any degree of success.

2. Budget resources. Programs are expensive. Generally speaking, implementation requires adaptations and organizational changes that entail high operating costs. This is perhaps the main stumbling block for compliance programs. From a cost-benefit perspective, compliance is difficult to defend because it does not generate income, open up business opportunities, or solve operational business problems per se. The benefit of having a compliance program is only evident when problems arise. Compliance becomes visible when it comes to avoiding a fine or dealing with an investigation by a regulator. In the past, the compliance function was downplayed. In this sense, compliance usually has relatively low or insufficient assigned budgets, which limits and influences the program's implementation.

3. Time resources. Compliance programs take time to implement, and organizations tend to change slowly. Radical, sudden transformation rarely occurs, which often affects implementation processes. As noted earlier, compliance programs require the support of senior management and the commitment of middle managers, but also sufficient time for organizational adjustments and rearrangements to percolate. Implementation rarely sticks to timelines. Launching a program simultaneously as the organization continues with its tasks is a complex exercise requiring patience and discipline to supervise the implementation. The problem is that teams responsible for implementation often share their time with other activities, which limits compliance program implementation.

These three resource constraints undoubtedly influence the implementation of programs beyond the evaluation criteria the DOJ recommends for evaluating their effectiveness. Reality prevails over planning. This does not, however, mean that change efforts are not desirable or even necessary. As already pointed out in the first chapter, compliance emerged as a response to organizational management problems in regulatory compliance and ethical behavior. From this point of view, no one, in their right mind, could oppose the attempts by compliance to bring about change. However, what is argued here is that this reform process does not take place smoothly, no matter how advisable it may seem. The limitations pointed out here in terms of resources are only part of the challenges faced by anyone responsible for running this type of program.

c) Incentives and Disciplinary Measures

The renowned sociologist of organizations, Amitai Etzioni, distinguished three means (mechanisms) whereby organizations ensure compliance with their internal rules to achieve their objectives (Etzioni, 1964). These mechanisms are as follows:

1. Coercive power is based on physical resources of surveillance and punishment, which are designed to instill fear in the members of an organization of engaging in a lack of compliance and being surprised at the lack of negative consequences this may have for them (such as dismissal, reporting to the authorities).
2. Utilitarian power is based on material resources (salary, benefits), designed to influence the evaluative framework of individuals so that they place what is understood or defined as organizational interest above their interests.
3. Identity power is based on symbols, which are designed to guarantee the loyalty of individuals toward what is defined or perceived as the interest of the organization through the use of cognitive persuasion via symbolic language (such as rituals and ceremonies).

These three powers coexist in organizations, and those responsible for compliance implementation processes use them either consciously or unconsciously. Every program aspires to influence the behaviors of members of an organization to ensure regulatory compliance and ethical behavior at all times. In this respect, organizations use the three mechanisms Etzioni described without any magic recipe. No procedural manual indicates what combination of power should be used to ensure that an organization effectively implements a compliance program.

What we know is that organizations attempt to introduce compliance change processes by taking advantage of coercion, utilitarian incentives, and promoting identity. The results are mixed, and some organizations appear to be more successful in certain respects than others. Moreover, in this respect, the compliance discourse does not appear to have a single answer.

For the DOJ, another critical condition for implementing a compliance program is establishing incentives for regulatory compliance and ethical behavior. The DOJ states that it is necessary to observe whether the organization has clear disciplinary procedures, enforces them uniformly throughout the organization, and ensures that procedures are consistent with the violations detected and investigated.

The specific criteria recommended by the DOJ to consider the type of incentives that a program has established are given below:

- *Human resources process*: Who is involved in making disciplinary decisions, including the type of misconduct in question? Is the same process followed for each case of misconduct, and if not, why not? Are the real reasons for discipline communicated to employees? If not, why not? Are there legal or research-related reasons for restricting information?
- *Consistent application*: Have disciplinary actions and incentives been implemented fairly and consistently across the organization? Are there similar instances of misconduct that have been treated differently, and if so, why?
- *Incentive system*: Has the organization considered the implications of its incentives and rewards for the compliance program? How does the company encourage third-party compliance and ethical behavior? Have there been specific examples of actions taken (such as promotions or awards denied) as a result of ethical and compliance considerations? Who determines the compensation, including bonuses, and the discipline and promotion of compliance personnel? (US Department of Justice, 2020: 13–14)

This is perhaps one of the most important aspects in the discussion of the implementation of compliance. The compliance discourse assumes that unethical behavior or lack of regulatory compliance is the result of individual deviance from the norm or procedures. This view, which we can describe as individualistic, maintains that corporate crime is the result of "bad apples" in a basket of healthy apples: crimes are individual, and integrity is organizational. This is an extremely reductionist view. Experience has shown that organizations often reproduce – consciously or unconsciously – practices and routines that affect individual dishonest behavior and the organization as a whole (Arellano-Gault, 2020).

Let us consider the cases of Odebrecht, Enron, WorldCom, and Siemens, to mention just a few examples, as cases in which the crimes committed were far more than simply individual actions by bad apples. On the contrary, they were cases that showed that corruption or fraud was practiced systemically and that control and supervision processes were knowingly violated or manipulated (McLean & Elkind, 2013). These extreme cases have led to major corruption scandals and involved heavy fines and jail time for executives in these companies.

Nevertheless, the reality in other organizations may not be much different. The problem lies in the normalization of practices that lead to crime. Accordingly, we maintain here that during the compliance implementation processes, a system of "adequate" incentives does not suffice to regulate the behavior of the organization's participants. It is equally or even more critical to have full knowledge of the formal and informal practices. The organization used to do business.

This is no easy task, especially given the complexity involved in diagnosing all the practices that take place within an organization at the same time. Contrary to what the compliance discourse might argue, it is not a question of constraints caused by the lack of resources. The inability to diagnose a complexity is extremely diffuse and escapes any efforts at control.

In conclusion, we are trying to point out here that organizational behavior, particularly that associated with corporate crime or regulatory compliance failures, is much more than the sum of individual behaviors. In this respect, the power mechanisms used to discipline employees or reinforce their loyalty will be limited by the partial and biased knowledge that is invariably available of organizational reality.

These considerations are intended to highlight the aspects that influence and limit the implementation of a compliance program. Even in cases where the program has been carefully designed, its implementation will also have complications. Organizational reality escapes the possibilities of total control that sometimes characterizes the discourse.

Implementation is defined as a set of decisions designed to introduce into organization routines and processes that have not been carried out until then or were carried out differently. From this point of view, implementation becomes a propitious scenario for conflict to emerge. Beginning with the fact that organizations have limited resources (such as personnel, budgets, and time), the compliance process obviously encourages organizational resistance due to the rearrangements that a reform program of this nature undoubtedly entails.

Does this mean that any compliance implementation process is doomed to failure? Not at all. What is being argued here is not that compliance cannot work or become operable. The point is that the program will face challenges when the reform effort is launched, and the final result will be different from the program originally planned or designed.

In this respect, the effectiveness of its implementation will depend on many factors. Suppose by implementation effectiveness we mean the ability for things to happen and for the components of the compliance program to be incorporated into the organization. In that case, this will largely depend on the ability of the team responsible for implementation to deal with the limitations inherent in the process of implementing a reform process of the magnitude entailed by a program. This issue will be addressed in more detail in the next chapter.

3.4 How are Compliance Programs being Operated?

Even when a program is well designed and a major effort has been made to ensure its implementation, this does not guarantee that deviance from the original plans will not occur. As in the two previous stages, compliance programs face limitations and insufficiencies in their execution that modify their results.

This is a critical aspect for organizations because the way a program is implemented can make a major difference when it is investigated by a regulator or questioned by an authority regarding the possibility of having broken the law or committed a crime under the criterion of Respondeat Superior.

Organizational Guidelines state that prosecutors charged with investigating an alleged crime by a company should assess "the adequacy and effectiveness of the corporation's compliance program at the time of the crime, as well as at the time of deciding to make an accusation (US Sentencing Commission, 1991).

Given the retrospective nature of a compliance investigation, prosecutors must answer one of the most difficult questions when evaluating a compliance program after uncovering a corporate crime is whether the program was operating effectively at the time of the crime, especially when the misconduct was not immediately detected. To assess whether a compliance program is being properly implemented, the DOJ recommends considering the following criteria:

a) Continuous Improvements, Periodic Tests, and Revisions

According to the DOJ, a critical element to consider in determining whether a program is running is its ability to improve and evolve. Implementing controls in practice will invariably reveal areas of risk and potential adjustment. An organization's business changes over time, as do the environments in which it operates, the nature of its customers, the laws that govern its actions, and applicable industry standards.

Consequently, when evaluating whether a program is effective, the DOJ recommends considering whether the company has made efforts to review its compliance program and ensure that it is not outdated or out of step with organizational reality. To this end, some organizations survey employees to gauge compliance culture and assess the strength of their controls and/or conduct periodic audits to ensure that controls are working well. However, the nature and frequency of the assessments may depend on the size and complexity of the firm.

The specific criteria recommended by the DOJ to analyze the improvements of a compliance program are given below:
- Internal audit: What is the process for determining where and how often an internal audit will conduct an audit, and what is the rationale behind that process? How are audits performed? What types of audits would have identified issues relevant to the misconduct? Did those audits occur, and what were the

findings? What relevant audit findings and remediation progress have regularly been reported to management and the board? How have management and the board followed up? How often do internal audits conduct assessments in high-risk areas?

–   Control tests: Has the organization reviewed and audited its compliance program in the area related to misconduct? More generally, what tests of controls, compliance data collection and analysis, and interviews of employees and third parties do the company conduct? How are results reported and action items tracked?

–   Evolving updates: How often has the organization updated its risk assessments and compliance policies, procedures, and practices? Has the organization undertaken a gap analysis to determine whether particular risk areas are insufficiently addressed in its policies, controls, or training? What steps has the organization taken to determine whether policies, practices, and procedures make sense for particular business segments and subsidiaries?

–   Compliance culture: How often and how does the company measure its culture of compliance? Does the company seek input from all employees to determine whether they perceive middle and senior management's commitment to compliance? What steps has the company taken in response to its compliance culture measurement? (US Department of Justice, 2020: 14–16)

The problem with periodic tests and reviews is that they often become ad hoc audits to legitimize the program's existence and justify the associated costs. Nevertheless, even when reviews are conducted honestly, the chances of identifying control gaps are limited if they are done using the conventional approach of reviewing general or superficial aspects of compliance mechanisms. Compliance programs usually meet the minimum requirements that allow a certain degree of implementation to be shown. For example, they usually have relatively straightforward policies and procedures, they are assigned people responsible for the compliance area and so on. But the problem may lie in the characteristics of the routines and tasks performed. Deviance from protocols or the shortcomings of oversight and control are usually found in micromanagement details (Hargie & Tourish, 2009).

Most organizations rely on internal audits, similar functions, or external consultants, to periodically assess the performance of their compliance programs. Typically, these efforts involve verifying that the necessary compliance procedures are in place. This is an excellent first step. However, just as financial audits are not designed to identify fraud, corruption, or money laundering (Singleton & Singleton, 2007), a standard compliance audit may sometimes fail to uncover problems even when conducted by independent third parties.

To gain deeper insight into whether and how their compliance procedures are being circumvented, organizations should move from compliance auditing to compliance stress testing. Compliance stress testing applies an investigative mindset to the compliance program itself, identifying and testing weak points to test a company's ability to detect and mitigate risk. Beyond merely confirming compliance through procedures, stress testing goes a step further to determine whether risks are actually being addressed. Have red flags in the credentials and documentation required been identified and acted? Have transactions flagged as potentially suspicious been reviewed and escalated? Have quality control procedures checked for weaknesses that lead to product failure?

In the compliance discourse, compliance programs are essential to ensure compliance with regulations and avoid illegal practices. To function as intended, compliance programs themselves must be subject to review and scrutiny. In practice, evaluations are problematic. Although compliance stress tests can provide a more rigorous means of identifying and remediating weaknesses, this depends on several factors. These include – very importantly – the fact that the organization wishes to submit to the stress of controls. In our experience, these exercises can become spaces for rivalry and conflict for one simple reason: no one likes to be singled out or shown up in a control failure or deviance from processes. Compliance programs are therefore not rigorously evaluated, severely limiting their adaptation to the risk scenarios organizations face.

b) Compliance Investigation

When preventive mechanisms have failed to prevent regulatory failure or unethical behavior, the organization is expected to be able to detect the failure and investigate it. In this respect, for the DOJ, another important element to consider when evaluating the performance of a compliance program is whether protocols are actually in place to conduct internal investigations into any complaint or suspicion of misconduct by the company, its employees, or third parties.

In the compliance discourse, organizations are therefore expected to have a functional investigation structure, in other words, the means to document the response the organization gave regarding the shortcoming detected, including the disciplinary or corrective measures adopted. Many companies do not have sufficient teams to undertake compliance investigations internally. These tasks often remain in the hands of other areas of the organization, such as internal or legal control, or are conducted by a third party or consultant.

In any case, in the discourse, the organization is expected to be able to investigate and reach conclusions that will enable it, in turn, to make corrective disciplinary decisions. The specific criteria recommended by the DOJ for analyzing the protocols of a compliance program are:

- Investigations with appropriate scope by qualified personnel: How has the company ensured that investigations have had the proper scope and been independently, objectively, and properly conducted and adequately documented?

   – Response to investigations: Have investigations been used to identify root causes, system vulnerabilities, and accountability failures, including those between the oversight manager and senior executives? What has been the process for responding to research findings? How high up in the company do the research findings reach? (US Department of Justice, 2020: 16)

The problem with internal compliance investigations is that they are not a minor issue. Assuming that they are carried out internally, there will always be reasonable doubt whether they were conducted with the necessary care and attention these matters require. Let us recall that a lack of compliance implies the commission of a potential crime. The investigation must therefore be carried out in such a way as to document the findings and preserve the evidence so that it can be presented to a judge or an authority. This capacity requires human resources with training and experience in this investigation. The fact is that not all organizations have these competencies internally. When evaluating how a program is being executed, one of the central points is to determine who is doing what in terms of the investigations. Having a compliance area with two or four officials dealing with an array of issues makes the investigative aspect of the program ineffective.

Many organizations deal with the situations they detect through consultants, and this could be a better option. However, the costs associated with a forensic or compliance investigation are a factor worth considering. There is a broad market for providers of this type of service, with tools and trained personnel. Good providers can therefore be found at relatively affordable prices. However, not even the most experienced forensic investigator will be able to solve the case assigned to them unless they have access to the necessary information and a proper understanding of the organizational context in which the events to be investigated took place (Simeon & Simeon, 2018). What we mean by this is that even in hiring a consultant, there will be constraints that may influence the operation of the compliance program, creating deviance from the established plans.

That said, it is logical to think that the purpose of organizations is not to investigate possible crimes. Organizations exist to achieve the purposes for which they were created. In this respect, expecting potential noncompliance to be investigated internally seems pointless. Nevertheless, the Respondeat Superior principle holds organizations accountable for their actions and those of their employees. Organizations are therefore justified in and obliged to prove that they have investigated the possible failures of which they are aware.

In this respect, organizations must investigate noncompliance, especially when there is no reasonable doubt that something is wrong. The question is not whether they should investigate. We wish to stress that investigations involve tasks that are often not even considered in compliance plans. As the organization assumes the costs of investing in human capacities and resources to have the necessary means of conducting investigations, some problems will be solved. Although, internal investigations and corrective and disciplinary action decisions will undoubtedly not go smoothly.

c) Analysis and Correction of Compliance Failures

Finally, another of the critical aspects for evaluating the effectiveness of a program concerns the mechanisms the organization has established to analyze and correct the lack of compliance that has occurred, especially those that entailed the commission of a crime.

In this regard, the compliance discourse is usually extremely emphatic about the need to analyze the causes that gave rise to the failures detected and to review all the aspects of lack of control that could directly or indirectly have affected the commission of a crime. Special emphasis is placed on the need for any compliance event to trigger corrective and disciplinary measures that will allegedly enable the organization to resolve control weaknesses and hold the individuals involved in the detected events accountable.

In this respect, the DOJ recommends the following criteria to determine how mature the implementation of a compliance program is:

- Root cause analysis: What is the company's root cause analysis of the misconduct in question? Were systemic problems identified? Who in the company participated in conducting the analysis?
- Previous weaknesses: What controls failed? If policies or procedures should have prohibited misconduct, were they effectively implemented and were functions that had ownership of these policies and procedures held accountable?
- Payment systems: How was the misconduct in question financed (e.g., purchase orders, employee rebates, rebates, petty cash)? What processes could have prevented or detected improper access to these funds? Have those processes been improved?
- Vendor management: If vendors were involved in the misconduct, what was the process for vendor selection and did the vendor undergo that process?
- Previous indications: Were there prior opportunities to detect the misconduct in question, such as audit reports identifying relevant control failures or reports, complaints, or investigations? What is the company's analysis of why such opportunities were missed?
- Remediation: What specific changes has the company made to reduce the risk that the same or similar problems will occur in the future? What specific solution has addressed the issues identified in the root cause and missed opportunity analysis?
- Responsibility: What disciplinary actions did the company take in response to the misconduct, and were they timely? Were managers held accountable for misconduct that occurred under their supervision? Did the company consider

disciplinary actions for supervisory failures? What is the company's history (e.g., number and types of disciplinary actions) in disciplining employees for the types of conduct in question? Has the company ever fired or disciplined anyone (reduced or eliminated bonuses, issued a warning letter, among others) because of the type of misconduct in question? (US Department of Justice, 2020: 17–18)

The underlying problem these evaluation criteria are attempting to solve is to know how the organization is responding and punishing the forbidden behaviors or lack of regulatory compliance detected. We must not forget that compliance arises primarily as a response to management problems in terms of self-control to ensure compliance with laws and promote ethical conduct within organizations. In this respect, compliance proposes establishing a control mechanism that will enable the organization to prevent, detect and respond to the offenses that may be committed on its behalf.

This issue is not new in the world of management. The problem of ensuring that an organization meets its objectives and is accountable for its actions has been present since the creation in 1602 of the Dutch East India Company, the first corporate organization as we know it today. Compliance is perhaps one of the most recent responses to this problem.

The approach proposed by the compliance discourse is the establishment of controls that experience – and rhetoric – have cited as the best practices for reducing risks. One of these control mechanisms involves analyzing and correcting the lack of compliance. However, in practice, it has been observed that efforts to correct the situations that gave rise to the compliance problems are limited. This is due to genuine ignorance of the issues that led to the problem. Except for cases in which the scope of the problem is so great that enormous efforts are made to investigate it, most compliance issues occur in the dark, and their solution is partial and barely publicized.

How many crimes related to compliance matters are committed each year in the corporate world? Surely hundreds of thousands of events, with varying severity and responsibility, although only a portion of them are thoroughly investigated. Although there are no statistics in this regard, experience has shown that only a tiny percentage of the investigations conducted in an organization culminate in a detailed root cause analysis. Limits on resources (such as budgets, staff, and time) play a crucial role in enabling organizations to conduct extensive reviews of what gave rise to compliance issues. Let us not forget that most cases begin with small irregular acts, which evolve into a serious matter. When a critical compliance issue is investigated, it is usually observed that they are problems that have been in the organization for a long time (years or even decades) and that, over time, they have acquired a degree of normalization in the company. Let us recall, for example, that Bernard Madoff's Ponzi scheme was developed over almost 30 years or that the infamous corruption scheme in Odebrecht was implemented over at least 15 years (Smith, Valle, & Schmidt, 2017).

Accordingly, when a compliance case is investigated, the reconstruction that needs to be done to identify the root cause is complex. Someone skilled in corporate "archaeology" must know how, when and who started the compliance problem. Moreover, these situations sometimes occur within the very dynamics of organizations that make it virtually impossible to determine the root cause of the problem in a timely manner.

This is important to highlight an essential issue: the efforts of organizations to correct or remedy compliance issues may be limited insofar as the intended analysis of the ultimate causes that gave rise to it is complex in itself. Evaluating a program's effectiveness based on how much it has corrected and learned from past situations is, therefore, at the very least debatable and indeed a long way from its intended purpose.

These considerations are designed to show that compliance programs are also implemented with biases or limitations in their actual operation. Some of these obstacles are inherent in the programs (such as limited resources). In contrast, others are due more to the complex reality of organizations (such as the normalization of inappropriate behavior or the institutionalization of criminal routines). In contrast, still, others have more of a political nature (such as deliberate decisions not to comply or only partially comply with the compliance program).

Indeed, organizations are complex spaces where decision-making occurs as part of contingent events that modify action strategies and tactical control plans. In this respect, it is unlikely that an action plan – whatever it may be – will be able to be implemented without undergoing alterations or deviations from the original plans. Is this necessarily bad? Not at all. In our experience, "lucky" deviance has been observed, in other words, unanticipated consequences that, far from becoming a problem, solved situations that had been regarded as insoluble until then.

The latter suggests that compliance programs are implemented with an indefinite combination of deliberate acts and fortuitous situations. Consequently, programs are executed in a complex environment and, as such, create organizational ambiguities that are beyond the conscious, rational control of those responsible for compliance. The result is that compliance programs, no matter how carefully they are executed, will invariably have limitations in their operation.

This point is not a minor matter, especially if one considers that having an "effective" program, that is, one that is actually implemented, is a necessary condition for companies being investigated for corporate crimes to be able to appeal for less harsh or costly sentencing. This creates a twofold tension among those responsible for compliance: on the one hand, they are obliged to respond to the requirements established by the regulator in terms of compliance (such as the DOJ guidelines) while, on the other, they have a specific organizational reality that does not mechanically respond to the action plans implemented.

Compliance officers must therefore have a profile that will not only enable them to address regulatory and ethical behavior issues, but also to exercise strong managerial skills, with enormous political capacity, so that things will happen even without sufficient resources, making it possible to combat institutionalized inertia and strike the necessary balance between controls and profits. A Herculean task.

3.5 What Results Have Compliance Programs Achieved to Date?

Just over 30 years have elapsed since compliance programs were institutionalized in the discourse as an effective means for organizations to deal with corporate crimes. However, numerous corporate scandals have shown that the promise of compliance is far from being achieved. From Volkswagen's cheating in pollution emission tests to cartels' money laundering in HSBC, the corporate world has shown that the problem of deception and lack of scruples remains one of its main problems.

It is surprising how many resources are invested annually in compliance efforts. A corporate organization spends, on average, several million dollars a year on compliance, whereas in highly regulated sectors, such as banking and financial services, costs can be even higher. Why is so much money invested in something failing to deliver the expected results? To some extent, compliance programs have become a kind of insurance policy. Companies invest in them not because they are thought to be effective (Raustiala, 2000), but because there is a fear of being exposed to more severe sanctions or shouldering a more significant burden of responsibility in the event of being investigated by a regulator.

Previous chapters had already explained how and when compliance programs emerged. At this point, it is only necessary to remember that, in the wake of a series of corporate scandals in the United States in the 1970s and 1980s, industry groups banded together and adopted internal policies and procedures to report and attempt to prevent misconduct. Those efforts helped appease US lawmakers, who were attempting to regulate and more severely penalize companies implicated in fraud and corruption scandals. This led to the notion of self-regulation through codes of conduct and compliance programs to mollify the authorities. Over time, this argument evolved into the promise that compliance programs would solve the problems of regulatory noncompliance and unethical conduct within corporations.

The point of inflection came in 1991 when the United States Sentencing Commission (USSC) (1991) offered companies a substantial reduction in fines if they could demonstrate that they had an "effective compliance program" in place. The idea was that not having a program creates too high a risk. This risk is increasingly serious if one considers that from the time of the globalization of the compliance discourse (in the 2000s), increasing numbers of countries have legislated legal frameworks under the same criteria, in other words, to apply more moderate sanctions or even forgive companies if they can prove that, at the time of committing the crime of which they are accused, they had an effective compliance program in place. This legal criterion has created perverse incentives, meaning that many programs merely control simulations, front programs, whose real objective is to avoid sanctions rather than correct corrupt practices.

The DOJ has recognized that organizations often create compliance programs to act as façades. In its 2008 review of "Principles of Federal Prosecution of Business Organizations," the DOJ specifically asked prosecutors "to determine whether a company's compliance program is merely a 'program on paper' or whether it was effectively designed, implemented, and reviewed" (US Department of Justice, 2020: 9; *Justice Manual* 9–28). However, it is often challenging to distinguish substantive programs from façades since evaluating a program takes time and experience.

In this context, the DOJ prepared and published the document Evaluation of Corporate Compliance Programs (Grubman & Tanner, 2018) in 2017, with the criteria for evaluating compliance programs reviewed in the preceding sections of this chapter. According to Hui Chen and Eugene Soltes, the authors of these criteria, the document was not intended to be used as a checklist for the effectiveness of compliance programs (Chen & Soltes, 2018).

However, corporations quickly began to use the document as a manual for creating their own "effective compliance programs." In fact, some firms have gone so far as to believe that if they can provide an answer to every question in the document, they can guarantee that DOJ's expectations are met. This has led to absurd situations. For example, companies selectively select data to support the notion that their programs are effective without realizing that the problems that have been recapitulated here strongly affect the final result of compliance programs.

Hui Chen and Eugene Soltes (2018) make an important point about how DOJ evaluation criteria have been misleadingly used. These authors note that one criterion in the DOJ document asks how the organization evaluates the quality and effectiveness of the compliance training program. In this regard, they point out:

A survey by Deloitte and *compliance week* suggests that the method of choice is to measure the completion rate of training and consider training to be effective if enough employees (perhaps 90% or 95%) complete it. However, that metric fails to reflect the quality of training (how appropriate and valuable the content is) or its effectiveness (how much employees learn and put into practice).

Companies rely on completion rates not because doing so is the "right way" to measure success but because their goal is simply to prove to regulators that they have accomplished the task – meaning that they can check the training box. Although some companies surely offer their employees effective compliance training, we have seen many more tricked into believing their training is satisfactory simply because a high proportion of employees have completed it (p. 120).

This example leads to the crux of this discussion: one of the main reasons organizations keep increasing the amount they invest in compliance is because they cannot tell what works and what does not. Investing in compliance is, therefore, the fastest way to maintain the illusion that risks are being managed and mitigated. In this respect, in many organizations, reinforcing compliance has become synonymous with hiring more personnel, buying more sophisticated software, or creating more policies and procedures simply to appear honest and self-regulated without really caring whether these efforts are redundant, expensive, or futile.

This discussion inevitably leads us to the question of how the effectiveness of a compliance program is defined. In other words, what type of information is a program said to be effective or not? If, as has been argued here, organizational reality imposes deviances and insufficiencies on compliance programs, then it is important to understand how this argument of alleged efficacy is built. According to the consulting firm Deloitte and *compliance week*, only 70% of companies attempt to measure the effectiveness of their compliance programs. Moreover, of those that do, only a third are confident or extremely confident they are using the correct metrics (Deloitte, 2017).

Experience has shown that companies often deceive themselves (Langevoort, 2016). Compliance programs are often presented as highly functional, even though they are not. An organization can have all the pieces in place to demonstrate a good compliance policy and controls until a serious crime or reputational scandal erupts. Only then will the organization discover that its compliance program was not as robust as once thought. What mistakes do organizations usually make when they look in the mirror? Hui Chen and Eugene Soltes (2018) suggest four errors whose precision and relevance make them important to revisit:

1. Incomplete Analysis Criteria

Organizations often delude themselves into thinking that they are assessing the effectiveness of their programs by looking at incomplete information. For example, one of the criteria suggested by the DOJ to evaluate the effectiveness of a program is to check whether the organization has applied disciplinary measures for noncompliance. In this respect, it does not suffice only to say that a certain number of employees have been disciplined, and it is also necessary to see that number in its context. Saying that five employees were sanctioned is not the same as saying that five out of fifty employees who violated compliance policies or procedures were disciplined. Nor would it be the same to report that five employees were sanctioned when those truly responsible or those of a higher rank go unpunished. In this case, the effectiveness indicator is relative to the context in which events occur. Looking at a piece of data in isolation can lead to self-deception because it means failing to see the totality or severity of the problem.

2. Invalid Analysis Criteria

Organizations also deceive themselves when they use invalid information to assess the effectiveness of their programs. For example, in response to the DOJ's question about how the organization has measured the effectiveness of its training program, companies often focus on the percentage of employees who have completed training courses. That is a mistaken criterion. Although completion percentage may be relevant for certain controls, it is not a valid criterion for evaluating the effectiveness of a program. Training should be judged on its content or, better still, on the understanding and implementation of the valuable skills learned to address real ethical dilemmas or situations that have already occurred in the organization. Assessing effectiveness using invalid criteria often diverts attention from what is truly important and overlooks more relevant aspects for evaluating a program.

3. Mistaken Analysis Criteria

Organizations also lie to themselves when they use misleading information to evaluate their programs. For example, one of the criteria suggested by the DOJ for evaluating the effectiveness of its program is to ask how the organization has evaluated whether compliance policies and procedures have been effectively applied. Organizations often fall prey to misleading criteria by responding with evidence that employees have signed an acknowledgment that they have read and understood the company's policies and code of conduct. Although this confirmation may provide legal grounds for terminating an employee who violates a corporate policy, it does not necessarily demonstrate that employees have translated knowledge of the policies into everyday work practices. Employees may sign an acknowledgment that they have "read and understand" corporate policies without ever actually reading or understanding corporate guidelines. In the worst-case scenario, which happens with alarming frequency, there are implicit or informal agreements within the organization that it is unnecessary to follow the compliance policies or controls. Evaluating the effectiveness of the objectives of a compliance program with ambiguous analysis criteria, in other words, those with multiple interpretations, prevents one from obtaining an accurate evaluation of effectiveness. On the contrary, it can lead to false expectations of control and consciously or unconsciously induces compliance failures that cause scandals or riskier situations.

4. Self-selection Bias

Organizations also deceive themselves when they use invalid information to assess the effectiveness of their programs. For example, when a compliance officer wishes to assess the effectiveness of their corporate anonymous whistleblower line (the ethics hotline), they can rely on surveys to tell them how comfortable employees are with using the mechanism. The problem with these types of surveys is that they can be skewed. Suppose the survey is not implemented by adhering to the methodological aspects of statistical sampling and well-designed items. In that case, this can lead to nonrepresentative results or misinterpretations and, therefore, false conclusions. When evaluating a program's effectiveness, it is also necessary to consider the type of information used and be aware of the type of bias it may contain.

All these considerations reinforce our core argument: the promise that compliance programs are a solution to administrative problems involving regulatory noncompliance and unethical behavior is problematic. The evidence shows that programs' design, implementation, and implementation face multiple obstacles that limit their effectiveness.

Furthermore, organizations can deceive themselves if they evaluate their programs using incorrect information. This point is hazardous, especially since many organizations could falsely expect control and compliance based on an alleged reality that does not exist. The consequences can be deadly, and multi-million-dollar fines and all kinds of penalties are a real danger.

Nevertheless, what is most worrying here is that the compliance discourse has created its traps. Faced with the possibility of obtaining the regulator's blessing through "effective" compliance programs, the infinite possibility of simulation has been institutionalized. Noticing mistakes and correcting them is presented as the logical, expected response. However, experience tells us that error-based corporate policy often multiplies; it never returns. The greater the investment and the more severely the ego of the compliance program sponsors have been compromised, the more unacceptable withdrawal becomes.

References

ACFE. (2021). *2020 ACFE Report to the Nations: Insights and Lessons on Occupational Fraud.* Retrieved from https://www.withum.com/resources/2020-report-to-the-nations-insights-and-lessons-on-occupational-fraud/ (accessed April 15, 2022).

Arellano-Gault, D. (2020). *Corruption in Latin America.* New York: Routledge.

Barnard, C. (1938). *The Functions of the Executive.* Cambridge: Harvard University Press.

Bribery Act. (2010). c. *23, § 7 (2)(U.K.).*

Chen, H., & Soltes, E. (2018). Why Compliance Programs Fail and How to Fix Them. *Harvard Business Review,* 96(2), 116–125.

Crozier, M., & Friedberg, E. (1980). *Actors and Systems: The Politics of Collective Action.* Chicago: University of Chicago Press.

Davis, W. B. (2009). The Importance of the Due Diligence Investigations: Failed Mergers and Acquisitions of the United States' Companies. *Ankara Bar Review,* 2(1), 5–17.

Deloitte & Compliance Week. (2017). *In Focus: 2016 Compliance Trends Survey.* Deloitte. Retrieved from https://www2.deloitte.com/content/dam/Deloitte/us/Documents/governance-risk-compliance/us-advisory-compliance-week-survey.pdf (accessed April 15, 2022).

Deloitte. (2017). *Compliance week. In focus: 2016 Compliance* Trends Survey. Deloitte.

Etzioni, A. (1964). *Modern Organizations*. Englewood Cliffs: Prentice Hall.

Grubman, S. R., & Tanner, G. A. (2018). The Department of Justice's Evaluation of Corporate Compliance Programs. *Criminal Justice*, 33(1), 23–25.

Hargie, O. E., & Tourish, D. E. (2009). *Auditing Organizational Communication: A Handbook of Research, Theory and Practice*. Routledge/Taylor & Francis Group.

Justice Manual. 9-28.000 Principles of Federal Prosecution of Business Organizations, Justice.

KPMG. (2022). *A triple threat across the Americas: KPMG 2022 Fraud Outlook*. KPMG. Retrieved from https://assets.kpmg/content/dam/kpmg/xx/pdf/2022/01/fraud-survey.pdf (accessed April 15, 2022).

Kroll. (2021). *2021 Anti-Bribery and Corruption Benchmarking Report*. Kroll. Retrieved from https://www.kroll.com/en/insights/publications/compliance-risk/anti-bribery-and-corruption-benchmarking-report-2021 (accessed April 15, 2022).

Kroll. (2017). *Global Fraud & Risk Report. Building Resilience in a Volatile World*. Retrieved from https://www.kroll.com/-/media/kroll/pdfs/news/press-assets-2016-17/kroll-global-fraud-report-2016-2017.pdf (accessed April 15, 2022).

Langevoort, D. (2016). Self-Deception and Regulatory compliance. *The Regulatory Review*. Retrieved from https://www.theregreview.org/2016/08/02/langevoort-self-deception-and-regulatory-compliance/ (accessed April 15, 2022).

Magallanes, A., & Sierra, D. (2020). Latin Lawyer: Litigation, *Referencia México*. Retrieved from https://www.vonwobeser.com/images/PDF_news/2020_2/LL_Litigation-2021_MX.pdf (accessed April 15, 2022).

Makkai, T., & Braithwaite, V. (1993). Professionalism, Organizations, and Compliance. *Law & Social Inquiry*, 18(1), 33–59.

March, J. G., & Olsen, J. P. (1996). Institutional Perspectives on Political Institutions. *Governance*, 9(3), 247–264.

March, J. G., & Olsen, J. P. (1998). The Institutional Dynamics of International Political Orders. *International Organization*, 52(4), 943–969.

McLean, B., & Elkind, P. (2013). *The Smartest Guys in the Room*. New York: Portfolio.

O'Shea, A., Bourtin, N., & Lewis, A. (2020). DOJ Updates Guidance on the Evaluation of Corporate Compliance Programs. *Harvard Law School Forum on Corporate Governance*. Retrieved from https://corpgov.law.harvard.edu/2020/06/20/doj-updates-guidance-on-the-evaluation-of-corporate-compliance-programs/ (accessed April 15, 2022).

Raustiala, K. (2000). Compliance & Effectiveness in International Regulatory Cooperation. *Case Western Reserve Journal of International Law*, 32(3), 387–440.

Sarbanes, P. (2002). *Sarbanes-Oxley Act of 2002*. In The Public Company Accounting Reform and Investor Protection Act. Washington DC: US Congress (Vol. 55). United States.

Simeon, E. D.; Simeon, E. I. (2018). Auditing and Fraud Control in Corporate Organizations. *Auditing*, 9(8).

Singleton, T. W., & Singleton, A. J. (2007). Why Don't We Detect More Fraud? *Journal of Corporate Accounting & Finance*, 18(4), 7–10.

Smith, M., Valle, S. & Schdmit, B. (2017). No One Has Ever Made a Corruption Machine Like This One. *Bloomberg*. Retrieved from https://www.bloomberg.com/news/features/2017-06-08/no-one-has-ever-made-a-corruption-machine-like-this-one (accessed April 15, 2022).

US Congress. (2010). *Dodd-Frank Wall Street Reform and Consumer Protection Act, 2010*. One hundred and eleventh Congress of the United States.

US Congress. (1977). *Foreign Corrupt Practices Act of 1977*. 15 U.S.C. 77dd-1, et seq. Government Printing Office.

US Department of Justice, Criminal Division. (2020). *Evaluation of Corporate Compliance Programs* (June 1, 2020). Retrieved from https://www.justice.gov/criminal-fraud/page/file/937501/download (accessed April 15, 2022).

US Sentencing Commission. (1991). *Guidelines Manual. §3E1.1* (Nov. 1991). Manual ("JM"), Retrieved from https://www.justice.gov/jm/justice-manual (accessed April 15, 2022).

Weick, K., & Sutcliffe, K. (2007). *Managing the Unexpected*. San Francisco: John Wiley & Sons.

Wilkinson, B. A., & Oh, A. Y. K. (2009). The Principles of Federal Prosecution of Business Organizations: A Ten-Year Anniversary Perspective. *NYSBA Inside*, 27(2).

Chapter 4
Can a Compliance Program Really Transform an Organization?

4.1 Introduction

As mentioned in the previous chapters, compliance is an organizational tool that attempts to modify the behavior of the people comprising a company, a government agency, or a nonprofit. It is also a political and administrative project requiring leadership, communication, negotiation, implementation, and evaluation conditions. In this respect, compliance programs are transformative projects from and for organizations. The point is that organizational change cannot be achieved by will alone, through regulations, or by assuming that orders or rules can exclusively shape people's behavior. As Chapter 2 discusses, organizations are an arena, meaning that organizational change is achieved within a systemic logic. In other words, the final effect of the desired change ends up being the product (or by-product) of the interactions and interrelationships between people, rules, structures, events, accidents, and events in the environment. That is why the change in an organization usually does not occur linearly, nor are these changes uniformly adopted by all members of organizations. Or at least not with the same net effects.

However, in the burgeoning literature on compliance, it is generally assumed that the organizational changes these programs entail within an organization can occur smoothly and be promoted by using standardized strategies (recipes) and basically by imposing a series of normative guidelines and oversight structures. Moreover, there is a tendency to assume that these recipes apply in the same way in all types of organizations through the catch-all term "good practices," as if there were an exact science of compliance. The view of compliance standardized through a logic of oversight, audits, codes of conduct, and control systems has become the conventional wisdom on launching a program as though it were a standardized, uniform process.

Along these lines, it is possible to speak of a compliance industry. In other words, a carefully thought-out business of advising on and selling "good practices," in which various groups and organizations have emerged as the holders of the expert knowledge that can be easily transmitted on how to design and implement compliance programs. The good news is that there is a compliance industry: knowledge and experience are created, and organizations are supported and guided through their design and implementation process. Nevertheless, it is also essential to describe the interests that this industry creates to produce a vision and a linear, overly optimistic discourse of the possibilities of transforming organizations instrumentally. In short, the compliance industry always begins with a view of organizations as monoliths (Chapter 2).

https://doi.org/10.1515/9783110749113-004

Advancing a compliance process demands changes within organizations, such as transforming structures, modifying the responsibilities of certain members, and including various actors with influence inside and outside the organization. It also requires the generation and strengthening of information, monitoring and oversight systems, and profound axiological changes on the part of each of its members, since "an organization is as attached to compliance as its least attached member" (Biegelman & Biegelman, 2010). Compliance must therefore be a totalizing program in the organization, in which all members are recipients and active participants in its implementation and observation. Easier said than done.

However, this contrasts with the reality of organizations, which, as Arellano-Gault (2010) explains, are social constructs contingent on the interactions between their members, both among each other and with their context. Organizations can be seen as arenas, in other words, as the result of the interaction (whether harmonious or conflictive) between the organization's various groups. These groups do not enjoy the same resources and capabilities and instead interact in asymmetric relationships, in which some strategically maintain spaces of uncertainty to preserve their status quo within the organization (Crozier, 1964). Within an organization, members may be more interested in complying with the established compliance parameters since it increases their share of power. Logically, other groups will strategically and actively or surreptitiously oppose them.

Likewise, implementing a compliance program involves a considerable investment of resources, which many organizations may have difficulty sustaining. In any case, developing and implementing this type of program has practically become an obligation. These programs will have to be tailored to the restrictions on economic, personal, and even physical resources that are experienced in practice.

This chapter focuses on analyzing why compliance should be seen not as a standard process of an organization but rather as a permanently evolving project that seeks constant change in organizations. In other words, as described in the previous chapters, there will be no change in an organization that does not require a regulatory process and involves the conviction and negotiation for it to be sustained and adopted. In the case of compliance, the specificity of the problem to be addressed is critical. As seen in previous chapters, the forces that lead to deviant behavior, rule-bending, fraud, and willful intent are permanent and endogenous to any organization. Compliance is an ongoing process that requires continuously recreating and rebuilding its bases, in keeping with the process of adopting and adapting the premises that each organization (and its members) adopts in practice.

Underlying this discussion is the question in the title: Is it possible to bring about the changes stipulated by compliance programs in organizations? How can this be done? In an initial reflection in this chapter, we can say that owing to the nature of compliance (as a political and administrative project to achieve change), the effects will not be exactly as expected within organizations. As dynamic arenas of relationships between people and groups, the dynamics and logic of interaction will steer the organizational adoption of compliance through adaptations and counterarguments. If, in addition, the compliance project is perceived by the people in the organization as an external imposition, the dynamics of adaptation and adoption can be radical and involve resistance or, at least, subterfuge. However, this does mean no changes will materialize in line with expectations. Nevertheless, because of this difficulty, a compliance program should not be seen as a linear process with a beginning and an end but rather as a flow that requires constant adaptations and tactical reforms.

This chapter analyses the key compliance instruments and their ability to transform organizations. To this end, Section 4.2. reviews the basic assumptions of compliance as a mechanism that is increasingly required in any type of organization. Although compliance literature contains various assumptions, only the main ones will be considered in this exercise. These include robust information systems for shareholder, manager, and director oversight, and internal and external audits, as well as the construction of shared value systems, promoted and supported by the main agents of the organization, from managers to board members, as well as all the members of the organization in general. The classic mechanisms for setting behavioral guidelines such as codes of conduct and values will also be examined. Moreover, there will also be references to leadership that focus on promoting ethical actions, appropriate behavior, and supporting cultural change within organizations. Finally, classic instruments include developing systems to control risks to ensure their identification and management, which involves using whistleblowing channels and detecting inappropriate or corrupt behavior. Based on a description of these elements, a brief criticism is made of the tendency to see them as a list, a checklist of mechanisms whose mere existence is assumed to make compliance a reality in the organization.

Section 4.3 examines another of the fundamental changes proposed in the compliance industry in greater depth: the inclusion of new actors within the organization, such as ethics managers. It also describes the changes that emerge in organizational structures due to the inclusion of these new roles, such as the increase in the obligations and responsibilities of executive chiefs, directors, and managers in various aspects. This gives rise to points that will guide the discussion: How do these changes impact the rest of the organization? How do these new roles interact with previously established ones? Which is the impact of these new responsibilities and powers on directors, CEOs, and managers? These answers highlight some of the problems of including these new organizational actors, in addition to acknowledging the capacity of managers to comply with the changes required by compliance programs.

The chapter ends with ideas on how to achieve the organizational change expected from compliance. It assumes that since programs are increasingly based on normative parameters, standardized practices, abstract policies, and general regulations, the anticipated changes will probably not occur as expected and, in extreme cases, will not even materialize. Due to the complexity of organizations, which are arenas in which various actors with different interests interact (as pointed out in

Chapter 2), changes do not usually occur linearly. Transforming organizations involves having the vision and ability to overcome the various obstacles that the dynamics and context of each organization impose on attempts to modify the balances that have already been established. They are balances, for better or for worse, but ultimately balances.

Organizations are often unable to comply with the organizational assumptions made by compliance programs due to a lack of resources, severe shortcomings in terms of the structure of the organization, and, many times, a lack of commitment from key groups owing to the difficulty of undertaking reforms and complying with new regulations, maintaining the traditional operational load and a lack of clarity regarding time and resources, capacity building and commitments from the management side to modify their routines and prerogatives as well.

Implementing compliance programs as a checklist can have a boomerang effect over time.

4.2 Compliance: Factors and Assumptions for Change

As mentioned in Chapter 2, compliance is a tool that seeks to transform organizations while becoming an inherent element of them. In other words, rather than being a practice or process that occurs only once, it attempts to be structural, a continuous function that will become an inherent part of the nature of the organization. Furthermore, even one is capable of reproducing itself as a standard practice within the organization. This means that for an organization to be aligned with compliance programs and policies, it must undergo a series of incremental changes yet aspire to modify the functions that have been stabilized and accepted in the organization for a long time. Compliance is therefore unlikely to be initially regarded as natural or even functional.

On the contrary, groups and individuals within the organization will see several functions considered basic and effective being disrupted. For many people, these programs designed to achieve change may seem costly and even unnecessarily intrusive. This is probably one of the most important practical principles when designing and implementing compliance programs: they are contradictory in many ways. The fact that an organization is attempting to create spaces, rules, and routines for people to act ethically obviously sounds like a good idea. Nevertheless, as we have already seen, things become more complicated when substantial practical elements become evident: Who decides what is right or wrong? Who will be responsible for oversight and making judgments about it? What happens when a chain of organizational processes, interactions, hierarchies, practices, and symbols are alleged to cause or initiate apparently unethical behavior? How does one resolve, in practice, the clashes and contradictions between criteria that the organization itself requires to be positively evaluated (e.g., being effective vs. being transparent, or being loyal and trustworthy vs. being a whistleblower)? A naive view of compliance would be content to assume that it will become just another smooth and without conflict function of the organization. The actual process and the experience accumulated to date suggest something entirely different.

In the literature, some factors are highlighted to guide and encourage changes in areas of organizations in which specific skills, practices, and strategies must be developed to promote robust and effective compliance programs are emphasized. It is important to note that these factors are established from a normative perspective. In other words, guidelines, general recommendations, and standards are drawn up, which, if adhered to, will ensure greater success in implementing a compliance program. One of the downsides of this normative view of an intricate process such as compliance is that the proposals prove to be very general and, at the same time, ambiguous. They are more like proverbs or general advice rather than applicable guidelines for coping with the variability encountered in practice. Ultimately, the changes proposed by a compliance program will elicit not only agreement but also conflicts, doubts, and varying interpretations about the intentions and viability of the ideas to be implemented. Ignoring these elements tends to limit the real possibilities of organizational change.

The traditional factors and assumptions put forward to encourage compliance are intended to establish behavioral models for the members of an organization (especially managers and senior officials such as boards of directors or directors), as well as shared axiological hierarchies. In addition, they highlight the development of new systems and structures for formulating information, the start of top-down communication, and the constant monitoring of practices within the organization. They also stress the need to institutionalize risk identification and management processes. In this respect, organizations must incorporate these elements internally and cope with the pressure of corporate practices' regulations, rules, and standards.

There has been a broad discussion about the principal factors that promote compliance in organizations. This section will address just four of them that are substantive for the development of compliance: the development of information systems; the establishment of value systems; ethical leadership and commitment on the part of managers to comply with standards and values and lastly, the establishment and strengthening of monitoring systems such as whistleblowing and complaint procedures. In the compliance literature, these factors and assumptions are crucial because they, in turn, produce a series of effects that contribute to other substantive factors. For example, when organizations develop robust information systems that produce quality information, internal and external audits are more accurate in identifying fraud and bad practices. Likewise, the systematic production of information on the organization and its context facilitates the identification of the risks it faces, thereby making their mitigation more effective. In a second example, if, within the organization, directors and managers show leadership designed to promote ethical behavior and a commitment to strengthening compliance in the organization, then further-reaching actions are taken to transform the organizational structures and dynamics.

These four factors and assumptions that promote compliance are briefly described below. The possible contradictions, paradoxes, and problems faced by these factors in organizations are subsequently analyzed. To this end, we consider organizations as arenas in which multiple actors have interests that do not necessarily coincide and may be affected by changes driven by compliance.

4.2.1 Information Systems Development

Information is an invaluable resource for companies. However, obtaining it is neither cheap nor easy (Leech & Thomson, 2008). On the one hand, when it comes to information about the organization itself, its complexity makes it difficult to accurately identify all the tasks, interactions, and decisions made by its members. On the other, information on the context in which the organization is located is not easily obtainable either because organizations create particular meanings and logics that frame the information in a way that fits the organization's parameters, symbols, and perceptions. External information can therefore be diffuse, which is why it does not help identify relevant context elements.

Paradoxically, information is a crucial asset for companies because of its multiple applications and uses. In terms of compliance, the most important ones are as follows: it provides knowledge to stakeholders and shareholders on the state of the organization, its areas for improvement, and the risks and problems it faces. It makes it possible to have a more accurate, clearer picture of an organization's resources, which the latter can be used for planning. It promotes openness, transparency, and accountability, which are crucial elements for public agencies and corporations. It facilitates access to oversight, continuous monitoring, and internal and external audits and encourages diagnoses and assessments of the organization's context.

In the compliance industry, information is fundamental since its central elements determine how relevant information is identified, captured, and communicated, as established by the Committee of Sponsoring Organizations (COSO) 1992 and Enterprise Risk Management (ERM) (Tarantino, 2008). Along these same lines, adequate information is essential within the entire organization, from the top-down and bottom-up. In addition, robust, quality information contributes to identifying and mitigating risks and evaluating these actions. Thus, information is a critical factor in decision-making.

However, information also constitutes a substantive factor for accountability, transparency, and internal and external oversight. Having accurate, accessible information enhances the confidence of shareholders and citizens. As a result, external auditors can more clearly evaluate performance, contributing to a positive image of the organization, thereby increasing its value or legitimacy. In this respect, the lack or poor quality of information is associated with opacity, the increase in discretionary spaces that allow harmful practices such as fraud, embezzlement, conflicts of interest, and the alteration of accounting books, as in the case of Enron (McLean & Elkind, 2013).

The importance of information makes the development of robust information systems a key factor in compliance programs. The causal relationship is clear: if an organization has more effective information systems, it is easier to determine and report whether it is complying with the regulations. However, this requires building capacities and structures that organizations do not develop either suddenly or methodically.

In this respect, implementing information technology systems (ITS) is widely linked to generating relevant information for organizations (Tarantino, 2008; Collet, 2008; Koo, 2008). IT assumes that information can be generated quickly and efficiently, is communicated instantly, and is accessible to all actors inside and outside organizations. Even more importantly for compliance, comprehensive ITS systems provide information flows that can be automated so that the data obtained can be consulted in real-time, reducing the scope for discretion in handling and managing sensitive information. Technological advances strengthen models such as Enterprise Content Management (ECM), which focuses on reducing the risk of altering or destroying documents and emails (Koo, 2008), such as collaborative work in virtual clouds or shared information systems such as blockchain (Montalvo, 2020).

Implementing information systems requires a series of resources and conditions. First, systems need to be embedded in compliance programs in which the relationship and functionality of the system are determined. Setting up a new system also implies innovation risks (Pope, 2016). In other words, changing the status quo requires the collaboration and cooperation of multiple actors who can intervene. Moreover, the structures of organizations must be modified since new agents emerge to manage these models, such as IT managers, who will be analyzed in the following section. Finally, the implementation and maintenance of these efficient information systems necessarily involve a substantial investment of money, personnel, and attention by members, regardless of the size or sector of the organization.

4.2.2 Value Systems

Values are crucial factors in successfully undertaking a compliance program. Organizations with value systems that are shared and accepted by their members are less likely to experience acts of corruption or harmful practices. In this respect, it is essential for all the actors in an organization to know, share, create and act in alignment with the designated values. Since these values are decided from the top-down, managers and senior officials are the first to promote and follow the established ethical guidelines, codes, and practices.

Value systems and ethical codes reinforce regulations and guidelines since they ensure that all actions and decisions pursue the moral standards guiding the actions of organizations. Indeed, value systems are related to concepts associated with compliance, such as good governance (Claps, 2008) and corporate ethics (Tarantino, 2008), because values and ethics shape the image of organizations, as well as the perception and reputation of stakeholders (Silverman, 2008). A socially constructed value system is therefore essential to the development of compliance.

This system is often constructed from the top-down, with senior staff such as managers and directors determining the organization's values, without lower-ranking employees' participation. Values and ethical codes are communicated and learned by all members as part of a socialization process. In this respect, directors and managers serve as examples of how the ideal model of the organization should behave. Other members imitate these behaviors because it is assumed that those higher up in the hierarchy elicit feelings such as admiration, respect, and leadership (as explained later).

The development of a value system creates organizational culture. Silverman (2008) notes that for the culture and values of an organization to have a significant impact on compliance programs, managers and directors must support the programs and actions designed to promote ethics and have the will to provide the necessary resources to comply with compliance initiatives and publicly reinforce the desired ethos of the organization. Defining the values of an organization is therefore linked to its mission and vision, which can be instituted by certain members of the organization so that these values are assumed to be shared by all members. Likewise, the will to contribute resources must materialize in concrete actions. Specifically, the formulation of communication strategies regarding values and their importance, generating incentives and sanctions for their adoption from the highest to the lowest position, establishing mechanisms for training and evaluating personnel practices to determine whether they follow ethical standards, and creating or providing capacities for areas and personnel that are specifically responsible for the promotion, communication and supervision of adherence to values, such as the establishment of a Chief of Ethics and Compliance Officer (CECO) which will be addressed in more detail later.

All these adjustments are a priority because they are related to or impact other factors. One example is that these value systems show what the behavior of directors and managers should be like, which is closely related to leadership, an essential element for implementing this type of program. Another example is that monitoring and reporting systems are reinforced if values are socialized and internalized. This is how the various systems contribute to each other, achieving a central compliance objective: its automatic, continuous reproduction.

4.2.3 Leadership

A crucial factor in the implementation of these programs is the leadership of the senior staff of organizations. The determination of leaders to implement the necessary changes, and encourage their peers, is key to whether a program will be effective. In this respect, changes are more likely to occur if there is a commitment from directors and managers. At the same time, for these transformations to be maintained, this commitment must be lasting. This is not easy because leadership must be expressed through everyday actions.

According to the compliance literature, leaders are responsible for continuously demonstrating their support. They must show commitment and impeccable behavior, act as mentors and guides for their colleagues, and encourage the path of transformation by showing the will to implement complex information systems and strengthen reporting systems and ethics programs. Leaders play a key role in compliance since they are the central actor who allows change, and lack of leadership makes it impossible to set all the factors required to achieve compliance.

Leadership is translatable to will and commitment, rather like the political will to implement public policies (Post, Raile, & Raile, 2010; Brinkerhoff, 2000). This will materialize in different ways, such as the creation of organizational culture (Silverman, 2008), committing to act impeccably and always in accordance with the ethical standards of the organization; assigning the necessary resources to meet the requirements of compliance programs; promoting a climate of trust, in which all members participate and contributing to the achievement of compliance objectives. It also involves undertaking the necessary transformations to align operations with compliance programs; facilitating the implementation of information, monitoring, incentive, and compensation systems, as well as sanctions, even for themselves, since this is where the strength of the message about the importance of behavior attached to values and ethical practices lies. The will of leaders can constantly be observed because it is expressed in decisions and habitual actions. In other words, will is not reflected in discourse or empty promises.

A leader's behavior is always under scrutiny from their colleagues and subordinates. A leader's message through their actions is continuous because compliance is not just an occasional tool but is expected to be reproduced until it is so stable that it is regarded as an inherent feature of organizations. The leader must make their message convincing and, even more importantly, consistent, ensuring compliance is perceived as a substantive aspect of organizations.

In addition, leadership is a key factor in creating effective organizational environments for the promotion of ethics and compliance, mainly because it has a significant impact on the behavior and attitudes of the members of an organization (Treviño, Weaver, Gibson, & Toffler, 1999). Along these same lines, for the institution of specific areas for the management of ethics and compliance, one of the main points is to grant sufficient authority and responsibility to a leader to enable them to discharge their responsibilities. This is the only way to reduce negative behaviors while increasing an ethical culture (Ethics Resource Center [ERC], 2007). Leadership, therefore, impacts some of the other factors mentioned and is perhaps the predominant factor.

4.2.4 Monitoring, Surveillance, and Control Systems

One of the main strategies of compliance programs is to implement and strengthen monitoring, oversight, and control systems. These systems are specifically designed to perform two tasks. This strategy establishes continuous evaluation mechanisms to determine whether decisions and practices adhere to the organization's normative frameworks, regulations, values, and codes of conduct, such as performance evaluations. The second involves promoting reporting mechanisms, such as whistleblowing platforms and channels. Additionally, internal and external audits can be included as oversight practices that the organization must adopt.

The importance of these systems lies in the fact that they contribute to risk identification and mitigation since they make it possible to focus on the areas in which the practices that lead to possible problems and acts of corruption arise. It is possible to intervene in these sectors quickly, strengthening the organization's compliance. The resources produced by the organization also strengthen these systems. As a first example, evaluation systems are linked to training, where the values comprising organizational culture are communicated and learned. The effectiveness of reporting wrongdoing is anchored to a positive organizational environment, so that middle- and lower-ranking members feel confident that they will be attended to and that their reports will have consequences, and that their sanctions are as credible as they are equitable for everyone regardless of their position in the hierarchy. Reporting channels are supported by ICT systems that ensure the protection of the privacy of whistleblowers and speed up the communication process. Internal and external audits take advantage of high-quality information systems since this provides them with critical information on the organization more easily and quickly.

The ethical policy clearly outlines the expected standards of business conduct and the actions to be taken in case of a breach. Monitoring systems underpin other essential factors for compliance, although they also produce effects such as continuous control or an increase in the confidence of internal and external actors. The Organization for Economic Cooperation and Development (OECD) and the Basel Institute on Governance argue that high-level reporting mechanisms, among other things, "create better levels of trust and transparency for firms." The development of effective, credible monitoring systems undoubtedly enhances transparency, as well as accountability.

Internal and mainly external audits increase an organization's reliability, trustworthiness, and legitimacy. Audits have achieved prominence due to the growing importance of the auditor's work, whether internal or external, and the skills required to meet the demands of this role (Edelblut and Murdock, 2008). Auditors must also abide by ethical codes of conduct (ERC, 2007) and obey regulations such as COSO 1992 and the Sarbanes-Oxley Act. The credibility of auditors is a highly prized variable that translates into the legitimacy and validity of an audit. Accordingly, auditors also end up adhering to the compliance programs established by organizations.

Once the four factors have been analyzed, this table shows the relationship between them and their assumptions regarding how they contribute to the changes required to achieve compliance. In Figure 4.1, the four factors are described.

4.3 Organizational Paradoxes of the Factors and Assumptions Underlying Change

As mentioned earlier, compliance programs are based on factors and assumptions that promote change. The transformation that leads organizations to compliance occurs due to adhering to this checklist. Many of these factors and assumptions are obviously underpinned by the view that Chapter 2 called "the organization as a monolith." As discussed earlier, organizations are not monolithic actors, so this conceptualization of compliance fails to capture the complexity and nature of organizations as social entities, arenas comprising strategic actors who interact not only to achieve the goals of the organizations but also to attain their interests and give meaning to their actions. Thus, the analogy of the organization as an arena in which different actors and coalitions interact, negotiate, and cooperate provides a complete view of them but also shows that changes do not occur in a linear, orderly, and simple manner.

Reform or change projects not only consist of establishing new patterns of behavior and premises in the interactions that will gradually replace previously established balances. For this reason, organizational changes encounter obstacles and limitations because they require creating new balances that disrupt different actors' power relations, interactions, and the status quo. Along these lines, resistance to change arises, not solely due to an irrational rejection of "the new," or the challenging tools of change that may even be perceived as necessary. Instead, resistance to change is due to the organization's interventions altering the spaces of uncertainty, balances, and interactions established by its members (March, 2008a). Once again, changes are organizational and do not occur due to mandates. This is not a normative or discursive issue. Instead, these are political projects in which consensus must be generated through the various actors and coalitions to convince, cooperate, and negotiate the new rules, parameters, and balances (Hochwarter, 2012).

Likewise, change in the behavior of actors is not a purely individual decision since the impact of that change is relevant in the interaction that occurs with other

Leadership

If leaders are committed, act impeccably and encourage other members then they can boost all necessary changes to achieve compliance

[assumption]

Commitment and willingness to undertake actions, allocate sufficient resources to meet with the requirements of the programs of compliance, act as role models, guide and promote the compliance-oriented changes

These elements promote the development of:

Monitoring systems

consists in:

Strategies and practices aimed at establishing control mechanisms to examine that the decisions and practices are attached to regulatory frameworks, regulations, values and codes of conduct of the organization

[assumption]

Monitoring is reliable since they contribute to quickly identifying risks. In addition, there is a reliable environment for members to report harmful practices

Value systems

consists in:

Values, behaviors and shared ethical standards socialized that make up the culture of the organization

[assumption]

The values are determined by managers and are transmitted to the rest of the members, who through training, the example of directors and managers, as well as codes of conduct, accept and internalize them

Information systems

consists in:

Strategies and practices for the generation, management and exchange of internal and external information of organizations

[assumption]

The information produced by organizations is trustworthy if it is framed in a program of compliance that establishes guidelines on how to collect, transmit and use the information

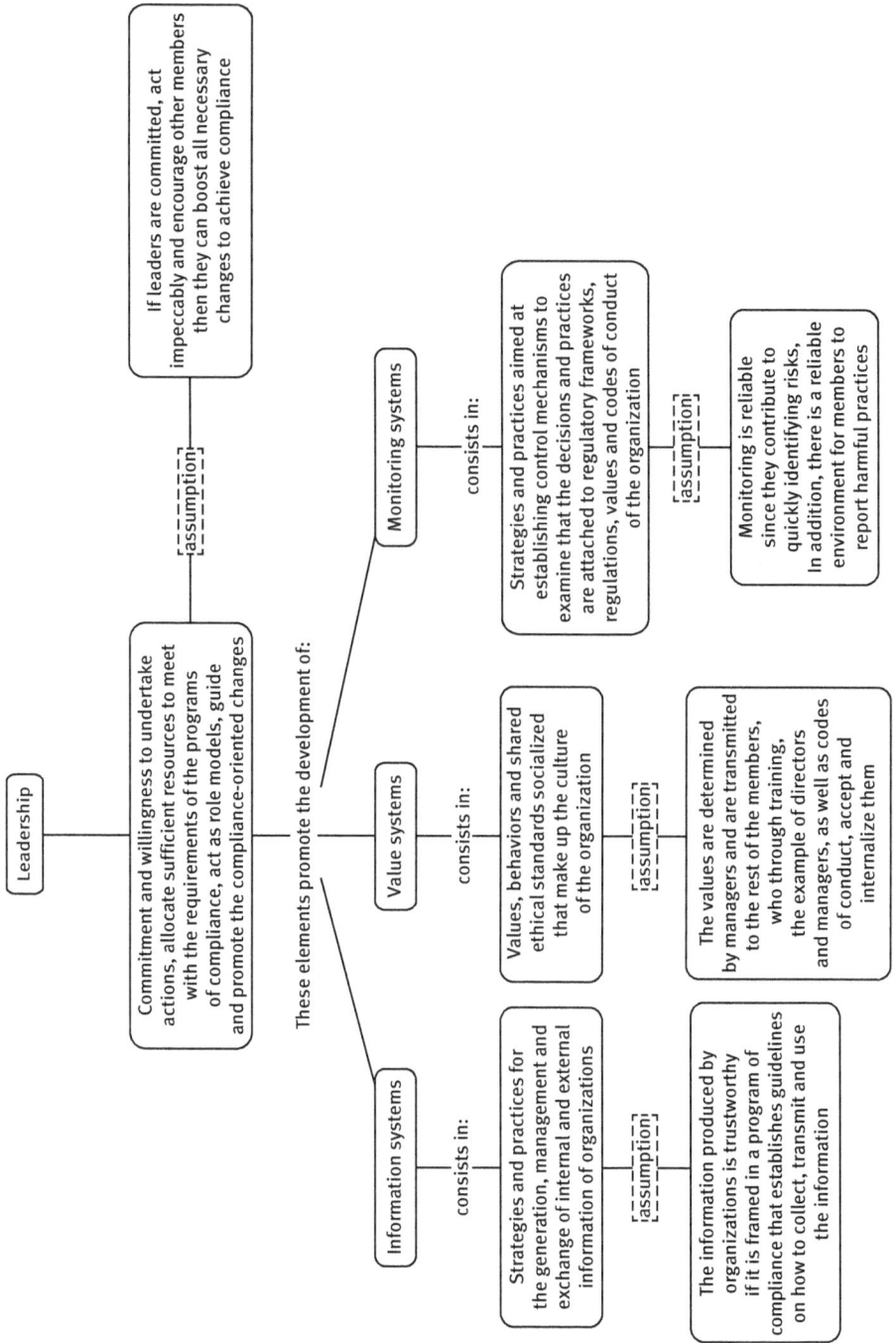

Figure 4.1: Four factors and assumptions for the change necessary for compliance.

people. Behavior is fundamental, but in organizational contexts, the interactions that arise within them are even more important. It is worth recalling that organizations are built on the interactions and logics of their members. Changing behaviors is essential, but it is even more crucial to reflect on whether these changes in behavior manage to impact balances and are capable of formulating new ones (March, 2008a).

In contrast, change factors are proposed in compliance literature, accompanied by assumptions that must occur for an organization to comply with the programs designed. The factors described are based on precepts that implementing these factors can be established through manuals, policies, and standardized practices, in a one-size-fits-all approach. However, organizations are not identical to each other, even those that belong to the same sector. There are considerable differences within public agencies, like those between a public company and an office within a secretariat and between a transnational corporation and a local, medium-sized company. Beyond these apparent distinctions, in every organization, the interactions and balances that originate are anchored to history and the social and cultural context itself, so that general intervention may not achieve the expected effects and, in some cases, have contradictory effects. With projects designed to achieve change, it is essential to evaluate the net effects (Arellano-Gault, 2010).

For each factor and its assumption, the criticisms, limits, and obstacles found in the literature on organizational analysis discussions are given below. Each of them shows the structural flaws of these factors that hamper the implementation of changes to adhere to compliance programs. Likewise, it will help us reflect on these alleged changes' feasibility and net effects.

4.3.1 Information Systems

Information systems assume that the information produced by organizations will be reliable if it is framed in a compliance program that sets guidelines on collecting, transmitting, and using the information. For the construction of these systems, all the members collaborate in different ways, whether in the construction of the platforms and mechanisms of the system, the supply of information, its review, processing and ordering, or the communication and exchange of data with both members and external agents. In this process, all the actors must comply with the ethical and quality standards established by the company's compliance program, which assumes that the systems are robust and reliable.

There are two general criticisms of this assumption. The first lies in what Crozier and Friedberg (1980) call strategic games. These games consist of actors constantly striving to control areas of uncertainty to have some power within the organization. As the actors strategically achieve greater control of more areas of uncertainty, their influence and power are likely to increase, which enables them to control and steer the dynamics of the organization toward the achievement of their goals. The power of these areas of uncertainty is achieved through the control of information, for example, through the opacity of the tasks of an actor or coalition, the undertaking of essential processes that are only undertaken by specific members, the concealment or ignorance of the resources required to accomplish specific tasks. In this case, sharing information with the rest of the organization implies losing control of these areas of uncertainty, which undoubtedly alters the balance of power within the organization. Since the implementation of information systems reduces the control of these areas of uncertainty, members of the organization may be unwilling to use them. In this respect, actors within the organization will not necessarily commit to complying with information system requirements. Instead, they will provide the minimum necessary information, share partial information and block the channels for exchanging information, exactly the opposite of what is expected for compliance.

The second criticism is that information produced by organizations is created through a crucible based on the meaning constructed within them (Weick, 2001), but is also influenced by group dynamics such as groupthink (Janis, 1972). On the one hand, the meaning created by an organization is a powerful mechanism that shapes the perception of reality. Meaning facilitates action, provides guidelines for behavior in response to an uncertain context, and establishes models of what is and is not correct. In this respect, sensemaking creates interpretations and definitions of reality, which at one extreme is extremely useful for organizations, but at the other, skews the interpretation of the context so that the information is framed in that direction. The consequences of sensemaking skewing prevent an organization from incorporating contradictory information into meaning, as a result of which it closes itself off to interpretations that prevent it from discovering the context in which the organization is located. Likewise, skewing neutralizes this function as a mechanism for risk identification, reducing the ability to recognize new risks or increase of others that have not been registered.

In other words, the organizational dynamics for incorporating and maintaining a compliance project are not exempt from the contradictions within the organizational dynamics. The case of groupthink is straightforward: launching a compliance project requires cohesion, and consensus decisions can produce the strength and motivation to launch a major effort to begin change and maintain it. On the other hand, too much cohesion can lead to groupthink: a resistance to obtaining better information, examining conflicts, and looking for alternatives when things are not working out. In groupthink, decision-makers close themselves off and create a veil that blinds them to making better decisions, admitting mistakes, and looking for alternatives. Cohesion enables organizations to make decisions and find agreements, fostering mutual empathy and support. Nevertheless, any compliance project risks becoming a sham or a formal, cosmetic effort when groupthink occurs. In the face of failures or resistance to the project, people can succumb to a closed logic of denying errors or forgetting that projects, in a real organization, in an organizational arena, require constant adaptation and negotiation.

Assuming, as is often done, that all members of an organization are willing to collaborate with information, share it, and improve it because that is simply the way it is stated in the organization's discourses and in the rhetoric of compliance projects is usually a serious mistake that will generate more negative consequences. The reality within an organization is that some coalitions and groups can cooperate and even agree with the general project of change that a compliance program implies. However, they will do so within various participation schemes, negotiation, haggling, coordination, and even sabotage. Information management is undoubtedly a key or strategic element for any group in an organization. Creating a groupthink logic and closing off dialogue or searching for options in the face of resistance to change from a compliance project is a common mistake that can lead to failure.

4.3.2 Value Systems

Value systems are a fundamental part of compliance programs since they establish the bases of behavior and the values that guide the actions and decisions of organizations. The assumption behind this idea is that values are substantially determined by the directors of an organization and are transmitted to the rest of the members, who, through training, the example of directors and managers, as well as codes of conduct, accept and internalize them. In this vision of value systems, middle- and lower-ranking members are the recipients of the values defined in the strategic planning process by senior management (directors and managers). The socialization of these values occurs through mechanisms of learning and the imitation of the behavior of the leaders of the organization. Accordingly, most members act as recipients of the values they must pursue.

This powerful assumption can be discussed through two significant criticisms, one at the group level and the other at the individual level. At the group level, the role played by members as passive actors in the delimitation of values is questioned. Bryson (1988) states that in the strategic planning process where the mission, vision, objectives, and values of the organization are defined, the inclusion of all the actors that are part of the organization enhances the process since it allows the incorporation of different visions, needs, and interests. Conversely, if members fail to participate actively, they do not feel identified with the established values, which impacts their acceptance. For values to permeate, they must be accepted, understood, and reproduced by all the actors. One of the most important means of achieving this is through the groups themselves within the organization. Groups and teams, both formal and informal. The key is that since teams and groups are so important, the variation and negotiations in which teams engage are critical to the final result of any organizational modification or reform project (Vigoda-Gadot &

Vashdi, 2012). However, the compliance literature assumes that values are only communicated and reinforced so that they are learned and internalized by people who regard themselves as individuals, not as part of formal and informal groups or teams.

This does not necessarily happen because the actors have individual logic regarding feelings, intentions, and "backstage" senses (Goffman, 1967). Members may pretend to believe in (and act on) certain values, particularly if they are not convinced that they are relevant or appropriate. Goffman (1967) explains how people create a façade with acts and expressions designed to elicit a specific reaction in their audience. In this way, members can function according to the value systems in the presence of their colleagues, auditors, and evaluators, even though their behavior has not actually changed, nor do the values permeate their conduct. As such, compliance with these systems is likely to be a mere façade, meaning harmful practices will likely remain. For this reason, the actors need to believe in the values that the company pursues genuinely. In the creation of these systems, the participation of members is a key factor.

4.3.3 Leadership

Leadership is the most significant factor for compliance, so the assumption on which it is based is substantive. In general terms, the presence of a committed leader, who is willing to take action to achieve change and commit resources, who acts impeccably and, in the process, encourages other members to do so, will ensure the program's success. A leader has wide-ranging responsibilities in the operational and administrative spheres, spread over various sectors of the organization. The leader must show willingness that must be expressed in various ways: in the allocation of resources, the reform of mechanisms and systems, the commitment to ethical action based on values, and the sustainment of the effort and commitment over time.

In this regard, the leadership factor is related to will and commitment, similar to the concept of political will, a fundamental element for undertaking policies that require support (Post, Raile, & Raile, 2010; Fritzen, 2005). In this respect, political will and leadership are slippery concepts that are difficult to measure and verify. In the case of leadership, it is assumed as an element present in the day-to-day running of the organization, meaning that it is examined insofar as the leader complies with the attributions that have been set out. The leader, therefore, seems to be under constant scrutiny since leadership is a visible characteristic one day but may not be obvious the next. Does this mean that the leader is not living up to expectations? Can leadership, as a variable, in fact, be objectively measured?

The leader is entrusted with so many attributions and responsibilities that they may be unable to fulfill them all due to budgetary, time, or capacity constraints, or even because they have limited rationality (Simon, 1947). A leader may realize that the changes required by a compliance program are too costly, so are they a good leader because they choose not to commit funds that will not achieve a solid result, or are they a lazy leader because they failed to implement possible actions to undertake the process to achieve compliance? The answer to this question poses a dilemma: the leader is pressured by their own conflicting responsibilities. As March (2008c; March & Weil, 2005) points out, an area rarely explored in the leadership literature is understanding the extremely contradictory logics leaders experience in this capacity. The pressures that need to be overcome between their private and public lives and the balance required between power, subordination, and innovation, come with high expectations (many of which are unrealistic). These include the pressures to maintain unity amid a diverse, heterogeneous organizational arena and the demand to be different, brave, yet at the same time, reasonable and focused. With elements like these, it is unrealistic to think that leadership is something that can be programmed in a compliance process based on a checklist.

As a final critique is that according to the assumptions of change, the leader must discharge all their responsibilities to promote compliance and perform efficiently in the functions of their position. This naturally prevents leaders from achieving optimal results in their set tasks and in their compliance responsibilities. Prioritization becomes a central strategy when company objectives and compliance are put in the balance; the latter is less of a priority. This is a serious problem in terms of compliance, as it requires the constant strengthening of leaders and decision-makers to ensure compliance actions are implemented.

4.3.4 Monitoring Systems

Monitoring, surveillance, and control systems are essential mechanisms for risk identification and mitigation and evaluating and preventing unethical practices that affect the organization's compliance. These systems are connected to information and values like a puzzle, so the monitoring mechanisms are reliable if these pieces are robust. Moreover, as the leader promotes a trustworthy environment, members feel confident to use specific channels to report behaviors that do not adhere to the codes of conduct and scale of values.

These monitoring systems must be neutral, automatic, and based on technical parameters, ensuring they are reliable. If they are subjective, with the interference of more actors, the process is flawed because evaluations and controls can be altered. This explains the paradox of these systems, which is summarized in what Merton (1940) observes: the existence of more controls leads to rigidity, affecting organizational functions. Additionally, the control and review of these systems always have a subjective component that can affect their reliability. This creates a paradox. In the case of reporting systems, what happens if the actor responsible for reporting is the offender? Likewise, reporting systems are based on power symmetry, an assumption that is difficult to sustain in reality. Organizations as arenas reflect the fact that there are interactions in which actors or coalitions are in dispute, revealing asymmetrical relationships (Cyert & March, 1963).

A paradox arises in internal control: how do actors implement surveillance mechanisms when those same mechanisms also monitor them? Given this situation, actors with more power and control might not impose more lax surveillance mechanisms to prevent themselves from being subject to sanctions. A paradigmatic case of this was Enron (McLean & Elkind, 2013), in which the director, together with the director of finance, was directly responsible for altering the financial reports. If a person wishes to report, how is this possible if the director is the main person responsible for this? Regardless of whether the environment is positive for reporting, the costs associated with reporting can discourage a whistleblower from doing so. Furthermore, what is to be done when a lower-ranking staff member reports one of the company's directors who enjoys broad legitimacy and credibility. Would the reporting mechanisms alone ensure that sanctions and punishments will be undertaken? In the case of audits, these are not infallible and have also failed to identify bad practices and fraud because the information is limited, and control can be simulated, especially in contexts where corruption is institutionalized, as happened in the case of Enron.

The power variable is an essential element that is not included in the analysis of compliance literature. For this reason, the factors and assumptions fall short in the face of the challenges posed by power asymmetries, the alteration of balances, and the strategic games that occur in an organization. Despite the myriad of regulations, regulatory frameworks, schemes, and sophisticated methodologies, monitoring mechanisms are not infallible. Examining their limits contributes to formulating other complementary tools that would improve the evaluation and surveillance of harmful activities for compliance. Likewise, one should recall that power is an inherent variable in organizations, which allows a better understanding of how these factors for change can be promoted more accurately, bringing us closer to an approach in which we analyze the net effects rather than the effects that the literature promises will happen. This section ends with Table 4.1 summarizing the factors and assumptions of change with their respective criticisms.

4.4 Compliance: New Roles and Effects

The shift to compliance requires factors that have assumptions, as well as new roles that can implement and drive the necessary systems. These new roles are also created in normative parameters that establish the functions, responsibilities, and interactions they must have so that the systems they lead can function effectively. Within the compliance industry, multiple roles (or positions) have emerged, with their different typologies and approaches, which are essential to triggering change. These new

Table 4.1: Factors, assumptions, and criticisms of compliance programs.

Compliance Factor	Assumption	Main Criticisms	
Information systems	The assumption of information systems is that the information produced by organizations will be reliable if it is framed in a compliance program that establishes guidelines on collecting, transmitting, and using the information.	1.	Actors and coalitions may be reluctant to share information that affects their control of the spheres of uncertainty
		2.	Sensemaking and group logic, such as groupthink, can skew the way information is generated, collected, and exchanged
Value systems	The assumption behind this idea is that the values are substantially determined by the organization's directors and are transmitted to the rest of the members, who, through training, the example of directors and managers, and codes of conduct, accept and internalize them.	1.	Actors who do not participate in the choice of values feel less identified and do not internalize them
		2.	Actors decide and act behind the scenes, creating facades according to their audiences, so they may not believe or internalize the organization's values.
Leadership	If the leader is committed, acts impeccably, and encourages the other members, then all the necessary changes can be promoted to achieve compliance.	1.	It is related to the will and commitment that is difficult to measure and verify in reality
		2.	Leaders must perform different functions that generate tensions between them, making it impossible to fulfill them
		3.	Limitations in terms of economic resources, capacities, time, and limited rationality
Monitoring systems	Monitoring is reliable since it helps identify risks quickly. In addition, there is a safe environment for members to report harmful practices	1.	Power asymmetries affect the effectiveness of reporting systems
		2.	Rigidity through controls and regulations slows down the functioning of the organization
		3.	Paradoxes: They may affect those who promote and control monitoring systems.

positions are based on the specialization and technical capabilities required in strategic areas of the organization. In this respect, managers of ethics management (Chief Executive of Ethics Office [CEEO]), compliance (Chief of Executive of Compliance Office [CECO]), communication (Chief of Executive of Compliance Communication Office [CECCO]), and information technologies (Chief of Information Technologies Office [CITO] have been proposed. Titles may vary within these examples, but the positions perform similar functions and have equivalent responsibilities.

One of these new roles is analyzed for this section: the ethics and compliance manager. This manager is one of the most innovative proposals and essential for compliance programs. First, a description is provided in order to subsequently reflect on the effects of this new role has on organizations. For example, what interactions are created between this new actor and executive directors and managers? What are the consequences of these responsibilities for the organization?

4.4.1 Ethics and Compliance Managers

The need to formalize actions intended to ensure ethical practices and compliance makes the creation of areas specifically dedicated to these functions a priority. In this way, a new role has been created to guide these new compliance-oriented units: the ethics and compliance manager (ECM), who has emerged to meet this growing need. However, their lines of action and hierarchy are not clearly defined, so they face problems legitimizing their authority or receiving resources. Despite the challenges facing the ECM, this new actor is significant if their responsibilities are established together with sufficient resources to strengthen the program that has been designed. In this respect, the ECM requires the support of the executive managers of the organizations. According to the Ethics Resource Center (2007), the value of the ECM consists in contributing to the establishment of a lasting, internalized ethical culture, helping other leaders in the organization to prevent misconduct, and providing solutions if it occurs, and providing a public demonstration of the organization's commitment to compliance.

However, a key point for the success of the ECM is that within the organization, it must have a precise, defined role. This implies striking a balance between adapting the needs and characteristics of the ECM with basic authority and the general tools that must be available to any manager in that position. To this end, the ECM must be accountable to the organization's directors. They must be independent and autonomous to avoid conflicts of interest and vetoes by actors in the governance structure. They must be linked to all operations to introduce an ethical culture that will include in the pursuit of the organization's goals, and their decisions and recommendations must be considered at all levels of the organizational structure. The ECM must have the necessary financial and human resources to promote ethical standards, educate and train all members, and respond to potential noncompliance practices.

The line of the hierarchy of the ECM determines the legitimacy and credibility this actor enjoys within the organization. Ideally, the ECM reports directly to the leaders and has direct access to information boards, financial reports, and other relevant information. In addition, they set performance goals together with the directors or governing councils. In the literature, the ECM is an executive management or audit committee member with technical-specialized knowledge in (corporate) ethics, compliance, and a commitment to integrity and ethical conduct.

Since the ECM has a clearly defined role, its functions are also specific. The main ones include supervising risk assessment; establishing ethics objectives in organizations, managing compliance programs, implementing initiatives for the promotion of values and an ethical culture; supervising the personnel of the ethical management area; informing directors, managers, and members of the board of directors about progress such as problems and the status of the program; implementing a program to measure and evaluate the actions undertaken in their area; and periodically monitoring these evaluations. This role is continuously evolving, while its functions, knowledge, and conditions are continually reviewed so that they can be successful.

Although this new role continues to be developed, it is in the process of being tested and improved. It is undeniably useful, but how can it be tested? The reality is that in the literature, the benefits of the ECM are hypothetical, based on abstract scenarios and causal relationships predicated on assumptions. For example, the ERC (year) argues that ECMs improve organizations in a legal, business, and philosophical sense. Although the evidence to support this argument is based on assumptions that do not necessarily imply that the ECM impacts the aspects mentioned above. For example, the ERC argues that "executives will find value in the presence of an ECM, for one fundamental reason: it is the right thing to do. This statement is open to debate since what is correct in one organization may not be so in another. Sensemaking emerges again as an element to consider because it defines an organization's perception of reality. The advantages of an ECM could be challenged if, in the organizational sense, the functions of this new role are believed to be unnecessary or overlap with preexisting roles with the organization's standards.

This reflection raises some controversial questions: is the ECM the only actor who can perform the functions attributed to them? Are the functions, characteristics, and responsibilities new, or are they merely divided among other positions and roles at present? What are the novelty and net value of the ECM? These questions require a systematic review since, in each organization, the conditions of the ECM vary, which is influenced by the organizational structure and the balances and interactions that shape both formal and informal institutions.

Like the factors and assumptions of compliance, the functionality and effectiveness of the ECM depend on a series of conditions, which will not necessarily occur as expected, nor will they be attached to expectations. The autonomy required for an ECM reveals a paradox: autonomy must be provided by an actor with power, who must atomize that power to give it to a new actor. In this respect, an ECM's independence alters an organization's status quo. Directors do not only act because it is the right thing to do but also decide to balance their interests with those of the organization. An additional actor with so much power shifts the balance, and directors will not easily relinquish control. Consequently, ECMs will not have the necessary power or support to achieve their objectives.

The hierarchical line also constitutes a problematic element. The ECM is not part of the organizational hierarchy but acts as an independent actor who regulates and monitors separately from the others. ECMs do not have direct authority over the operational structure, and if they do, it creates an overlapping of authorities that results in confusion, duplication of activities, and conflicting mandates. Authority is a central element because if the ECM lacks the mechanisms to control and sanction the members of the organization, then their actions will be less credible and will not be followed. Equally, if the ECM can evaluate and impose penalties, it must be given teeth to coerce members into complying with compliance guidelines. However, enhancing these skills does not happen due to a mandate. Instead, it requires administrative reform that will create new balances so that a new area with unusual characteristics will set evaluation and measurement standards and sanctions and receive specific resources, with all the consequences arising from these changes.

Finally, the ECM within the formal organization allows the emergence of one of the main problems of the administration: multiple command units. What happens when the ECM's guidelines contradict those of the executive director? So, to solve this problem, it is assumed that the ECM manages to internalize ethical behavior and a commitment to compliance across the organization, although this may not happen. This is particularly true in cases where managers are not present in day-to-day operations, meaning that they have limited contact with compliance strategies and other members. The reporting of functions becomes embroiled in controversy, affecting compliance and the image and authority of the ECM. These paradoxes are not easily resolved but require coordination and a clear definition of roles.

4.5 How Can Change be Achieved for Compliance?

This chapter has described the premises underlying the change being proposed in the compliance industry. As we have seen, the assumptions encounter criticism, obstacles, and problems that must be considered, which affects the implementation of these factors. So how can compliance changes be strengthened? How can this political-administrative project be promoted? This section analyzes some of the elements that facilitate change. However, it should be clarified that the proposed proposals are general and normative since general actions are less effective than the strategies oriented toward the particular context of each organization. To this end, some recommendations for change are proposed. However, this introductory analysis suggests a future agenda to test the guidelines.

i. Include all the Members of the Organization in the Definition of Compliance Guidelines

In the analysis of change factors, one of the limits was that if the actors do not participate in certain processes, they will feel that the change is unrelated to them. Therefore, the project does not belong to the organization. The inclusion of more actors does not end with their giving their opinions. Instead, they must play an active role in the decision-making regarding the values pursued by the company, the objectives, change strategies, and their roles and influence on the compliance programs. All members of the organization do not merely act as individuals, and instead, they engage in interactions that build meanings and dynamics that comprise the logic of the organization.

Inclusion requires cooperation, negotiation, and dialogue. The actors that promote change must be willing to communicate continuously with the various coalitions and groups within the organization, who will be the subjects that experience and implement the proposed changes. The approval of the groups that will implement the changes significantly increases the likelihood of change. Compliance is therefore not a guided change, established from the top of the organization downwards, but must be seen for what it is: a political project that requires legitimation, support, and conviction from all the actors participating in it. The clarity in communicating the project is also beneficial because it ensures certainty for its members, reducing resistance to change.

The compliance project managers must create an open dialogue with all the members while incorporating them into decision-making. In that case, this will ensure the socialization of the program, which is an essential element for any compliance project. Through the attention and participation of the actors, the program becomes a shared general theme, which will be discussed. This will make it possible to find criticisms, problems, and obstacles that the leaders and managers could not have encountered due to their lack of knowledge of the organization's dynamics. Including more actors enriches the analysis and reveals the plurality of views and values for establishing shared systems among all members and tailoring them to those of the organization. It also helps identify the conditions of the organization, the actors' perceptions of change, and how they will behave once the changes are implemented.

ii. Convince Others of the Importance, Necessity, and Urgency of Change

Compliance as a political project requires legitimacy. Actors within the organization must be convinced that the change they will face is important, necessary, and urgent.

The actors responsible for managing the changes to achieve compliance must communicate the importance of an organizational culture that adheres to ethics and value systems and must also convince all members. This is linked to the previous point that the inclusion of actors is part of the dialogue and negotiation. In this process, the conviction on change results from the exchange between the actors responsible for the compliance program and the rest of the organization's members.

Kotter (1995) claims that if members of an organization do not believe that change is pertinent and urgent, it is unlikely to be taken seriously. It is therefore essential to create a perspective of urgency and of how essential it is to seek change and the consequences of failing to make it happen. One of the priorities of compliance programs is to persuade all members that ethical practices and values-oriented operational actions are essential to the organization's functioning. To this end, those responsible for compliance programs must make all stakeholders aware of why an organization must comply with compliance standards.

The mechanisms that can be used are training through courses in ethics, in which the importance of compliance is emphasized to improve the trust of the stakeholders and shareholders in the organization. Members of an organization are more receptive to changes if they are explained in detail, and people are told why they should be promoted. Along these lines, if the programs not only impose sanctions but explain the real benefits and their importance for the organization's survival, members will perceive that the changes make sense and should be made.

iii. Identify the Dynamics, Interactions, and Balances in Organizations

Since compliance programs are political-administrative projects, they seek to modify behaviors. The changes brought about by these programs alter the balances that exist within organizations. Before intervening in the established dynamics, it would be helpful to identify them. Knowledge of the logics of interaction established by organizations enables one to understand them to formulate change strategies focused on the structures to be modified.

In this respect, if these dynamics are noticed, changes are not planned in the abstract and instead integrate the organization's cultural and contextual elements. Complete knowledge of the balances in place is not required since some relationships occur in opacity and secrecy. However, it is still essential to know that these visible interactions occur. In identifying these practices, those responsible for compliance programs must interact with the rest of the members. Closeness, constant interactions, forums, and spaces for coexistence make it easy to recognize the main dynamics, relationships, and balances that shape the organization.

Using this knowledge will foster programs based on the actual context of the organization. It will also neutralize some of the limits found in compliance factors, for example, by anticipating the direction and logic of groups, identifying the characteristics of leaders, and discovering the values and practices established in the organization. Knowledge of the interactions within an organization should be sought at the beginning of the implementation of the compliance project but throughout its development.

iv. Show that Expected Results occur in the Short, Medium, and Long Term

Part of the second point is to convince people of the importance of the compliance program. It will be useful to prove that the changes produce concrete results in reality. One of the main criticisms leveled at compliance is that change may not show any progress as implemented. Paradoxically, directors and managers may lose confidence in compliance programs if they do not perceive a significant change, although this may also indicate their success.

Compliance programs will be more successful if they can clearly convey their short-term objectives and long-term vision. Although it is not easy to strike this balance, it is essential to prove its usefulness immediately to ensure that compliance programs receive the resources to implement the necessary practices to continue with the changes required. The success of any project is tied to the number of resources it can secure. In the case of compliance programs, although they must be autonomous, the allocation of their resources depends on the organizational authority (either the director or the board of directors).

Likewise, actors' commitment to implementing changes may decline if they do not believe their efforts will produce tangible results. Continuously published results should not only be sent to directors and managers but should also be made available to all members. In this way, transparency inspires both trust in and the credibility of changes. The more information is available, the easier it is to prove that the programs do indeed work and what their value is. Members will therefore understand the importance of compliance and be its staunchest champions. The argument for the value of compliance is not the fact that it should be done because it is the right thing to do but because it is useful.

References

Arellano-Gault, D. (2010). Reformas Administrativas y Cambio Organizacional: Hacia el "Efecto Neto." *Revista Mexicana de Sociología*, 72(2), 225–254.

Biegelman, M., & Biegelman, D. (2010). *Foreign Corrupt Practices Act Compliance Guidebook. Protecting your Organization from Bribery and Corruption*. New Jersey: John Wiley & Sons.

Brinkerhoff, D. (2000). Assessing Political Will for Anti-Corruption Efforts: An Analytic Framework. *Public Administration and Development*, 20, 239–252.

Bryson, J. (1988). The Strategy Change Cycle: An Effective Strategic Planning and Management Approach for Public and Nonprofit Organizations. In Bryson, J. (ed.), *Strategic Planning for Public and Nonprofit Organizations*. San Francisco: Jossey-Bass, pp. 35–74.

Claps, M. (2008). Public Sector Transparency—How Is it Regulated in Europe? In Tarantino, A (ed.), *Governance, Risk and Compliance Handbook. Technology, Finance, Environmental, and International Guidance and Best Practices*. New Jersey: John Wiley & Sons, pp. 485–492.

Collet, H. (2008). IT Controls Automation and Database Management: Defending Against the Insider Threat. In Tarantino, A (ed.), *Governance, Risk, and Compliance Handbook. Technology, Finance, Environmental, and International Guidance and Best Practices*. New Jersey: John Wiley & Sons, pp. 325–341.

Crozier, M. (1964). *The bureaucratic phenomenon*. Chicago. Chicago University Press.

Crozier, M., & Friedberg, F. (1980). *Actors and the Systems: The Politics of Collective Action*. Chicago: University of Chicago Press.

Cyert, R. M., & March, J. G. (1963). *A Behavioral Theory of the Firm*. Malden, MA: Prentice Hall/ Pearson Education.

Edelblut, F., & Murdock, H. (2008). The Role of Internal Audit. In Tarantino, A. (ed.), *Governance, Risk, and Compliance Handbook. Technology, Finance, Environmental, and International Guidance and Best Practices*. New Jersey: John Wiley & Sons, pp. 83–94.

Ethics Resource Center (ERC). (2007). *Leading Corporate Integrity: Defining the Role of the Chief Ethics & Compliance Officer (CECO). Chief Ethics & Compliance Officer (CECO)* Definition Working Group. Ethics Resource Center.

Fritzen, S. (2005). Beyond "Political Will" How Institutional Context Shapes the Implementation of Anticorruption Policies. *Policy and Society*, 24(3), 79–96.

Goffman, E. (1967). *Interaction Ritual. Essays on Face-to-Face Behavior*. New York: Pantheon Books.

Hochwarter, W. (2012). The Positive Side of Organizational Politics. In Ferris, G., & Treadway, D. (eds.), *Politics in Organizations* (27–65). New York: Routledge.

Janis, I. (1972). *Victims of Groupthink: A Psychological Study of Foreign Policy Decisions and Fiascoes*. Boston: Houghton Mifflin.

Koo, J. (2008). What to Look for in Enterprise Content Management for Compliance. In Tarantino, A. (ed.), *Governance, Risk and Compliance Handbook. Technology, Finance, Environmental, and International Guidance and Best Practices*. New Jersey: John Wiley & Sons, pp. 259–266.

Kotter, J. (1995). Leading Change: Why Transformational Efforts Fail. *Harvard Business Review*, March–April, 59–67.

Leech, T., & Thompson, J. (2008). A Risk-Based Approach to Assess Internal Control Over Financial Reporting (ICFR). In Tarantino, A. (ed.), *Governance, Risk and Compliance Handbook. Technology, Finance, Environmental, and International Guidance and Best Practices*. New Jersey: John Wiley & Sons, pp. 41–64.

March, J. (2008a). Understanding Organizational Adaptation. In March, J. *Explorations in Organizations* (106–115). Stanford: Stanford University Press.

March, J. (2008b). Rationality, Foolishness, and Adaptive Intelligence. In March, J., *Explorations in Organizations* (167–190). Stanford: Stanford University Press.

March, J. (2008c). Literature and Leadership. In March, J. *Explorations in Organizations* (434–440). Stanford: Stanford University Press.

March, J., & Weil, T. (2005). *On Leadership*. New York: Wiley-Blackwell.

McLean, B., & Elkind, P. (2013). *The Smartest Guys in the Room. The Amazing Rise and Scandalous Fall of Enron*. New York: Portfolio.

Merton, R. K. (1940). *Bureaucratic Structure and Personality. Social Forces*, 18, 560–568. https://doi.org/10.2307/2570634

Montalvo, H. (2020). Blockchain-Compliance, la Union Perfecta. *Legal Today*. https://www.legalto day.com/legaltech/novedades-legaltech/blockchain-compliance-la-union-perfecta-2020-07-17/

Pope. A. (2016). What's the Risk of Innovation? *CMS Wire*, Retrieved from https://www.cmswire. com/social-business/whats-the-risk-of-innovation/

Post, L. A., Raile, A. N., & Raile, E. D. (2010). Defining Political Will. *Politics & Policy*, 38(4), 653–676.

Silverman, M. (2008). *Compliance Management for Public, Private, or Nonprofit* Organizations. New York: McGraw.

Simon, H. A. (1947). *Administrative Behavior: A Study of Decision-Making Processes in Administrative Organization*. New York: Macmillan.

Tarantino, A. (ed.). (2008). *Governance, Risk and Compliance Handbook. Technology, Finance, Environmental, and International Guidance and Best Practices*. New York: John Wiley & Sons.

Treviño, L. K., Weaver, G. R., Gibson, D. G., & Toffler, B. L. (1999). Managing Ethics and Legal Compliance: What Works and What Hurts. *California Management Review*, 41(2), 131–151. https://doi.org/10.2307/41165990

Vigoda-Gadot, E. & Vashdi, D. (2012). Politics in and Around Teams: Toward a Team-Level Conceptualization of Organizational Politics. In Ferris, G., & Treadway, D. (eds.), *Politics in Organizations* (287–322). New York: Routledge.

Weick, K. (2001). *Making Sense of the Organization*. Oxford: Blackwell.

Chapter 5
So, What is to be Done?

5.1 The Challenges of Transforming the Organization through Compliance Programs

A compliance program is always a mechanism for organizational change. In other words, its introduction means that an organization adapts and adopts new routines, values, structures, and processes. But once the change process, structures, and compliance routines have been implemented, the central question is whether the expected changes have been brought about, even more importantly, whether the changes made will lead to the expected results. Launching a change process is relatively simple. The first challenge is to ensure it remains alive and operative and continues to be adopted in the day-to-day life of an organization. The second is to monitor and tweak it so that the changes ultimately reinforce the expected behaviors and the organizational culture it is expected to achieve.

Compliance programs promise and require organizations to change. It is their basic premise and their raison d'être. Unless a change is achieved, the modification of day-to-day routines and practices, the ideas, values, and expectations raised by any compliance program will end in nothing more than good intentions, but not in the systemic transformation (i.e., not only of each organization but of the set of political and economic organizations comprising society) one would hope to attain. Not to mention the significant cost compliance entails for any organization and society. So, it is essential to answer the question of organizational change. How is it started, guided, and achieved? Can it be designed and controlled? Is it possible to ensure that achieving the promised benefits will reward the costs of starting and maintaining the changes implemented by compliance? It is important to answer these questions. Particularly so if one does not subscribe to the view that organizations are monoliths. In that case, all that is required is to provide a list of good intentions and legislative instruments that are naively simple. However, doing so from a more realistic perspective of organizations as arenas require understanding the diverse, heterogeneous, intelligent, and emotional, organizational dynamics critical to change as a continuous, intense, conflictive, and changing process.

It is worth dwelling on this point since there are issues that may seem paradoxical when discussing compliance. For example, at one extreme, if a compliance program is entirely successful, does that mean it no longer needs to be maintained? This is because, under this extreme assumption, organizational behaviors and routines are already fully aligned and consistent with the organization's values in a perfectly legal, legitimate way, and there are no behaviors that can be regarded as deviant or improper. Although this theoretical abstraction is valid, it would seem to be just that: a purely theoretical possibility. Organizations are not precise, untainted instruments in

https://doi.org/10.1515/9783110749113-005

search of the promised land of order and cooperative behavior. They exist because plural, diverse, dynamic, emotional, and rational human beings exist. So how does one determine whether a change has been successful if organizations are living, shifting social entities?

From the perspective of the organization as an arena, it is essential not to speak of an organization in the abstract but of the people, groups, and teams that comprise it and make it alive and active. From this point of view, compliance programs appear to be here to stay. People have different values and interests, they are fallible, and organizational structures are built on the interactions and conflicts between groups and those who comprise them. What is proper or perfectly legal or legitimate is constantly in motion, being interpreted and reconstructed. Thus, "change should not be regarded as a property of the organization, but rather, the organization should be understood as an emerging property of change" (Tsoukas & Chia, 2002: 570). Therefore, from the organization's perspective as an arena, organizational change is a continuous, never-ending process in a permanent state of production and adaptation.

Under this logic of arena organizations, one can generally speak of two logics of change: planned, directed, controlled, orchestrated change; and spontaneous, unplanned change that emerges and is dynamically configured daily (Scott, 1998). The differences between the two logics are critical. Planned change assumes that some form of control can be exercised (Seo, Putnam, & Bartunek, 2004). Unplanned change accepts that the routes of change can be surprising. Planned change assumes that a relatively orderly orchestration of steps and processes is essential to guiding change. Unplanned change accepts that many of the results produced by change can be unexpected and even unwanted, which entails constantly reviewing the strategies and tactics sought. Finally, the effect of the change is predictable, contrary to the idea that the effects of change are always surprising and create dynamics that crystallize and are difficult to change. For this reason, in many respects, people speak of the essential capacity to "manage change": a compliance program can be agreed upon, legitimized, and designed well. Nevertheless, the compliance program and its embedding in the organization can be flawed without a change strategy and a grasp of the group and individual dynamics that will be unleashed to adapt, adopt, and even resist and boycott it.

5.1.1 Organizational Change: Changing People and Their Groups

Now that it has been established that organizational change is a continuum between what is planned and what is created in the dynamics of the interaction arenas that make up any organization, it is worth asking: what do the dynamics of change involve? It is undoubtedly a process that begins and ends with people. With the interaction of people, people and the groups, both formal and informal, to which they belong. Indeed, change is often conceived of as a matter of processes, rules, and structures. Of course, in an organization, these are critical variables for intervening in, arranging, and structuring people's behavior.

Nonetheless, rules, processes, and structures are the static moment of the organization. The initial photo raises the hope of creating order, obedience, cooperation, and coordination. But this static photo only represents the game board. People must be added to and placed on that board, together with the interactions of those people with others. A board can never be the right image for watching the movement of the game in action.

Organizational change requires seeing at different levels. Achieving changes in the organization must be undertaken by people and in the groups and teams of the organization itself. A compliance program can therefore be seen in the long term as a planned change at the level of the organization as a whole. However, in practice, the key is in the short and medium term. The changes that are created at that time are in the routines, relationships, interactions, and interdependence between people who also tend to be in teams or groups. A compliance program will be measured, over time, by the changes brought about in teams and their logic, in groups and their dynamics, and lastly, in the behavior of specific people.

Dansereau, Yammarino, and Kohles (1999) have extensively studied how groups are crucial to understanding how organizations operate. Additionally, their change dynamics are specific to each organization's situations and logic. For example, a homogeneous group differs from a heterogeneous group whose members are interdependent or a heterogeneous group of highly independent members. A homogeneous group ideally exists when all or nearly all members are fused together and function as a unit. Conversely, a basic, heterogeneous group comprises people who, although they do not pursue the same values or interests, are nevertheless in a relationship that makes them interdependent. They should be together and cooperate for assorted reasons but based on heterogeneity, they are understood and accepted to a certain degree by its members. Moreover, highly heterogeneous groups can also be found of interdependent subgroups or individuals, yet in a less intense way that enables them to remain as a group consisting of independent parts that can be distinguished from each other. Lastly, there are also groups comprising independent units that act on their own without reference to the group as a whole.

To illustrate the dynamics and logics between groups, Drazin, Glynn, and Kazanjian (2004) propose three forms of change that involve organizational logic: change through the establishment and elaboration of logic, change by breaking away from and replacing existing logic, and change through logics that incorporate change as a basic premise. So, in addition to being a process that can be both planned and unplanned, organizational change attempts to affect behaviors in a heterogeneous arena of groups with varying degrees of homogeneity, interests, and strategies. All this only complicates the logic of change. Even change processes that are urgently required in some way, such as the implementation of a new process in a certain area or a modification of the organization's compliance structure, will have to be embedded in these logics of a change that to be effective, will have to pass the scaffold and the organizational test. In other words, no organizational change process is devised, arranged, and implemented as though one were typing instructions into a computer. Organizational changes and compliance implementation processes are no exception: they involve working with people, their positions, values, and resistance.

As a crucial step, it is essential to recover the logic of organizational change in a more realistic, more substantive way. It can be highly unproductive and ineffective to assume that changing an organization to design and implement a compliance program can be achieved by creating a project, promoting certain modifications of structures, and imposing certain modifications of rules and processes. In the case of compliance, then, it is practically mandatory to understand the change process as being filled with specific challenges and complications. This implies the construction of new processes and structures and their embedding in routines and practices, in the organization's culture and values, seen as a whole.

In short: organizational change is only achieved through the genuine modification of the behavior of its groups and individuals. In an organization seen as an arena, the reasons why people and groups modify their behavior to create new routines and practices are not necessarily linked to a project or series of procedures that are imposed by management or through documents and standards. As we saw in chapters 2 and 4, individuals and groups negotiate their way, haggle, and adapt changes, orders, and routines. They do all this to achieve a new equilibrium agreed over time that will enable the organization to maintain its activity in a stable, constant manner. Studies have systematically found that organizations do not always welcome innovation and novelty. Novelty may be viewed unfavorably compared with the past routine and stability agreed upon on that set of habits and dynamics. The stories and sagas of an organization matter, and the past is not so easily dismissed. The structure of an organization is a "time capsule" of logic and knowledge at the time of its construction. An organizational logic lends purpose and meaning to an organization's structure, providing members with norms and interpretive schemes (Scott, 2004).

Unless we are talking about an organization that has already virtually collapsed, people in organizations remember and defend the sagas of the past that have enabled an organization and its people to cope successfully with the environment (March, 2010: 76). Organizations must continuously balance "exploitation" and "exploration." In other words, a balance between knowing how to improve on what has worked well in the past and expending energy on the search for new ways of exploring reality. These forms of exploration, however, are costly and can lead to flawed solutions and major failures (March, 1991). Every change project, then, is a process of risk, calculating potential costs and benefits and controlling and accepting the unwanted consequences of the action. It is difficult then, within a logic of compliance, to get bogged down in a linear, top-down vision. Probably not very productive if compliance and its structures and principles fail to change the way groups and individuals build their participation in the organization. The consequences of a relevant compliance effort that fails to prevent the worst consequences of people's misconduct, significant flaws in their behavior, and the group dynamics that allow and normalize such behavior can be dire.

How, then, could the most consistent vision of organizational change be described from the point of view of compliance? Tsoukas and Chia's (2002) arguments are an excellent start. Rather than seeing change as orchestrated from above, Orlikowski (1996) frames it as one based on the ongoing practices of organizational actors embedded in their adaptations and experiments. People in organizations deal with everyday contingencies, breakdowns, exceptions, opportunities, and the unintended consequences of decisions and actions taken (Orlikowski, 1996: 65). So, change cannot be conceived of as the property of the organization. Instead, the organization is an emerging property of change. Change is the condition of the possibility of the existence of the organization itself. How people incorporate and adapt to change and how organizational systems change their interrelationships and configurations end up being the basis of the net effects of change. In other words, the organization is an attempt to sort out the flow that involves the action of people (action is always situational and always contextual), channel it toward certain ends, and give it a particular shape by stabilizing meanings and practices. The organization is a pattern that is constituted and configured as a result of the change. From this perspective, the organization is an achievement that must be constantly maintained and stabilized. First, it is a set of socially defined rules to stabilize an ever-changing reality by making human behavior more predictable. Second, the organization is a result, a pattern, emerging from the thoughtful application of people in local contexts experienced on a day-to-day basis. Although the organization aims to stop change, it is also the result of the change (Tsoukas & Chia, 2002: 580).

Therefore, a reform and compliance program requires combining two logics of change that are usually seen as separate or contradictory: planned change and spontaneous, unplanned change. Planned change is assumed to be a conscious process conceived and implemented by certain knowledgeable people in a position of sufficient power to instill change. This type of change is devised as an effective, explicit one, with a clear vision and knowledge of the path to follow. It is obviously supported by a normative scaffolding, with defined, transparent processes explained ex-ante. Based on a precise diagnosis of the situation, it proposes and attempts to implement a series of steps to seek to achieve a well-identified, desired goal. Conversely, unplanned or spontaneous, constant change may or may not be driven by identified individuals. Generally, change of this type is not initiated or developed on purpose, and the direction it takes is generated by the dynamics and correlations of forces within the organization. And, of course, by various contextual contingencies and circumstantial situations. The result is therefore unpredictable and can even lead to unwanted effects and transformations that are not sought, expected, and often not regarded as positive, at least by certain parts of the organization (Poole, 2004: 4).

However, these two abstract ways of looking at change are extremely useful for identifying the expectations and axioms underlying the proposals built on transformations such as compliance programs. The contrast between planned and unplanned change enables us to observe and discuss fundamental assumptions, such as the importance of justifying the degree to which change and innovation can be choreographed. It allows us to see the degree of control and even transparency of change strategies without overlooking the degree of control expected of the process. In practice, it is evident that the degree of control over a change process such as that sought by compliance programs is not absolute. Organizations seen as arenas involve a broad process of communication, persuasion, negotiation, and bargaining. Even if they are implicit rather than planned processes, these communication processes can follow a master plan, but they must constantly complement with adjustments and discussions within the distinct groups for various purposes. This basic master plan must understand and interpret the idea and the values of change from within the group; each group needs to understand and interpret how the overall change will affect day-to-day work, the dynamics of the area, and established processes. Ideally, groups are required to plan their internal changes, envisage, and design modifications and adjustments. They must adopt and adapt new practices on a day-to-day basis. These practices may be completely new. Some will be adapted, others adopted, and still others overtly disruptive of the customs of groups and areas, which is an issue that will have to be addressed. Likewise, it is worth identifying the differences between the change processes. McGrath and Tschan (2004) differentiate between operational, developmental, and adaptive processes. Operational processes consist of the ways groups do their work. Development processes involve the way the group as an entity changes over time. Every group has a history, which evolves through its relationship patterns involved in its formation and functioning. These processes include the effects of practice/experience, learning, and transformation. Adaptive processes are related to the way groups react to events and contingencies.

Indeed, a general change process begins when it is designed and proposed. It will depend on many internal dynamics of groups, teams, and areas that cannot only change due to these rules and overarching visions. It will have to become involved in the various processes of change and internal adaptation, one of whose basic variables is not the large, orderly structure change wishes to create but the mezzo and micro affectations these expectations imply in the relationships, rules, norms, and customs of the group, area, or team. Furthermore, as if that were not enough, it will have to be aware of how this general proposal for change will affect the interrelationships and correlations of forces between the groups in the same organization. The possibilities of this process are multiple, and groups can ideally seek the full adoption of proposals for change planned from above.

Nevertheless, they have other options. They can attempt to adapt. In other words, they can adjust various change aspects to make them more viable or feasible for the practices, knowledge, and skills already in place. This adaptation may require haggling and negotiating. The results of these negotiations depend on the strength, the ability to impose or resist, and the reasonableness of the proposed adaptations. This adaptation game can also be played in several ways. Engaging in an open, public, explicit negotiation process is possible. Still, there can also be strategic acts. In other words, processes in which the various parties calculate the clash of objectives and expectations in asymmetric information frameworks. The various groups have information advantages or disadvantages concerning other groups. Besides, the various groups use these asymmetric issues to gain the upper hand in negotiations.

The dynamics of organizational change, whether through a compliance program or otherwise, requires dealing with a fundamental reality: it is the people and their groups that will change, adapt, modify, or resist change. Also, they do not only do so through simple rational calculations, of short-term benefits and costs, as the theory known as "rational choice" claims (Arrow, 1974). They also do so because, in the face of an uncertain reality and a dynamic environment, their learning and reflection tools differ from those of simple rationality. In their analysis, people consider more productive heuristics in the face of change and its uncertainties. For example, logics of what is appropriate: given the past of the organization, the balance that has been achieved, but also given the changes in the environment or threats (e.g., from an organization with serious problems of misconduct or even fraud), what are the most sensible, viable, least disruptive agreements that would allow a feasible change and controllable or at least identifiable risks (March & Olsen, 1995; 2011)? The logic of the appropriateness involves admitting that people can experience a logic of change with significant degrees of confusion and uncertainty regarding many things: what change seeks, its likelihood of success, and the way it will negatively affect routines and practices, including understood values. A person coping with a process of change in an organization and compliance with a program is no exception; they observe that many things are happening simultaneously. Expectations, orders, technologies, and practices are shifting. Opportunities and risks are created, and new people join the organizational equation. Solutions are typically much more discursive than they would seem. In other words, solutions are slightly connected to the problems; people and results are combined or mixed in unclear ways (March, 1994: 176). How, then, do people cope with processes of change? With uncertainty, sometimes anguish, juggling different issues simultaneously, seeking to understand and simultaneously intervene in the ideas of change and the processes and routines that they will cope.

As one can see, managing change is not a simple matter, and it entails order, processes, transparency, rules, and steps. Also, and substantively, it calls for a rare skill: leading the different processes and logics of change between groups, teams, and people, so it requires a managerial capacity, no doubt, but also a political one. Thus, it can have serious limitations to assume that a compliance program will be adopted merely because it is rational, technically correct, or imposed as a hierarchical order.

An example is a proposal by Deetz (1995), who points out that an open, deliberative process based on a conception of "strong democracy" is a fundamental means of achieving change in an organization. Thus, change can occur through the empowered participation of all members, and change is a force in its own right. When change is produced, grows, and is promoted, the ability to control this change is reduced and modified. The same is true of the process of adaptation and even resistance to change: the process acquires its logic, legitimacy, and strength.

5.2 The Art and Politics of Organizational Change: The Perspective of Change from the Groups in an Organization

From a management point of view, a compliance program implies modifying the political status quo of an organization. In that manner, it is relevant not only to alter the budget structure but also the chains of command, linearity of the hierarchy, incentive structure, and, in general, organizational sensemaking. It is an art because it requires attention skills, imagination, and capacities. It is a political change not only because there is potential conflict involved between groups and individuals but also because preferences, values, and expectations are at stake, even beliefs. In a compliance program, this is extremely clear: the ways the organization has dealt with behaviors and expectations do not appear to suffice. When a compliance program is promoted, this is tantamount to an admission that the organization may have serious flaws and allow misconduct on the part of its people and groups. A compliance program, at the bottom, is the powerful questioning of the direction of an organization, its history, several of its decisions, and routines. Hence the need for change, for a main, profound change. An example discussed in Chapter 4 is the role of leaders as managers and CEOs who must function as agents of change. These actors must embark on a crusade in which the organization's culture must be renewed. However, when these strategies conflict, they are often resisted and will never be fully adopted (Hatch, 2004).

A compliance program is part of an organization's political change and requires politics to be implemented. Convincing is required, but also strategic maneuvering and tactical capabilities. People must be prepared to create compromises, negotiate, haggle, induce, encourage, and even force. This combination will make it possible to ensure proper, effective implementation of changes in the behavior of people and groups that are not cosmetic or short-term changes but relatively stable and even internalized ones.

Henceforward, to operationalize this perspective, it is essential to maintain the overall image that has been used in this book: that of the arena organization. From this perspective, the organization is not a monolith, a homogeneous entity with a single mind or rationality. Organizations comprise different people who belong to and build groups and teams. These groups and teams can be homogeneous or highly independent yet deal with the specific situations of their work in particular contexts. These groups and teams interact, negotiate, haggle, and have spaces, capacities, and resources that they control and use in strategic negotiations.

5.2.1 Toward a Theory of Organizational Change for Compliance

In short, the logic of organizational change through compliance has key features: a) introducing and creating a compliance program entails a process of organizational change; b) a change process that directly affects the image, values, and beliefs that may be firmly embedded and legitimized in the organization; c) the proposed change is not only disruptive but also uncertain. In other words, it is not exactly known how to transform behaviors and values with simple instruments, nor is there clarity about the systemic changes a compliance program will have as a consequence; and d) any process of change implies achieving adaptations, negotiations, agreements, and battles between groups and agents inside and outside the organization.

Given these critical dynamics, any compliance process requires a robust and solid theory of change. The theory is not an abstract expression of ideas but rather an expression of concrete causal chains to achieve a type of change that is as close as possible to what is expected, given the four characteristics or logic expressed above.

The vision and theory of change appear as a substantive aspect for understanding how a process such as the one required by compliance programs can be implemented and directed. In other words, we are talking about a process of change that must be both planned and spontaneous; orderly and yet with substantive flexibilities; unified yet capable of adapting over time, understanding, and considering the actions, reactions, and systemic logic experienced by an organization.

In this respect, exploring whether a synoptic vision of change can be the solution is attractive. Although change is a complex process, midway between being planned and unplanned, a comprehensive approach that seeks to understand the forces and time frames entailed by a change process can greatly assist. Synoptic views make it possible to regard change as an intricate event, processed by key situations, variations, causal antecedents, and consequences. It is also a perspective that tends to be abstract. It is a vision that approaches change from an external perspective, typically interpreting the process as a series of scenarios, stages, or states analyzed in various time frames. This type of vision has helped obtain snapshots of the different moments and dimensions of organizations in the process of change (Miller, 1982; Miller & Friesen, 1982; Tushman & Romanelli, 1985; Donaldson, 1999). However, despite these advantages, a synoptic view of change has certain limitations. Given the tendency to see general processes as enormous forces that accumulate and shape reality, it also tends to lose sight of the microprocesses that can ultimately be critical. It tends to reduce the importance of the role that the action of people and groups and coalitions trigger through their decisions and nondecisions. In short, they reduce the importance of the impact of action and the concrete, contextual situations people and their groups overcome, interpret, and intervene. These issues are the flow without which major trends and variables would not exist.

Although a synoptic view of change is valuable and necessary, it does not suffice. Human agency, in other words, the actions and inactions of people, are crucial to understanding how organizations, institutions, and groups change and transform. Contrary to synoptic vision, micro and even antisynoptic vision is indispensable. Individuals and groups face and must deal with the flow that is the reality of everyday life. They are obliged to cope with the contextual and situational conditions that require them to interpret all the time, making sense of what they face every day. As Weick (2001) says, people need to answer the question: "What am I experiencing and facing, here and now?"

Therefore, the logic of change is inserted and generated in local spaces (groups, departments, and offices). A decision or an order becomes relevant or irrelevant in these local spaces. From this micro or antisynoptic view, organizations are more than just a permanent or guaranteed fact. Instead, they are flows people promote every day, making them a reality in interaction, in the choices that are interactively negotiated and agreed upon through the implicit rules observed at the local scale. Boden (1994) argues that when an organization is observed from the outside, it appears to be a phenomenon controlled by general, almost mechanical rules and regulations. But if one devotes more time and attention to the details, the microactions and decisions reveal something quite different. What emerges is a delicate process of adjustments and readjustments recreated in systematic interactions between people located in various structural spaces within an organization (Boden, 1994: 42). In short, organizations do not merely exist; they exist through multiple actions and interactions.

It is a fact that the leaders of an organization wishing to implement a compliance program must become involved in a project of changes that are specified, legitimized, and undertaken in practice. This requires plans and processes. However, it is also essential to remember that organizational change occurs without necessarily following the effects and patterns of an intentional action program. This results from individuals and groups attempting to adapt to new experiences and realize new possibilities. It is relevant to show that interventions from the management or leadership of an organization cannot be regarded as events exogenous to the organization. They are also people and groups attempting to bring about change, using arguments and rhetoric to convince those who are questioned and defend specific interests. They cannot be seen as the unconditional champions of the "organizational goal" as if that goal were the exclusive possession of one or two groups. The manager is just as much an agent of change as everyone else. The difference, in the end, is the hierarchical authority but not the monopolistic possession of the organization's objectives. Nor are they the only ones with legitimate interests within the organization. In any case, management can appropriate certain declarative powers, a key issue but not the only one to achieve change in organizations (Taylor, 1985; Taylor & Van Every, 2000).

Curiously or even paradoxically, however, a compliance program must address the complexity of the change process through simplified strategies and processes. It must be sufficiently clear and communicable to have a minimal probability of being implemented in such a way that the enactment of the compliance program has some likelihood of achieving something. Simplification can help as it produces economies of scale, allowing redundancy in processes that reinforce changes. In addition, it creates trust in people within the organization (Michaud & Thoenig, 2003: 3).

The change required by a compliance program can be sought at two interrelated levels. It is a first-order change where the aim is to modify the skills or abilities of people within an already agreed arena that establishes negotiated and accepted reference frameworks. Second-order change, on the other hand, seeks to transform these frames of reference and renegotiate new schemes of action (Seo, Putnam, & Bartunek, 2004: 78)

It is logical to consider change processes as long-term strategies with punctuated equilibriums at various times. In other words, in lengthy organizational processes, moments of intense change are produced, followed by spaces of stability in a lengthy process of negotiations and rearrangements that enable people to learn and adapt to the processes of change and managers to maintain spaces for modification and transformation (Abernalthy & Utterback, 1978; Tushman & Romanelli, 1985).

Change requires strategy, meaning, and orientation. However, is this strategy planned, simple, accurate, conscious, and flawless? Mintzberg and Waters (1985) have long argued that it is also essential to understand that strategies emerge. In other words, the order observed in an organization is likely to have arisen from actions and accommodations that are not strategic-planned but rather strategic-emerging and unintended. It is important to recall that organizations are people and groups behaving, creating in games and through actions, arenas of interactions, and interdependencies. An arena is therefore not designed or planned but a stable structure capable of producing results thanks to the agreement and constant renegotiation of these interrelationships and interdependencies.

It is important to make this point clear since it is essential for a compliance program. The organizational order, which regards the organization as an arena, is a result of both the action and deliberate decision of the management and members of an organization and the dynamics, interrelationships, and interdependencies negotiated and recreated on a day-to-day basis. And, of course, of the context, time and events, accidents, and situations. The result of a compliance program, then, will be the result of a mixture of these elements. Furthermore, it would therefore be extremely limited to think that a change strategy is a simple, direct course that emerges from the minds of the managers or authorities of an organization. The strategy is that course, plan, or program proposal, which, at the same time, considers the importance of the emerging strategy. It is a strategy that implies sustained attention to punctuated equilibriums, the emerging strategies of groups and individuals, and the conflicts and modifications created by the constant change in the context.

A strategy is seen as a linear plan; a process of sequential steps is a contradictory route that will cause the change process to erode over time, given its inability to constantly intervene in the dynamics that the organizational arena is undergoing to trigger once the change process is proposed and begins to be implemented. Additionally, this is the key to a change strategy for a compliance program. Rather than thinking of the change journey as a navigation route, it is a process more akin to wayfinding (Chia & Holt, 2009: xi). The change strategy is something that begins with an intention and a plan, an exact process. However, it is only known and understood as it is applied and progresses.

At one extreme, this argument can be understood this way: organizations as living and dynamic social creatures will find their way, with or without a planned strategy. The continuous interaction and interdependence that is constantly created and co-created between people construct order and a sense of organization without the need for a plan or program. Of course, this is an exaggeration: organizations are also made up of people and groups that seek to lead, convince, endure, and win. Proposing a compliance program and convincing people of the changes an organization must undergo to implement it involves a combination of the two logics. The current equilibrium of the organization may be stable and even legitimate, but it can lead the organization to experience many problems, including compliance failures.

The crux of the matter is that the change a compliance program requires will not be successful merely because it is necessary or rational. Alternatively, it is based on a strategy of reasonable and technical change, created from the highest sphere of the organization and with substantive political and economic support. The compliance change plan and program require an additional critical ingredient: it anticipates the constant interventions that will have to be undertaken due to the micro dynamics and adaptations people and groups will conduct and promote in the process. Many adaptations are explicit and transparent, while others are opaque, strategic, and even based on boycotting and resistance.

5.2.2 The Risks of Change (and Overoptimism)

James Scott (1998) has summarized a series of experiences illustrating the extreme view of trying to make all reality "manageable." Although Scott is talking about governments and their organizations, the central argument is sobering for any organization. The main issue then is that in the face of the challenges every organization must face, it is essential to make reality itself operational. To this end, an analytical operation is required: to make reality itself manageable, reducing its complexity by making it manageable. Its elements must be identified, broken down, and then made operational to make reality manageable. In other words, one must assume that there are instruments for intervening in it. It can therefore be assumed, to continue with the case of compliance, that a change program can be built on the assumption that people obey orders from their superiors simply out of loyalty, fear, or due to incentives. What if reality is less manageable than expected? An overly optimistic vision of a simplified reality under the assumptions of its manageability can run out of weapons to cope with uncertainty, the resistance of people or systems, and the strategies people and groups use to resist, adapt, and interpret instructions. Regarding reality as manageable can create an aura of infallibility in the designers and implementers of change. This infallibility blinds them to their mistakes, overly optimistic decisions, and miscalculations in the face of a much more dynamic reality (Arellano-Gault, 2022).

Over-optimism regarding the possibilities of controlling change can therefore lead to self-imposed blindness. In other words, reformers create an argument, an ideology, and a need to succeed that prevents them from paying attention to the factors that can subvert the change they are proposing. Sieber (1981: 55) identifies seven logics change processes that need to observe to be able to react in time to prevent the objectives of change from paradoxically producing its opposite: a fiasco.

a) Functional disruption. The reality, or what people understand as it, is a composite of multiple determinations. Likewise, intervening in it will always contain a degree of uncertainty: the actual effects will often be seen over time since any intervention upsets the functional balance of reality.

b) Exploitation. Any intervention alters the balance of costs and benefits, burdens and resources of actors and agents. These agents respond, react, and can gain advantages in unforeseen ways.

c) Displacement of ends. In Merton's classic argument (1942), the processes confronting a complex system become paramount, creating perverse incentives to obtain security via these processes rather than based on results. In other words, faced with the uncertainty of achieving goals, agents protect themselves by emphasizing the achievement of the processes.

d) Provocation. This is the exaggeration of passion or desires, ideology or values, as indispensable vehicles for achieving results. This can lead to exaggerations in terms of trust, the search to force equilibriums, or even people beyond the logic or the results observed.

e) Classification. This involves forcing reality to behave based on classification models that have been created for specific purposes. As Scott also observes, classifying imposes a type of order with specific aims in response to a social or ecological reality that is, in fact, much more complex and intricate.

f) About commitment. This is the illusion that they have the resources, time, and capacities to intervene while overlooking details and their importance for achieving goals.

g) Appeasement. In practice, an intervention becomes a means of reassuring or demobilizing certain agents to gain support or reduce their resistance. This can lead to problems not fully addressed, accelerating or exploding with worse consequences.

A compliance program always involves a process of significant organizational change, with long-term logics that cannot be achieved except through actions and decisions in the here and now. This implies a process of constant attention to detail from a vision that avoids seeing deviations from the path as pathologies or abnormalities. These deviations are probably due to endogenous processes and the dynamics of the groups and individuals themselves seeking to make sense of and interpret the situation. Also, a pathology-based vision is the surest way to fall into decision traps and self-imposed blindness like those posited by Sieber. Since this blindness to substantive processes of organizations is neither understood nor analyzed, it makes managers of organizations unable to cope with the challenges of changing organizations to implement innovative ideas and programs such as compliance.

5.2.3 Organizational Change Seen in its Human and Group Dimension: Uncertainty and Dynamism

No matter how solid a plan is, how well defined the arenas and groups are, with their interests and capacities, and how rigorous the logic and rationality of a compliance project are, there will always be exceptions, unpredictable dynamics, and clashes and conflicts. Change processes can be extremely distressing and messy. A compliance program undoubtedly requires a strategy. However, not necessarily or exclusively a strategy is considered an ex-ante, integral, and unconscious design. A strategy also emerges and is constructed whenever people and groups need to calculate and recalculate their intentions, arguments, and actions based on the reactions and counter-reactions of other groups and people (Clegg, Courpasson, & Phillips, 2006). Strategy means achieving the desired goals when those goals depend on the action or inaction of other agents and groups over which one has no control. A strategy cannot be based on an abstract decision logic, a plan, or a prediction. Although those elements may be important as a foundation, the key is how the environment, groups, and individuals react and act (or fail to act). New reactions are required to these reactions. This is what strategy as something that emerges looks like.

How is this possible, and what does it imply? A compliance program, for example, entails a powerful dichotomy: preventing misconduct (and even punishing it) through the appropriation of the values of compliance by individuals and groups.

Nevertheless, as discussed in chapters 2 and 3, people must cope with an organization-'s day-to-day, operational and action reality. The organizational world is, therefore, less controllable and orderly than organizational textbooks assume. Does this mean then that there are no possible, useful tools in such an unpredictable, changing world? The answer is no, and these are tools. One must admit that in an organizational world, there is an imperfect order, in constant construction, and not designed. This order was not merely the result of an organizational design. Therefore, constructing a new organizational order cannot assume that it can be designed either. At least not entirely.

Organizations are, in many ways, an order that has spontaneously emerged. Instead, an order resulting from the interaction and interdependence of people and their groups is faced with a highly mobile, changing environment. An order emerged more to prevent uncertainty (Cyert & March, 1963) than to end or eliminate it (which is actually impossible). Avoiding uncertainty is a wonderful emerging strategy: the point is to trap uncertainty (Luhmann, 2010), sifting it through heuristics, habits, experiments, and learning. Rather than an engineered world, organizations are a mixture of design, structure, and interrelationships between people and groups transacting with the environment (Simon, 1983; Nootebom, 2009).

This is why changing organizations is so difficult, an undertaking with a high likelihood of failure. An organization is an extremely stable, spontaneous order because it is created by the constant emergence of traditions, values, routines, and practices that have gradually been woven into a sturdy fabric. As seen in chapters 2 and 3, the problem is that the order created or emerged may be creating an equilibrium producing significant internal conflicts and conflicts with the environment. The case of compliance is classic: international standards and the pressures of the context to break with routines and practices that can lead to acts deemed improper are becoming more assertive. However, although the context changes, the created order that worked in a given context will be the first port of call. In other words, organizations will seek to adapt rather than transform themselves. In the face of the uncertainty that change implies. In the face of an uncertain, dynamic world, an idea of change guided by the assumption of control based solely on a predesigned strategy sounds patently illogical. In this respect, Tsoukas and Chia (2002) argue that as human agents perform routines, they constitute possible sources of change. In other words, even the routines assumed to be the most stable elements of organizations are potentially unstable.

How should one deal with a process of organizational change as required by any compliance program or policy? A good start is by understanding the different forms of knowledge and action that a dynamic, uncertain world imposes on people and groups who nonetheless seek and trust they will be able to affect, intervene and direct this world. In Eudemian Ethics, Aristotle distinguished three types of valuable knowledge in reality: episteme, techne, and phronesis. Episteme is the generalizable knowledge usually achieved through processes such as science in an attempt to generate a universal, abstract, and complete understanding of the world. It is generally systematic knowledge that can be documented and replicated beyond the particular contexts in which it is produced. Techne, unlike Episteme, focuses on a more precise, specialized type of knowledge: more than general knowledge, techne must intervene in specific objects whose characteristics as specific objects make them particular elements. Techne is a situational and object-dependent knowledge addressed in a specialized way. Techne is handy for constructing objects: physical or social instruments ranging from a screw in a table to a structure or rule in an organization. Competent, specialized people create structures and rules. Both episteme and techne are abstracted from a fundamental element: action. What happens on a day-to-day basis? What happens in operation must be abstracted because it and its environment must be controlled and standardized to prevent deviations. However, many of these standards or controls tend to be unable to foresee changes, accidents, and variations. Action, the world of action, usually has its logic and dynamics.

A famous boxer once said, "Everyone has a plan until they get punched in the mouth." Any project's plans are shaken once people enter the world of action. The world of action is "becoming," something that can only be understood exactly if one continues to act. A person in the world of action understands firsthand the strength and importance of relationships of interdependence (with reality and with other people). Phronesis does not require plans or forecasts but a mental state that allows the person to have or acquire resourcefulness: the ability to adapt and understand each of the situations they face. Phronesis attaches great importance to situations that are concrete and contextual. They can be stable, but also accidents, revolutions, or mistakes. Stupidities, problems, emotions, chance, and disorder are not denied in the situation. All these elements can happen. How then does a rational person or group deal with the situation? By acting with the awareness that they are dealing with situations where flexibility is required to use available resources in ways that may be novel and different (Dunne, 1997).

Changing an organization entails planning, designing, proposing, and assuming. But it also involves acting and in action, which endures practical rationality. Acting, therefore, implies attractiveness. Moreover, in order to become, it is essential to understand and know how to be in conditions of interdependent relationships (Dunne, 1997: 263). Does this imply that phronesis, in the process of organizational change, involves letting go of trends, floating, and going where the wind blows? The answer is a resounding no. For this reason, various organizational change processes with highly normative, evaluative visions such as compliance flounder or fail to achieve their ultimate consequences. To be successful, achieve its objectives, and at the same time have the capacity to cope with its behavioral dynamics, an endogenously integrated organization must be embedded in the organization itself. Changing an organization implies acting and understanding the arenas, the interrelationships, and interdependencies. To achieve what? To become.

Therein lies the rub. Become what and why? Aristotle himself makes it clear that it is impossible to seek excellence in phronesis, unlike techne. By way of example:

the Nazis may have excelled in their techne for conducting the Holocaust. Nevertheless, that was hardly phronesis. The becoming of the Nazis was destined to fall off a cliff, eventually. Phronesis is intimately linked not only to action per se but also to the underlying reason for the action: knowing how to be with others and become in an interdependent world, that is heterogeneous, diverse, plural, and dynamic. It is conflictive and therefore requires constant reassessment in which action and reality can lead to a different result from the one a person is seeking or claims to be seeking if they do not have phronesis.

Let us take a closer look. In the case of techne, knowledge can lead to evil, error, and deception: a person wants to achieve something different from what they are explicitly seeking. In the case of phronesis, this is unlikely to happen: action reveals the real intention, what a person wants to become. A person can attempt to convince others that there is a particular goal, but phronesis, acting in the situation, reveals what one wants to be (rather than just do). For this reason, a change project is seen for what it is in action: either because of its erroneous techne or its vision of what it wants to be or become. A compliance program that is satisfied with the form and the creation of structures, the signing of codes, and the rhetoric of change and honesty, will reveal its limitations once it is implemented and its lack of a becoming that is consistent with its aim, so false phronesis (Dunne, 1997: 267).

This view of phronesis is both fascinating and substantial. The combination is essential: acting in practice, coping with situations in their logic, and learning by doing. However, not like a weathervane, pushed every which way by the chaos and complexity of reality. But instead, by dealing with that situational reality, in action, with a vision and a sense of becoming. In the case of compliance, what is that vision of becoming? That is a critical question. It is strategic in a concrete sense: not only as a vision or plan but as becoming in the situation, in action, interdependence, and interaction. Every action inevitably happens in a context in motion, with the past and the specific history of the people and groups involved in the action: an action is always imbued with the past that has also permeated our practices and habits, structures, and rules. A compliance program that is not clearly aware of this reality is probably lost without a strategy or the possibility of leveraging phronesis.

Thinking that organizational change is automatic or a matter of rules and processes would seem to be a fundamental mistake. Ultimately, a compliance program wants to break away from a stable, accepted dynamic to create a new one, which is also stable and accepted over time. Lewin (1951) proposed pragmatically analyzing the change in three critical and complex phases: unfreeze, movement, and refreeze. Unfreezing implies a thoughtful, systematic process for disrupting the stabilities and inertia that make the organization, its groups, and people what it is today. It should be clear that unfreezing implies a risk or a problem since it creates an inevitable destabilization in people, groups, and their behavior. Channeling this destabilization is essential. You cannot risk setting the organization and its parts in motion without understanding or at least being aware of new, experimental processes that can cause confusion, resistance, and fear. Moving the organization is a phase that is filled with uncertainties: new processes are learned, changes are made that do not yield clear results, and new uncertainties are produced. The movement phase involves learning and modifying. By then, people will clearly understand how and when to create the new stability (unfreezing). In practical terms, this is an extremely idealistic phase. But from an operational point of view, it involves constantly asking oneself: Is this equilibrium being created and crystallized as the one we expected? Because organizations and their groups, as we have seen, in their logic of negotiation, struggle and agreement, create stabilities. Furthermore, they will not necessarily be the expected or planned ones. Understanding how and in what way a phase of new stability is achieved will significantly help to create the options to intervene in time before the arrival of the refreezing phase.

The change process is a process of action rather than just planning. It entails a constant commitment to contingency, vicissitudes, the dynamics of people and their groups in their operations, and their appropriation of ways of acting and dealing with everyday reality. At the operational level, speaking of the first-order change differs from a second-order change. The first-order change seeks to increase the skills of people and groups to solve problems within an accepted, negotiated arena of organizational logic. But if we are talking about a general transformation, which most compliance programs wish to achieve, thus this implies changing the frames of reference of groups and their members (Argyris & Schon, 1978). In other words, changing an organization implies changing the behaviors of its groups and individuals. However, at the same time, changing behaviors has a clear cognitive dimension. Learning different processes and new values is not just a question of will. It is also a question of the practice and exercise of various skills and expert ways of dealing with situations generated in practice. Cognitive change is a change that constantly challenges what has been learned, what is assumed to be stable and adequate. At the same time, learning implies, at various times, destroying or challenging what is accepted as stable or normal (Fiol & Lyles, 1985).

5.2.4 So, What View of Change is Required for a Successful Compliance Program?

A dynamic, human, political, or group vision can be a good option. Organizations are constantly changing, adapting, stabilizing, and encountering new instabilities. The punctuated equilibrium view is helpful in this regard: although change is a constant, it is not homogeneous. During periods of stability, periods of transformation and then restabilization are created (Abernathy & Utterback, 1978; Gersick, 1991; Miller & Friesen, 1980; Tushman & Romanelli, 1985).

The punctuated equilibrium view allows one to challenge the more uncomplicated view of organizational change that generally states a similar idea to the following:

1. The organization (be it a group, subunit, or entire organization) is in a state of homeostasis where there is alignment between environment and structure that produces an acceptable level of performance. This is the current instantiation of its logic.
2. An exogenous change occurs that results in decline in performance to an unacceptable level. The old logic no longer works.
3. Management attempts to rectify the situation, instituting a set of structures and technologies that constitute a new logic.
4. The organization, or its employees and middle managers, resists change due to inertia or self-interest. The new techno-economic logic contradicts the normative logic of the past.
5. Management overcomes resistance or inertia through change management techniques, some of which are drastic.
6. The organization is resurrected in a new form, better adapted to the environment's needs, and performance is restored. A new techno-economic and normative logic are now in place (Drazin, et al., 2004).

Punctuated equilibrium avoids oversimplifying the change process as a unitary, planned, and directed process. Change, therefore, has phases, disruptions, interrupted processes, and surprises. It is unlikely to be a gradual, cumulative process and can be sudden, surprising, and even dramatic.

5.3 The Dos and Don'ts of Change through a Compliance Program

Any proposal for change in an organization implies a series of strategies that aim to intervene in the organization's dynamics, logic, or culture. This statement makes more sense if we analyze organizations as arenas, as has been pointed out throughout this chapter. Change projects occur in spaces where they are not simply imposed rationally and accepted across the board but must include negotiation, dialogue, cooperation, and even conflict resolution processes with groups or coalitions that are part of the organization and maintain a balance within it. However, these balances are not of any kind but of power. Every organizational change project is an inherently political project.

In this respect, organizational change projects are anchored and built on narratives, discourses, symbols, and analogies. A change project is driven by discourses that seek to legitimize it within the organization and thereby convince the various groups of the need for change. Brunsson (2009) illustrates this by analyzing organizational reforms, noting that they tend to be one-sided. Reforms take up a single set of coherent values and perceptions of the world, in contrast to organizational practices that often deal with inconsistent values and perceptions between groups.

The change represents a political project that seeks to intervene in all the logic within the organization. In this respect, a vision that considers that change can be affected from the top down and can also be conducted through formal mechanisms such as the implementation of manuals, standards, or codes, loses sight of the complexity of organizations. Change is seen as a political project indeed adds key elements that are not opposed to technical mechanisms but complement them with political ones. Organizational change is linked to discourses and how attractive or legitimate they may be for the various coalitions within an organization. Change programs provide discursive resources to make certain things possible (Tsoukas & Chia, 2002). In this respect, discourse cannot be separated from the change that is being proposed. Especially when that discourse attempts to intervene in the way it acts within the organization, in its culture, and in its logic of what is appropriate. It would be pertinent to include in the theory of change the role of organizational culture in the processes of manifestation, symbolization, realization, and interpretation (Hatch, 2004).

Within the compliance literature, change is regarded as a purely technical-rational element in which the organization must modify substantive factors of its own structure. Additionally, these changes occur in a generalized, uniform way through regulations, good practices, audits, codes of conduct, control systems, and internal audits. Likewise, it is considered that a solid compliance program can be promoted through robust leadership that champions the project, sharing it without apparent conflict with the rest of the organization. However, this vision ignores the political element of change projects. In this widespread view in the compliance literature, little is said about the necessary reflection and inclusion of an essential variable: the political nature of compliance programs. As explained in the first paragraphs, this nature is linked to power, a relevant variable but extremely difficult to incorporate into organizational change, so sometimes it is not incorporated, thereby overlooking a fundamental dimension. In this regard, McGrath and Tschan (2004) consider the dynamics of the groups, stating that they create and maintain taboos regarding the transmission of information that appears to endanger the structure of the group or the characteristics that are important to it. Groups provoke, maintain, or inhibit individual energizing processes through the exercise of influence or social power, both directly and indirectly. In this sense, an individual's change projects are disrupted by the meanings generated within the group they comprise. When an organization is viewed as an arena, the differences between the groups and coalitions mean that the changes sought do not occur as expected.

Compliance as a political project does not escape this logic. Change strategies and elements go through a group sieve and may contradict the status quo of that group, affecting their reception and adoption. Thus, compliance is not a program that can simply be implemented and internalized since, as discussed in Chapter 4, individuals and groups maintain their own logic, resist, negotiate with norms, and act according to their interests. So, given this political dimension, is change possible?

The answer is yes, but this is precisely why it is essential not to ignore this dimension and instead to acknowledge its importance. This is mainly because this will encourage more solvent and realistic change programs with a greater likelihood of success. How can this dimension be successfully included? There is no single answer because all organizations are different. However, some general recommendations can be offered that may be useful, as well as suggestions on what not to do when implementing a compliance program. To this end, it is important to remember two things: every organizational change project is a political change. Therefore, as a change project, compliance is also political.

5.3.1 Mistakes in the Implementation of Change in Compliance Programs

In the spirit of providing general guidance, we will refer to Kotter (1995) and his study on how to lead change within an organization. Although the author offers a series of steps and rules, this normative element is less important than the fact that he raises a substantive question: What are the forces within an organization that oppose change? This question tacitly assumes that there must be politics, leadership, and risk for change to occur within an organization. It is worth distinguishing between the notion of leadership that must act with an awareness of its limited power and the one proposed by the compliance literature, to which plenipotentiary powers are attributed since the leader is capable of acting without the need to incorporate any another actor. Their position and mandate suffice to champion change.

Likewise, Kotter (1995) acknowledges that change is traumatic since it affects the agendas, the arenas of certainty, and the power dynamics of people within an organization. Change is not accepted or embraced without resistance, nor does it occur as expected. On the contrary, it must be admitted ex-ante that change will not go as planned. Some groups will attempt to boycott change if it affects their interests and benefits, while others will partially adopt it. Groups that consider that their status quo will benefit from adopting the change programs will accept the new guidelines, discourses, and logic. However, to know the particular way each group will act, it is essential to initially acknowledge the existence of these groups and be open to admitting that our change project will not be as envisioned. Compliance literature does not incorporate this reflection, assuming that the organization is an entity whose members act rationally, are willing to change if it is promoted from above, and will support any reform based on a technical-rational logic, such as the implementation of information and monitoring systems. Likewise, the values of an organization can be selected by actors who can socialize them through courses and workshops without the active participation of the rest of the members of an organization (Silverman, 2008). This implies that members of an organization will internalize values they may not share and with which they certainly do not identify.

Given the challenges and dilemmas of change, leaders who promote it tend to make eight classic mistakes. In each mistake, the importance of power is recognized as a fundamental variable for achieving change. In that respect, change implies costs that must be considered before launching any project. First, each error is pointed out, and a brief reflection is provided on how this error is present in the compliance literature.

The first mistake is to be too lenient. In other words, if the change is not seen as necessary or urgent for the organization's existence, its members will be unlikely to believe it is necessary and fail to implement it. In this respect, it is essential, in the construction of the discourse, to convince others that change is urgent and fundamental and to explain the possible implications of failing to implement it, such as, for example, the possibility that the organization will disappear. Consequently, change programs are discursive, as Brunsson (2009) points out. Discourse produces ideas and norms about possible, desirable organizational forms. The work of a leader must not only be oriented toward creating a convincing discourse on why this form of change is the best and conveying the importance of adopting it promptly. If the discourse is not well-argued, it is difficult to transmit, and if there is no awareness of its relevance, it will be assumed that there is no point in changing. Majone (1989) refers to this in the context of using evidence and arguments in the choice of public policies.

This error materializes in the compliance literature because it is assumed that the compliance program is presented as a rational change that must be incorporated to improve compliance with regulations and avoid problems related to risk or acts of corruption. However, although normatively, all organizations should comply with the corresponding regulations, develop systems to identify and mitigate risks or have mechanisms to reduce the possible occurrence of acts of corruption, it does not suffice to argue that change is necessary for it to be supported by all members of an organization. As Kotter points out, a process of argumentation and conviction about the urgent need to implement a compliance program must also be implemented. Along these lines, within the compliance literature, it is assumed that the aim of adopting a compliance program is in itself a sufficiently solid reason for leaders to promote it with the rest of the members and that, as passive recipients, they will understand the importance of adhering to the provisions and proposed changes without the need for any kind of discourse to explain the relevance of the change they will undergo. The first error suggests that this considerably limits the success of a compliance program since people unless they are aware of the possible consequences – particularly negative ones – of not changing, will do little to follow the change guidelines and therefore not adopt the compliance program.

The second mistake is failing to create a powerful coalition to support change. As has been explained, understanding organizations as arenas enables one to analyze them as spaces in which various coalitions or groups come together, discuss, negotiate, agree, and cooperate. Thus, organizational change is not implemented in a purely homogeneous group although it is part of an organization, but rather any change project intervenes in separate groups, each with its own logic, dynamics, values, objectives, purposes, and interests. Therefore, a leader cannot undertake change without first determining whether they have the support of coalitions that will help them implement their proposal.

This implies that the leader must negotiate, dialogue, and ease elements of the change they are proposing to achieve a consensus with some of the preexisting coalitions or negotiate to build a sufficiently solid coalition and able to unite common interests to promote a shared change project. In any case, none of these options is easy since they require calculation skills. Skills to calculate costs, whereby the leader constantly assesses how much they must give up, how much they can trade, and the extent to which they can strike a balance in the project between what they want to change and what can actually be changed. If the leader is too rigid, coalitions are less likely to accept proposals they regard as an imposition. At the same time, if the leader is too lenient when the change project is eventually undertaken, it may be very different from what was planned and will become a project implemented by a dominant coalition.

The main source of this mistake in the compliance literature is that compliance programs fail to regard coalition support as relevant. Moreover, it is not included within the substantive elements for implementing a compliance program. The leader alone promotes the necessary changes through their actions, as well as the establishment of codes and manuals, the facilitation of workshops, and the development of new areas, positions, and systems. Although, in some cases, the importance of having specialized managers is mentioned, they are not necessarily members of coalitions that promote change. On the contrary, they are usually external members who, through their knowledge, functions established – paradoxically by the leader – have sufficient legitimacy and reputation for implementing compliance program strategies.

An example of this is mentioned in Chapter 4 on the role of managers of ethics management (Chief Executive of Ethics Office [CEEO]), compliance (Chief Executive of Compliance Office [CECO]), communication (Chief Executive of Compliance Communication Office [CECCO]), or information technologies (Chief of Information Technologies Office [CITO]). All of them are actors who are inserted into the organization. However, their influence within it is minimal since they do not form part of any coalition as they do not have any relationship with the other members. The rank or specialization of these actors is not sufficient conditions to ensure that they have enough influence to initiate change. In this respect, compliance programs are boycotted or partially implemented without the participation of coalitions or the creation of one that defends change. Social and political aspects are not mandated but created through interaction.

The third mistake lies in being unable to say what change will lead to. In other words, there is a failure to create a vision that motivates and unites several groups with a significant expectation of improvement. Without this vision, the cost of change and change itself is considered unnecessary. Providing a roadmap that will illustrate the benefits of change is therefore essential. Thus, members of the organization lend meaning to change and contribute by being convinced of the need to support and maintain change actions, despite the costs entailed by leaving their logic and arenas of uncertainty. This mistake is intricately linked to the first one. Formulating a discourse that legitimizes change is essential, which explains why this form of change is better, more useful, or more effective than others. However, leaders themselves are sometimes unsure why a change proposal is a better option and the precise results that will be obtained. Brunsson (2009) observes that reformers who incorporate the value of ambiguity and complexity formulate reform proposals that prioritize clarity and simplicity. Leaders must therefore focus on promoting concrete actions with clear meanings and results that are easily measurable and observable. Otherwise, doubts increase, and commitment decreases.

In the compliance literature, the vision is imposed by leaders who are agents of change (Treviño, Weaver, Gibson, & Toffler, 1999). This vision is handed down to all members without asking them whether this project seems adequate, credible, or desirable. In this respect, the vision of compliance proposed by those at the top of the organization may not elicit a legitimate expectation for the rest of the members and may be scorned, criticized, or simply misunderstood. The normative element of compliance assumes that since compliance is desirable and positive, any organization that implements certain conditions will be able to convince its members of its necessity and importance. Also, all actions are thought to be self-contained, and it is assumed that their importance will automatically be understood through their development. For example, although information systems can be extremely useful for identifying risks and fraud, it is essential to explain their importance. They may not on their own reflect their value and impact on the improvement of an organization. Compliance programs must spell out why they should be implemented, clarifying their importance, effects, and benefits to convince all those who will be part of it.

The fourth mistake is linked to the previous one: failing to communicate the vision. Since there are different coalitions, interpretations are also heterogeneous and can significantly vary. It is therefore essential to clearly communicate the vision, even the costs that are not easy to convey. Without a clear understanding of what is expected of the change project, groups may lose interest in continuing with compliance programs or interpret contradictory elements of the program that has been designed.

In this respect, compliance programs rarely include costs in their discourse, merely echoing the benefits of compliance elements. One example is that when a new compliance-oriented department is proposed, the general costs for its establishment are not examined. Costs may involve cuts to other areas, changes in personnel from reassigning workers to laying off workers, and sunk costs once these proposals fail. In the compliance literature, failure is not discussed since there are a series of steps that, if properly conducted, will ensure the success of the programs.

Nor is there a review of costs, which are not only incurred on one occasion but continuously.

The fifth mistake concerns problems arising when unsurmountable vision obstacles remain. Accordingly, change is impossible if a person is unwilling to shift the balance of power if consensus is not constructed to modify these logics of power and authority. Therefore, to return to the second mistake, it is essential to create empowered change groups that can promote and negotiate modifications to obstacles and power structures. In this respect, the balances of power that must be intervened in must be identified. This is sometimes not easy since some equilibriums are deeply rooted and exert considerable influence. In others, the leaders of change themselves do not wish to alter their logic of power or those of their coalitions. This leads to a paradox: why change something that will affect or not be in the particular interests of an actor or group? Why modify the organization if a group loses its arenas of uncertainty and power? Both questions are central, the answers are far from simple, and sometimes they do not have one. This enormous limitation dashes the hopes of a purely objective and technical compliance program.

In other words, how can one guarantee that a leader who can be constantly watched by monitoring systems, by the constant attention of his peers and subordinates, is indeed willing to implement all this? This would appear to be a contradiction considering that the members of an organization are seeking to expand their arenas of uncertainty through opacity (Crozier, 1964). Compliance programs do not resolve this key paradox. It should be noted that essential assumptions of compliance rest on this paradox. As noted in Chapter 4, leaders must have the will and commitment to be those who initiate change and defend it, serving as impeccable examples for the rest of the members. So, if a compliance program relies on leaders showing a willingness to change, which will undoubtedly reduce their power in an organization, why should they? This seems contradictory since power does not come from the formal structure but is generated by interactions, sometimes informal ones.

This can be extended to coalitions. If the support of coalitions is required to undertake a change project, why would they accept changes that entail more costs than benefits? Once again, this goes back to the discussion of equilibriums. To what extent is it possible to negotiate, give in and cooperate? A leader who wishes to implement a compliance program cannot afford to overlook these skills. Otherwise, they will fail because they will not mobilize the power logics that structures the organization.

The sixth mistake involves failing to make short-term benefits evident. The view of change is often long term and more of a dream and an aspiration. However, change must be perceived in specific short-term benefits that are clearly and readily observed. This favors commitment since it gives a sense that efforts are genuine, reasonable, and concrete. So, if efforts are sustained, there will be even more benefits. In this respect, if no change is achieved in the preliminary stages, members will think that it is pointless and does not improve the organization. Brunsson (2009) points out that reforms usually take so long that people often forget the results, which means a new reform has begun. This situation turns administrative reforms into endless routines without real changes or results.

In the case of the compliance literature, this mistake can be seen in two ways. The timing is not apparent. Although time is the "ether" of change (Scott, 2004), it is not included in the discussion on the implementation of a compliance program. In this respect, what is the nature of time within compliance? Is there an approximate time a compliance program takes to be implemented? There is no standard for this question because not all organizations are the same, but the question could be rephrased: are there deadlines in a compliance program? Can anybody be sure that a program yielded short-term results, and if so, how? One problem with the compliance literature is that it views the necessary factors for a program. What needs to be done first to create a new value system? How can the progress of such a system be measured? How can it be shown that there are indeed short-term results? What should they start with in constructing a new monitoring system, or should it be established as a whole?

Woodman and Dewett (2004) argue that effective organizational change requires system-wide efforts rather than piecemeal approaches and that changes to various aspects (or subsystems) of the system must be congruent. Compliance is a change project that permeates the entire organization, so its efforts are aimed at the entire system, as the authors note. So how does one measure, convey, and share the progress of a project seeking to change the organization as a whole?

The seventh mistake is thinking that success can be achieved quickly and easily. This is exacerbated when it fails to happen, and under pressure, victory is declared without achieving the expected change. Organizations are resilient; they resist. Organizations can change in the short term only to quickly resume their routines, dynamics, and logic. Change can be diluted over time to the point where the organization will return to its initial state in a couple of years. As has been shown, change is not simple, is not mandated, and is not achieved as expected. To think it can be achieved in a linear fashion is a serious delusion that disrupts the aspirations of change and the chances of success. Change is constantly up against coalition forces that seek to maintain the status quo, which is why they push back. The organization's practices are based on the interactions between groups and individuals, meaning that these logics are endowed with meaning that cannot be modified without further ado. This meaning helps deal with organizations' uncertainty and ambiguity (Weick, 2001).

In this respect, the compliance literature considers that implementing certain factors will be enough to think that the compliance program has been successful. However, on many occasions, the implementation of systems, the creation of new values, or the establishment of certain norms are not internalized and end up not failing to impact the behavior of members of its organization. Likewise, compliance implies an ongoing process rather than a single effort, as discussed at the beginning of this chapter. Compliance does not happen just once but is a permanent change project. However, paradoxically, the importance of compliance becoming a condition of the organization has been pointed out, although this should be achieved through a single definitive and totalizing intervention. So, it would appear that compliance programs declare victory too quickly. Instead, they should be thought of as permanent, ongoing efforts. Otherwise, their effect will be temporary, with minimal impact.

The last mistake is underestimating the importance of anchoring change in the organizational culture. Organizations are understood in practices and daily routines. If change is not observed there, then it has not taken place. It is essential to assign concrete efforts to intervene in the organizational culture. Culture involves what is called the nuts and bolts of an organization, which reveals the interactions between members and coalitions in practice. For this reason, it is the most difficult aspect to change, in addition to the fact that its importance is minimized. The daily routine is far from being the most striking element of an organization. Therefore, when a change project is undertaken, lofty goals are set, such as the objectives, mission, and values. All these are important, but an organization exists through its routines and the development, interaction, and gathering of its members. The organization is ultimately a by-product of these relationships between its members that are guided by their logic of what is appropriate, their dynamics, and balances of power.

The compliance literature tends to focus on modifying specific elements of the organization, particularly values, ethics, available information, and adherence to rules and regulations. However, there is barely any mention of how these factors impact routines and specific daily actions. The implicit causal relationship is that if value systems are changed, there will be more information; consequently, better monitoring will make behaviors change. All members of the organization will be less prone to acts of corruption, break the rules less, and report inappropriate actions. Once again, this does not necessarily happen because although the factors that promote better behavior exist; they do not suffice because what is required is for actors to be willing to function as expected, use the systems, internalize the values, and for them to report wrongdoing despite the power asymmetries.

Some of these actions that should occur remain nothing more than an aspiration, an entirely normative element. Unlike the spectacular change compliance programs expect, true change happens organically, incrementally, and inexorably through slip, drift, and natural spread. It is subtle, cohesive, often underground, heterogeneous, and surprising (Tsoukas & Chia, 2002).

Table 5.1 summarizes the mistakes and provides a brief explanation of how to correct each one and a clear description of what happens in compliance programs.

Table 5.1: Summary of classic mistakes, recommendations for their solution, and examples of what not to do.

Classic mistakes	What to do	What not to do
1. Being too permissive	– Communicate the importance and urgency of change, usually by pointing out the problems involved in not bringing about change	– Assume that all members of an organization understand the need and urgency of change – Fail to communicate the effects of not changing (especially if one of the consequences is that the organization will disappear)
2. The second mistake is failing to create a powerful coalition to support change	– Recognize the various coalitions comprising the organization – Establish negotiations, dialogue, and exchange with the most potent coalitions to increase the likelihood of the compliance program occurring – Clearly outline and establish balances of power that are neither too rigid nor too flexible	– Consider that organizations are homogeneous entities in which all members have the same values, interests, and objectives – Refrain from seeking support from any coalition that strengthens the change project – Assume that a leader can promote a compliance program alone
3. The third mistake lies in being unable to say what change will lead to	– Have a vision, a road map that details what is expected from the change and the benefits of this – Communicate and motivate several groups with a significant expectation of improvement	– Be unsure why a change proposal is better than the current situation – Not know what the expected results are – Create a discourse that does not include others and does not encourage them to believe that the change will be worth the cost
4. Failing to communicate the vision	– Recognize the different interpretations of coalitions – Communicate the vision, especially the costs	– Fail to convey what is expected of the change project – Homogeneously communicate the vision without thinking about the differences and discrepancies

Table 5.1 (continued)

Classic mistakes	What to do	What not to do
5. Preserving insurmountable obstacles to vision	– Be willing to shift the balance of power – Build consensus to modify the logic of power and authority – Create empowered change groups that can push for and negotiate changes to obstacles and power structures – In this sense, the balances of power that must be intervened must be identified.	– Be uninterested or unwilling to intervene in certain balances of power – Impose and change the logic of power without considering the importance of coalitions – Assume that a leader can promote a compliance program on their own
6. The sixth mistake involves failing to make short-term benefits evident	– Show that change is perceptible and measurable – Show specific, short-term benefits that are clearly and quickly observed	– Do not show any progress or result expeditiously – Be ambiguous about benefits without demonstrating progress in any way
7. The seventh mistake is thinking that success can be achieved quickly and easily	– Recognize that definitive change takes time – As has been shown, change is not simple, is not mandated, and is not achieved as expected – Recognize that there are unintended effects of proposed change projects	– Think that change can be achieved linearly – Believing that change is easily achievable and that there are no obstacles – Believe that change can be decreed – Fail to include the time variable in the development of a compliance program
8. The last mistake is to underestimate the importance of anchoring change in the organizational culture	– It is essential to assign specific efforts to intervene in the organizational culture – Recognize that the organizational culture is the most difficult to change but also the most substantive – Recognize that change is constant and requires ongoing efforts	– Minimize the importance of organizational culture, routines, and daily actions – Focus on modifying lofty aspects yet with a minimal impact on the adoption of change – Think that change can be brought about with a single intervention, without the need to continue

5.4 Final Thoughts

According to what has been analyzed, organizations are arenas where various coalitions dialogue, negotiate, cooperate, and come into conflict. Kotter's proposal contributes to this approach since the errors it cites tend to occur more frequently when organizations are studied as entities, instruments in which politics does not exist, the capacity for negotiation is unnecessary, and there is no explanation of the risks and costs associated with change. In this respect, examining the complexity of organizations enhances the analysis. It certainly complicates it, sometimes to the degree that is hard to grasp, but it also makes it possible to identify valuable lessons for change.

Compliance is a project regarded as rational, eminently technical, and highly normative. It focuses on explaining the importance of its implementation and the factors required for change. However, it is not considered a political project, despite the fact that every change project implicitly involves political conditions since it affects the balance and dynamics of power. Compliance programs must incorporate these elements. Otherwise, they will experience the tensions and paradoxes outlined in the previous chapter and explored in greater depth in this last section.

There is no manual on how to implement a compliance program perfectly. However, it is possible to offer recommendations on the classic mistakes that crop up when one tries to promote change within an organization. It is also possible to suggest ways to deal with them and which activities are best avoided. A compilation rather than a guide has been provided here. This must be a mandatory analysis for compliance programs since they are usually based on widely criticized assumptions and limitations when it comes to an understanding of the change conditions that are part of organizations. Organizations as arenas, of course. Change on its own is weak because it must percolate through various groups with its logic and meanings. Understanding this is key to thinking about more concrete ways to achieve successful, lasting change in compliance programs. Now, though, it seems we still have a long way to go.

References

Abernalthy, W., & Utterback, J. (1978). Patterns of Industrial Innovation. *Technological Review*, 80, 41–47.

Arellano-Gault, D. (2022). *Las trampas de la decisión. O por qué los gobiernos y las organizaciones marchan (casi) gustosamente al precipicio*. México: Fontamara-Universidad de Xalapa.

Argyris, C., & Schon, D. (1978). *Organizational Learning: A Theory in Action Perspective*. Reading, MA: Addison-Wesley.

Arrow, K. (1974). *The Limits of Organization*. New York: W. W. Norton & Company.

Boden, D. (1994). *The Business of Talk*. Organizations in Action. Cambridge, UK: Polity Press.

Brunsson, N. (2009). *Reform as Routine: Organizational Change and Stability in the Modern World*. Oxford: Oxford University Press.

Chia, R., & Holt, R. (2009). *Strategy Without Design*. Cambridge: Cambridge University Press.

Clegg, S., Courpasson, D., & Phillips, N. (2006). *Power and organizations*. London: Sage.

Cyert, R. M., & March, J. G. (1963). *A Behavioral Theory of the Firm*. Malden, MA: Prentice Hall/ Pearson Education.

Dansereau, F., Yammarino, F. and Kohles, J. (1999). Multiple level of analysis from a longitudinal perspective: some implications for theory building. *The Academy of Management Review*, 24(2), 346–357. https://doi.org/10.2307/259086

Deetz, S. (1995). *Transforming Communication, Transforming Business: Building Responsive and Responsible Workplaces*. Cresskill, NJ: Hampton.

Donaldson, L. (1999). *Performance-Driven Organizational Change*. Thousand Oaks: Sage.

Drazin, R., Glynn, M. A., & Kazanjian, R. (2004). Dynamics of Structural Change. In Poole, M.; & Van de Ven, A. (eds.), *Handbook of Organizational Change and Innovation*. Oxford: Oxford University Press, pp. 161–189.

Dunne, J. (1997). *Back to the Rough Ground*. Notre Dame: University of Notre Dame.

Fiol, M., & Lyles, M. (1985). Organizational Learning. *The Academy of Management Review*, 10(4), 803–813.

Gersick, C. (1991). Revolutionary Change Theories: A Multilevel Exploration of the Punctuated Equilibrium Paradigm. *Academy of Management Review*, 16, 10–36.

Hatch, M. (2004). Dynamics in Organizational Culture. In Poole, M., & Van de Ven, A. (eds.), *Handbook of Organizational Change and Innovation*. Oxford: Oxford University Press, pp. 190–211.

Kotter, J. (1995). Leading Change: Why Transformational Efforts Fail. *Harvard Business Review*, March–April, 59–67.

Lewin, K. (1951). *Field Theory in Social Science*. New York: Harper.

Luhmann, N. 2010. *Organización y decisión*. México: Herder.

Majone, G. (1989). *Evidence, Argument and Persuasion in the Policy Process*. New Haven: Yale University Press.

March, J. G., & Olsen, J. P. (1995). *Democratic Governance*. New York: Free Press.

March, J. G., & Olsen, J. P. (2011). *The Logic of Appropriateness*. Oxford Handbooks Online. doi:10.1093/oxfordhb/978019960445

March, J. (1991). Exploration and Exploitation in Organizational Learning. *Organization Science*, 2(1), 71–87.

March, J. (1994). *A Primer on Decision Making*. New York: Free Press.

March, J. (2010). *The Ambiguities of Experience*. Ithaca: Cornell University Press.

McGrath, J., & Tschan, F. (2004). Dynamics in Groups and Teams. In Poole, M., & Van de Ven, A. (eds.), *Handbook of Organizational Change and Innovation*. Oxford: Oxford University Press, pp. 50–72.

Merton, R. K. (1942). *Social Theory and Social Structure*. New York: Free Press.

Michaud, C., & Thoenig, J. C. (2003). *Making Strategy and Organization Compatible*. New York: Palgrave.

Miller, D., & Friesen, P. (1980). Momentum and Revolution in Organizational Adaptation. *Academy of Management Journal*, 23, 591–614.

Miller, D. (1982). Evolution and Revolution: A Quantum View of Structural Change in Organizations. *Journal of Management Studies*, 18, 116–138.

Mintzberg, H., & Waters, J. (1985). Of Strategies, Deliberate and Emergent. *Strategic Management Journal*, 6(3), 257–272.

Nooteboom, B. (2009). *A Cognitive Theory of the Firm*. Cheltenham: Edward Elgar.

Orlikowski, W. (1996). Improvising Organizational Transformation Over Time: A Situated Change Perspective. *Inform Systems Research*, 7, 63–92.

Poole, M. (2004). Central Issues in the Study in Change and Innovation. In Poole, M., & Van de Ven, A. (eds.), *Handbook of Organizational Change and Innovation*. Oxford: Oxford University Press, pp. 3–31.

Scott, J. (1998). *Seeing Like a State*. New Heaven: Yale University Press.

Seo, M., Putnam, L., & Bartunek, J. (2004). Dualities and Tensions of Planned Organizational Change. In Poole, M., & Van de Ven, A. (eds.), *Handbook of Organizational Change and Innovation*. Oxford: Oxford University Press, pp. 73–107.

Sieber, S. (1981). *Fatal Remedies. The Ironies of Social Intervention*. New York: Plenum Press.

Silverman, M. (2008). *Compliance Management for Public, Private, or Nonprofit Organizations*. McGraw-Hill: New York.

Simon, H. (1983). *Reason in Human Affairs*. Stamford: Stanford University Press.

Taylor, C. (1985). *Human Agency and Language*. Cambridge: Cambridge University Press.

Taylor, J., & Van Every, E. (2000). *The Emergent Organization*. New Jersey: Lawrence Erlbaum.

Treviño, L. K., Weaver, G. R., Gibson, D. G., & Toffler, B. L. (1999). Managing Ethics and Legal Compliance: What Works and What Hurts. *California Management Review*, 41(2), 131–151. https://doi.org/10.2307/41165990

Tsoukas, H., & Chia, R. (2002). On Organizational Becoming: Rethinking Organizational Change. *Organization Science*, 13(5), 567–582.

Tushman, M., & Romanelli, E. (1985). Organizational evolution: a metamorphosis model for convergence and reorientation. In. Cummings, L-; and Staw, B. (eds.), *Research in organizational behavior*. Greenwich: Elsevier Limited, pp. 171–222.

Weick, K. (2001). *Making Sense of the Organization*. Oxford: Blackwell.

Woodman, R., & Dewett, T. (2004). Organizationally Relevant Journeys in Individual Change. In Poole, M., & Van de Ven, A. (eds.), *Handbook of Organizational Change and Innovation*. Oxford: Oxford University Press, pp. 32–49.

Chapter 6
Conclusions: Driving Compliance Programs in the Real Organizational World

6.1 The Paradoxes of Compliance

The approach adopted in this book outlines a vision of compliance that is both complex and encouraging. It has attempted to show that to be effective. Compliance must understand various challenges that are not only important but can even sometimes seem like challenges that lead to insoluble obstacles. From this point of view, in this book, we aim to demonstrate that compliance faces at least two paradoxes.

6.1.1 The Paradox of Perpetuity

Paradox 1: The massive wave of global concern about probity and ethical failures in organizational behavior has shown that despite the enormous efforts made since the 1990s (such as laws, regulations, cross-surveillance, and new supervision technologies), fraud and corruption problems have persisted. In fact, there is even a sense that they have worsened. Thus, the more efforts are made (obviously at a greater cost), the clearer it becomes that illicit corporate practices, such as fraud and corruption, remain stable at least. It seems that they are a normal and even enduring part of social, political, and economic activities, despite the awareness that has been promoted of the severity of its consequences.

The paradox is obvious: the more the wave of concern about these behavioral and ethical failures grows, the more one sees that these failures are universal, able to adapt to regulations and new technologies swiftly, and can even be regarded as inseparable bedfellows of economic and political activities. With varying degrees of intensity, this is true for any organization, independently of the industry it works. Will acts like fraud and corruption ever be eliminated anywhere? Is society destined to have to live with these problems forever?

From a normative position, improper or illegal acts simply should not exist. However, this normative position, although necessary, is probably unrealistic and ineffective when creating proper instruments and viable strategies for dealing with the dilemma in question. For various reasons, improper and even illegal acts are and will be a constant, so the real goal should be to advance understanding of the reasons for this stability and the persistence of improper acts. This understanding will make it possible to continue learning and experimenting with instruments and increasingly effective ways of reasonably controlling them, thereby preventing their worst consequences.

https://doi.org/10.1515/9783110749113-006

Paradox 1 is quite clear. The more misbehavior triggers are understood, the more one realizes that it is not a problem of rotten apples. Fraud and corruption are organizational phenomena that can even occur without deceit. They can also be facilitated by rules and processes, both internal and external. Rules can be bent, and people can strategically learn to game the system. In addition to the broad array of spaces where wrongdoing can be created and sustained, it is imperative to mention the limitations of oversight and surveillance instruments. And above all, the limitations of the overseers. Indeed, oversight and surveillance always experience considerable instrumental, time, and capacity constraints on dealing with all the possibilities in the contemporary world to flout or at least bend the rules. Not to mention the classic contradiction: who oversees the overseer?

Paradox 1 calls for a fundamental change of perspective: there is no promised land. An overly optimistic vision can lead to despair. Like Sisyphus, thinking that it is possible the perfect honest organization (if such a thing were possible to define) only leads to failure in the attempt and to being endlessly condemned to watching the rock roll down the hill again. This Paradox encourages a less Manichean, more realistic conception of the organization's world. The border between honest and dishonest behavior is a socially constructed line, yet artificial and critical, so the line must be legitimized. Conceiving a "totally corrupt and dishonest" world would be just as impossible as conceiving the existence of a "perfectly honest one." Human beings are neither angels nor demons. There is no promised land, but adequate organizational space is only possible. This leads to the following paradox.

6.1.2 The Paradox of Duality

Paradox 2: Organizational studies have shown that the same logic and processes that enable people to cooperate and coordinate in an organization are the ones that create and constitute the sources of wrongdoing. From this point of view, the paradox is obvious: wrongdoing, including fraud and corruption, occurs using the same mechanisms of trust and discretion that make an organization viable. Misconduct or ethical failures are not exogenous pathologies, diseases that can be extirpated as though they were abnormalities. They are built and reproduced within the organizational sphere of people attempting to make sense, render the world intelligible, and find reasons to obey.

Paradox 2 implies a radical perspective: organizations consist of people behaving and interacting permanently. Such interaction requires a certain level of freedom and autonomy. These two elements are essential for organizations to exist and cope with their uncertain environment. Discretion is essential to understanding and making goals and objectives intelligible. The crystallization of any organization is largely based on these dynamics of autonomy and freedom. However, discretion is the source of both innovation and what could be regarded as wrongdoing. Social and organizational relations create order and cooperation. What Paradox 2 explains is that freedom and discretion, essential to creating cooperation and order, are also the sources of deviation and even the rationalization and normalization of questionable acts.

Perhaps an example will better illustrate this paradox. During the World Swimming Championships, 2022, an accident occurred during the competition. A synchronized swimmer fainted during her participation. The lifeguards were paralyzed, waiting for the judges' instructions to jump to rescue the swimmer. The athlete's coach, seeing the inaction of the lifeguards, jumped in and rescued the swimmer. Lifeguards followed established procedures, which involved inaction that could have been fatal. On the other hand, the coach's judgment led her to action. Nevertheless, it is paradoxical to think that the same freedom the trainer used is, in essence, the same freedom that could have made her not jump and, like the lifeguards, stick to the protocols.

This incident sparked an interesting debate. Should obedience to the rule or discretionary action be rewarded? An organization requires standards, rules, and procedures to achieve its goals. If everything were discretionary, deception could flourish at any moment, and controls could be weakened. On the other hand, discretion is essential to adapt and respond effectively to the uncertainty of the organizational environment. However, that does not prevent discretion from being used to obtain irregular personal benefits. That is the paradox of duality.

Comprehending these paradoxes will allow a more realistic understanding of compliance and its potential for organizational change. Compliance has been framed as an increasingly broad and ambitious instrument that seeks to create the conditions for modifying organizational behavior. From this point of view, compliance implies, in practice, choosing one of the following directions. The first is ineffective in the long term yet necessary in the short term: establish concern, oversight, and punishment for wrongdoing from within organizations. Indeed, punitive and normative arguments seek to impose oversight and even fear in people because of the possibility of being punished at all levels of the organization, including shareholders and the legitimate legal managers of an organization.

However, given Paradox 1, this normative face of compliance is both indispensable and insufficient. Although there is only a slim chance that more oversight and a greater likelihood of punishment will solve the problem in the long run, the situation would be even worse without such oversight and the possibility of real punishment.

Paradox 2, however, opens up another course of action. It is more complex and less instrumental, although probably more effective in the long term: compliance can become a tool for organizational change and transformation with an accurate, effective focus. It can do so precisely because it is an instrument capable of understanding that inappropriate behaviors are embedded in organizational processes, routines, and culture. As we have seen in this book, the theory of organizational change behind the logic of compliance is encouraging. Compliance requires an endogenous organizational change, making compliance logic necessary and intelligible for the organization from within.

Few instrumental visions of organizational change have the opportunity that compliance programs offer. Indeed, classic theories of organizational change generally begin with a normative and optimistic position: people in an organization will behave as expected in management because they are rational and, thus, capable of understanding that the achievement of the goals of the organization will be the basis for the achievement of their own goals. This is a rosy view, and it is empirically easy to show that it is unrealistic, as decades of organizational studies have shown (Poole & Van de Ven, 2004). Changing organizations would be relatively easy, and, as has been argued in this book, compliance implies changes that are by no means simple or without facing obstacles.

An alternative view of organizational change proposes a very different perspective: people in organizations decide, interact, and make mistakes (Courpasson & Thoenig, 2010). They are emotional and, thus, they can fail and make mistakes. Moreover, they have enduring and unavoidable cognitive biases, prejudices, and cognitive dissonances they desperately try to reduce. As discussed in previous chapters, reducing cognitive dissonance is a powerful need: failure of all kinds, particularly moral failure, is painful. So painful that people are willing to reduce the pain of being seen as corrupt, to create justifications for self-delusion, rationalizing negative decisions and effects as if they could actually be transmuted into positive (or at least justifiable) acts, or that they were not their responsibility.

Changing an organization cannot begin with a theory of change whose "raw material" is a human being who does not seem to exist: a rational human being who understands their actions and the consequences very well and who is in control of their emotions and feelings. The "raw material" that exists is another type of human being: a relational, emotional one with significant rational limitations and capable of constructing imperfect yet highly effective meaning and intelligibility. A human being who relates and creates interdependencies with others based on negotiations and dialogue (Gigerenzer & Selten, 2002).

How can we change organizations with this more realistic and intricate "raw material"? Being clear about the paradoxes that compliance implies, organizational change is possible assuming a set of strategies oriented toward political negotiation within the organization. These strategies are explained in the next section.

6.2 Strategies for Organizational Change in Compliance

Compliance as a goal has an advantage over many organizational change projects: its ethos and foundation are concrete and of immediate and obvious practical importance. In the growing context of oversight and punishment organizations are experiencing, as seen in Chapter 1, failure to achieve a certain degree of effectiveness in oversight, control, and organizational behavior change can be extremely risky. Companies experience this fear due to the authentic possibilities of punishment and fines with a high impact on their pockets and reputations. In all types of organizations, there is an enormous risk of seeing the foundations of their reputations and the trust of their consumers, citizens, and society, in general, being rapidly destroyed.

Compliance projects have complex, intricate, yet clearly identified goals. The issue, however, is pretty straightforward: the risk of an organization's partial and general failure is always present, given the dense social, group, and psychological dynamics of organizational behavior.

Compliance projects need a strategy to achieve their goals of organizational change. A strategy that moves away from visions such as "rotten apples" or the simplistic idea that organizational change can be imposed vertically with an exclusively normative vision. These views, as discussed in this book, overlook the richness of people's behavior and its effect on organizations. As discussed in Chapter 2, unlike the monolith organization, the arena organization is built and rebuilt by enacting accepted, rationalized, and normalized behaviors. This role is permanently embedded and created within the interdependent relationships that sustain any organization.

Visualizing an organization as an arena implies that organizational change requires rational and political leadership. Closely following Kotter's proposal (1996) and adapting it to the arena organization's central argument and the compliance project's specificities, we suggest four strategies or steps that summarize the idea of effective change by the organization. These strategies are not based on illusory hopes of a linear and purely instrumental process of change but rather on a process of establishing compliance as an endogenous part of organizational life. The strategies are:

1. Build a legitimate coalition of different organizational groups to support the compliance program at all the design and implementation stages.
2. Define a realistic agenda for the different stages to be accomplished, placing special emphasis on small gains so that organizational members can observe key changes.
3. Define the challenges and obstacles to modifying routines and practices to achieve the new behaviors that the compliance program requires to be successful.
4. Build a practical communication strategy not only because of the need to "comply with the compliance program" but to define specific transformations in the cultural mindset of the organization and routines and processes.

6.2.1 Strategy 1. Build a Legitimate Coalition

The first step is understanding that the arena organization is composed of an orderly structural scheme. The formal structure is just the basis on which specific aspects of authority, responsibilities, and duties are defined. The organizational structure is established daily through the acts, relationships, and interdependencies people legitimize through obedience, strategy, and even resistance. Organizations move through their groups and coalitions. They have different regulatory commands, legal and financial resources, and technical and leadership capabilities. A compliance project under the logic of the arena organization requires agreements. It will affect different coalitions unequally, both positively and negatively. It will affect highly established and legitimized or justified organizational agreements and meanings. A compliance project will therefore have a better chance of being accepted and implemented if built and founded through a broad, influential coalition. The coalition of different groups implies a governance process of the compliance project that establishes the rules of the decision game from the design, formulation, and implementation of the compliance program. Governance does not mean total participation or endless assembly; it must be clarified. Governance is who decides, how they decide, and how legitimate this division of labor between different people, agents, or groups is. Organizations will delegate much of governance to external actors, while others will prefer a more insider approach or a combination of the two. The point is that a compliance project implies an agreement and continued political commitment. It must be assumed that the ups and downs, negotiations, and renegotiations will be constant. Managing to stay on course despite a complicated process of changes, struggles, and bargaining is probably the most complex task for the success of a compliance program. Hence the importance of this first step.

6.2.2 Strategy 2. Define a Realistic Agenda

The second step underlines the idea that a compliance project implies a time commitment. This assumes that under the logic of the arena organization, the project envisioned from the beginning will remain intact until its implementation and evaluation are simply unrealistic. Under any governance dynamic (with low or high participation), a compliance program will have to adapt and change over time. The challenges will be seen more clearly once it begins to be implemented. The environment moves swiftly. The organization needs to continue operating while various issues are being transformed. Moreover, a compliance project will not only be adopted within organizational logic but also adapted: its viability implies its ability to change and be tailored to circumstances. Furthermore, the challenge is maintaining its essence and overall consistency while it is being adapted and modified. Achieving this is like steering a ship on the high seas on a long voyage punctuated by storms, frost, peaceful moments, accidents, and vicissitudes that it was able to circumvent to reach its intended destination. In other words, the process or path is as important as the goal. Ultimately, a compliance project seeks to become stable and endogenously embedded in day-to-day organizational logic. Keeping the hope alive, every compliance project elicits among people (in some, at least, others may fear it) entails intelligently managing the process. Small gains show the way and are not negligible. Not everything can be achieved, nor can everything be achieved quickly: some phases and stages can provide certainty, at least partially. The organizational battle involved in compliance is often a long-term one. Without a compass or guide, waiting to see long-term results can be highly demoralizing. Allowing the new organizational meanings to be tested and creating new routines that provide renewed and practical intelligibility for people and their groups can be a winning tactic.

6.2.3 Strategy 3. Define the Challenges and Obstacles

The third step expresses a stark, realistic position: a compliance program, like any change process or proposal, will have to experience an unavoidable truth, which is that reality will resist change. Much has been written about resistance to change as if it were a pathology or a perverse tendency of people to maintain the status quo. As if every change were always a good thing and every status quo or time-honored practice is less good, irrational, or wrong. The statement that reality is going to resist reflects another view of resistance. One in which people, groups, and the organization itself have found ways to make the challenges they face intelligible. They have learned to "play the game" so to speak. This learning to play the game accommodates several types of logic: from learning to play it to improving, developing, and enhancing it. They have also learned to game the system: they know how to exploit loopholes, practical flaws, and the limitations of the game's rules to use these systemic dynamics for their benefit. A compliance project needs to understand these logics of resistance: from noticeable efforts to ensure things do not change to the possibility that resistance makes sense given that it lays bare agreements and practices that have worked and can be critical. It is necessary to understand that it is human nature to game the system and spot weaknesses in the rules of the game (both the new and the old ones) to take advantage of their flaws and limitations. The Goodhart Law states: "When a measure becomes a target, it ceases to be a good measure" (Goodhart, 1984). In other words, any reformer or group wishing to make a change and propose a project may find that their project ends up being simplified and distorted. For example, a new rule seeking to increase strict compliance with a standard creates a compliance indicator. it ends up encouraging people to find ways to strategically increase the indicator regardless of whether it changes the intended goal of the new rule. Changing the reality of an organization is achieved through human, group, and social behavior. The unforeseen effects and consequences of any project involving change or compliance reform mean preparing and anticipating these unforeseen consequences is necessary. Definitely, it is not always possible to know what those unexpected consequences will be or the new perverse dynamics or unbalanced incentives that the compliance project will create. Although, one just has to be prepared to address them rather than assuming that a compliance proposal's simple rational logic or legitimacy will lead to success in its design and implementation.

6.2.4 Strategy 4. Build a Practical Communication Strategy

Finally, the fourth step proposed has been observed to fail in practice: the communication of change systematically. Communicating in the arena organization is more than rhetoric or good and innovative channels to transmit data or information. Communicating is a critical part of the very process of a compliance project. The challenges are enormous given the nature of oversight, surveillance, and obedience. As noted earlier, the inseparable bedfellows of compliance are punishment and oversight. as we have seen throughout this book, human and organizational behavior is full of details, biases, emotions, intentions, and failures. Therefore, it is impossible to speak of a battle between paladins and villains or bad guys against good guys. The essence of compliance speaks of human nature, which is relational, emotional, and has limited rationality. Punishment and oversight are only one aspect of compliance. They are essential aspects but far from being the only or dominant ones regarding long-term changes. The previous steps require key communication processes to be understood and implemented. Achieving agreements, garnering support, and convincing stakeholders involve an intelligent, skillful communication strategy. Maintaining that understanding and motivation over time, throughout each stage, also involves critical communication skills. The importance of communication in a compliance project is easier to understand if one accepts that there is not only a "top-down" process in this respect. Groups and coalitions inside and outside the organization will also have them, making this process less linear and one-way.

6.3 The Promising Future of Compliance

Weick and Sutcliffe (2007) proposed an apparent organizational paradox that fits perfectly into practical, realistic compliance philosophy. The proposal is an organization prepared to manage the unexpected. But, if something is unexpected, how can it be managed? Precisely because it is based on an axiom, a fundamental dogma. Human nature is both limited and dynamic. Social relationships are built, remodeled daily, and established through obedience, resistance, and strategy. Through their interaction, all these elements create systemic effects: the result of the interaction is a complex amalgam of interdependencies, actions, and decisions related to each other. And to a changing environment. The unexpected is as inevitable as death and taxes.

Understanding that what is unexpected, paradoxical, and quintessentially human is the basis of what makes an organization exist and change would, strange as it may sound, seem to be the most rational thing to consider. Thus, fraud and corruption are not exceptions but are normalized. People justify and rationalize them, and organizations produce them contradictorily through the same structures, processes, and routines that make them stable and functional.

Unlike many organizational change theories, the one that is most logical from the point of view of compliance is much better prepared to achieve what Weick and Sutcliffe propose: a highly effective, resilient organization (Highly Reliable Organization or HRO) (Weick & Sutcliffe, 2007: 147–148). This type of organization can learn from small changes, understand the contradictions of human behavior, and how people rationalize and normalize even improper or highly questionable (even illegal) acts and customs.

The path of compliance can therefore be brilliant: a view of a key aspect of organizations, their people, rules, and structures that are profoundly dynamic while at the same time worrying and critical to the future of the organizations themselves. The key is to accept and understand the rich and intricate human, social and group nature that defines the sometimes thin and always complicated line separating wrongful from permitted, right from corrupt, and ethical from fraudulent acts. However, that complex, difficult line is one that every organization (in fact, every society) needs to fight, discuss and learn to enact. Agree on. And legitimize. Compliance is a great tool that can help to establish, in an intelligent and humane, understandable, and adaptive way, the dividing line between what is ethical and what is wrongful, what is right and what is wrong. Not like in a battle or war. Militaristic metaphors are probably not the most appropriate ones here. Powerful, effective compliance should not be seen as a battle but rather as a transparently constructed agreement with responsible, shared governance within a richly diverse organization.

References

Courpasson, D., & Theonig, J. (2010). *When Managers Rebel.* Hampshire, UK: Palgrave.
Gigerenzer, G., & Selten, R. (eds.). (2002). *Bounded Rationality. The Adaptive Toolbox.* Cambridge: MIT Press.
Goodhart, C. (1984). *Problems of Monetary Management: The U.K. Experience.* London: Palgrave. https://doi.org/10.1007/978-1-349-17295-5_4
Kotter, J. (1996). *Leading Change.* Cambridge: Harvard Business School Press.
Poole, M., & Van de Ven, A. (2004). *Handbook of Organizational Change and Innovation.* Oxford: Oxford University Press.
Weick, K. & Sutcliffe, K. (2007). Managing the unexpected. San Francisco, Ca: John Wiley & Sons.

About the Authors

David Arellano-Gault is Professor at the Department of Public Administration, Center for Research and Teaching in Economics (CIDE) in Mexico City. He earned his Ph.D. in public administration from the University of Colorado at Denver. His research looks to critically incorporate the organizational variable to different governmental and public policy issues to understand such phenomena in a more practical and less normative way. His most recent book, *Corruption in Latin America*, was published in 2020. He is a member of the Mexican Academy of Science and serves in several editorial boards of journals including *Organization Studies*, *Organization Theory*, and *Public Integrity*, among others.

Arturo del Castillo is Associate Managing Director of Kroll, based in Mexico, where he leads the Forensic Investigations Practice. With over 20 years of experience advising clients across multiple industries on complex matters, Arturo has extensive international experience in the preparation of expert witness reports in the context of forensic investigations, as well as judicial proceedings for property damages.

He has advised global Fortune 500 companies in FCPA investigations and due diligence matters, and several others in the assessment of compliance risks, design internal controls and support to implement compliance policies and procedures. He also specializes in the design and implementation of compliance programs.

https://doi.org/10.1515/9783110749113-007

Index

https://doi.org/10.1515/9783110749113-008

www.ingramcontent.com/pod-product-compliance
Lightning Source LLC
Chambersburg PA
CBHW081105220326
41598CB00038B/7234